AF568156

Rural Development Policies and Strategies

Rural Development Policies and Strategies

Prof. Surinder Pal Singh

RANDOM PUBLICATIONS
NEW DELHI (INDIA)

Rural Development Policies and Strategies

ISBN 978-93-5111-484-0

Published in 2015 in India by

RANDOM PUBLICATIONS

4376-A/4B, Gali Murari Lal, Ansari Road
New Delhi-110 002
Phone : +9111-43580356, 011-23289044, 011-43142548
e-mail: sales@randompublications.com,
info@randompublications.com, randomexports@gmail.com

Reprinted 2025

Type Setting by : Friends Media, Delhi-110089
Digitally Printed at : Replika Press Pvt. Ltd.

Preface

Rural development generally refers to the process of improving the quality of life and economic wellbeing of people living in rural areas. It has traditionally centred on the exploitation of land-intensive natural resources such as agriculture and forestry. However, changes in global production networks and increased urbanization have changed the character of rural areas. Increasingly tourism, niche manufacturers, and recreation have replaced resource extraction and agriculture as dominant economic drivers. The need for rural communities to approach development from a wider perspective has created more focus on a broad range of development goals rather than merely creating incentive for agricultural or resource based businesses. Education, entrepreneurship, physical infrastructure, and social infrastructure all play an important role in developing rural regions.

Rural development aims at finding the ways to improve the rural lives with participation of the rural people themselves so as to meet the required need of the rural area. The outsider may not understand the setting, culture, language and other things prevalent in the local area. As such, general people themselves have to participate in their sustainable rural development. In developing countries like Nepal, India, integrated development approaches are being followed up. Rural development programs are usually top-down from the local or regional authorities, regional development agencies, NGOs, national governments or international development organizations.

The present book comprehensively addresses the basic concepts, elements, paradigms, policy instruments, strategies and programs of rural development. It emphasizes the pivotal role of human resources as both a means and an end of development. The book will be of immense use to policy makers, planners, social organisations and researchers.

Author

Contents

1

Strategies of Sustainable Rural Development in Asia and Pacific

Asia and the Pacific today is home to about 70 per cent of the world's rural population. Despite its declining share in national income, the farm sector remains the largest employer. But the per capita arable and permanent cropland availability in the region is only 0.16 ha, compared to 0.37 ha in the rest of the world.

An estimated 524 million of the 2.8 billion people in the region are undernourished, the bulk of them in the two most populous countries, China with 150 million food-insecure people and India with 212 million hungry. Hunger manifests itself in the very high child malnutrition and mortality rates in this region, with rates in some South Asian countries higher than those in sub-Saharan Africa. India has the largest number of hungry people in the world with nearly of half of all children under five being underweight. Most of the food-insecure people are in the rural areas, with small and marginal farmers, landless, women and children, indigenous people and rural persons with disabilities being the most vulnerable.

The widespread food insecurity in the region has economic implications as hunger is not only a consequence but also a cause of poverty, and a major contributory factor in undermining the economic productive potential of individuals, families and entire nations.

However, the region has also seen impressive gains in poverty and food insecurity reduction over the last three decades. Economic growth over the past decade, although uneven, has surpassed that of any other region in the world, enabling 270 million people to escape poverty between 1990 and 2004.

Yet, the region has more than half the world's extreme poor with an estimated 641 million people living on less than US$ 1 per day. Inequitable distribution of growth rather than macro-economic growth is the main cause of income poverty in the region. Rural women are among those most at risk of poverty with fewer livelihood chances, less occupational mobility, weaker skills and less access to resources and training.

The high levels of rural poverty and hunger in the region persist because of lack of secure livelihoods for the marginalized rural poor, lack of adequate non-farm rural employment opportunities, declining public investment in agriculture and rural development, lack of participatory decision-making and the inability of rural producers to take advantage of the new opportunities created by the liberalisation and globalisation of agricultural trade. While many countries in the region can mobilise internally the resources needed to meet sustainable development needs, the poorest nations lack adequate funds for their basic investment needs. Providing the poorest nations with access to developed world markets can be a highly effective way to generate the funds needed for investment in sustainable rural development.

The declining share of agriculture in national income is reflected in the increasing urban-rural migration, especially of young males and skilled workers, resulting in the greying and feminization of the rural sector. Continuing deprivation of women, marginal farmers, and ethnic and social minorities are undermining rural human resources.

Yet, agriculture remains the main livelihood provider in the region which is emerging as the breadbasket of the world. More than 50 per cent of the world's industrial crops are produced in the Asia-Pacific region. Enabling policy and economic environments have led to many success stories, including unique rural development models: from agro-industrial entrepreneurship, cooperatives, and rural financial systems to farmer field schools in integrated pest management.

There is growing inequity among countries in the region as well as at national and local levels. Average farm size is declining in many countries and increasing occupation of marginal lands is widening disparities in land and water distribution. While improved productivity and commercialization of agriculture have boosted rural incomes, policies tend to favour large producers and have not been fully sensitive to social and ecological concerns. Failure to consider equity in development and governance is marginalizing vulnerable groups, especially women, small producers and landless farmers.

There are estimated to be more than 200 million persons with disabilities in the rural areas of Asia and the Pacific who are among the most prone to food and livelihood insecurity. A large number of them are small and marginal farmers depending on agriculture. More rural work opportunities are needed for persons with disabilities in rural areas. Malnutrition caused by extreme poverty, road or machine accidents due to agricultural mechanization and commercialization, as well as violence and armed conflict are major causes of disability among rural people in the region.

The food needs of a growing population coupled with rising living standards and consumer expectations are adding to pressure on an already strained natural resource base. Pressure on land, forest, water and aquatic resources in Asia and the Pacific is the most severe compared to other regions in the world. More than 28 per cent of the region's land area - 850 million hectares – is affected by some form of degradation. Water and wind erosion, salinization and waterlogging have severely affected the productivity in large parts of Central, South, South-east Asia and China, reducing rural livelihood and income opportunities.

With forests on just 28 per cent of the land, Asia and the Pacific has the lowest per capita green cover in all regions. Besides their valuable environmental role in water conservation, sustaining agro-ecological health, natural disaster mitigation, including climate change processes, forests provide food, household energy and livelihood to hundreds of millions of people in the region. Commercial pressures have led to increased exploitation of forest lands, affecting forest dwellers and those dependent on forests, in particular women.

In recent years, in more and more countries in the region, local communities, local governments and civil society organizations are being delegated powers for sustainable forest management as the central part of the strategy for rural development and sustainable natural resource management.

Asia and the Pacific has the world's largest coastal area and nearly 40 per cent of the region's population lives within 100 km of a coast, their livelihood affected by large-scale commercial over-fishing and pollution of marine resources. The region's ecosystems which provide vital ecological and economic service to hundreds of millions of people, the majority of them rural and poor, are threatened by population increase, growing food demand and conversion for urban and industrial development.

Climate change threatens to undermine progress towards food and rural livelihood security in the region. Besides, the small island states in the Pacific which are threatened by sea level rises, crop, marine and aquaculture in several Asian coastal nations is also at risk. Land degradation, poor water management, rising pollution in urban areas, greenhouse gas emissions along with other factors could push more people into poverty.

Of all regions, Asia and the Pacific is the most exposed to disasters, ranging from wild fires, cyclones, landslides, floods and drought to transboundary animal and plant pests and diseases, war, civil unrest and economic crises. Building resilient rural communities and introducing improved agricultural practices will be crucial for cushioning the impact of disasters. In recent years, El Nino and the avian influenza outbreaks have caused huge losses to economy and threatened human life, especially in rural areas.

A livestock revolution is sweeping Asia and the Pacific having the world's largest animal population. Consumer driven demand has seen meat, milk and egg production grow at rates nearly four to eight times compared to the rest of the world. If this growth is sustained, the livestock sector has the potential to spearhead sustainable agriculture and rural development in Asia and the Pacific in the decade to 2015. However, unsustainable large-scale industrial livestock production practices are to blame for serious environmental degradation, including climate change. The growth in world trade of livestock products has exposed the region to increased risk of disastrous pest outbreaks and transboundary animal diseases that can undo gains in food and livelihood security.

As poverty and hunger are concentrated in the rural areas, revitalizing the rural economy is vital if the Asia-Pacific region is to make progress towards MDG 1, other MDGs for which hunger and poverty reduction is a condition, especially MDGs 4 and 5 as well as the relevant commitments in Agenda 21, the Programme for Further Implementation of Agenda 21 and the Johannesburg Plan of Implementation.

Inadequate policy support and investment in the agriculture and rural sector prevent small and marginal farm and non-farm producers from taking advantage of and complying with changing global and national market trends and conditions. This calls for institutional capacity-building in the agriculture and rural sector, for improved delivery of production support services and technologies, and strengthening of local institutions, in particular agricultural cooperatives. Fair trade is a tool for more equitable distribution of opportunities and benefits. This requires a supportive policy environment, empowering the poor.

Most Asia-Pacific countries are implementing some form of decentralization to empower local communities, recognizing the vital role civil society can play as a partner in meeting sustainable rural development challenges. In the world's largest democracy India, a quarter of a million elected village councils with over three million directly elected councilors, more than a third of them women, have been constitutionally recognized as a lay element of grassroots governance and entrusted with a range of sustainable agricultural and rural development responsibilities and functions. Decentralization has a key role in promoting sustainable agriculture and rural development objectives through improved planning, implementation and delivery of equitable local development programmes and essential rural services. Yet, genuine devolution of powers and funds for local development is lacking. As a result, the impact on poverty and hunger has been far from satisfactory.

Energy plays a central role in economic development and poverty reduction in rural areas. Inadequate or inequitable access to efficient, low-cost and sustainable energy affects the livelihoods of hundreds of millions of small farmers, landless and indigenous people in the Asian region. This is denying them livelihood opportunities through start up of small-scale rural enterprises. Currently, small-scale rural industries account for less than 10 per cent of total rural energy demand. Rapidly rising fossil energy costs for farm inputs, local transport and agricultural machinery pose a major challenge to small farmers' households. Small farmer-owned enterprises can play an active role in local demand-driven production and delivery of energy services.

About one billion rural people in the region depend solely on traditional energy sources. Between 80 to 90 per cent of Asia's rural household energy needs are met by wood fuels and crop residues.

The collection of biomass – mainly fuel wood – which is the main source of rural household energy, is primarily the responsibility of women and girls and is a burden on their time, energy and health. Informal income-generating activities by women are fuel-intensive, making them increasingly vulnerable to fuel scarcities and rising fuel prices. Lack of access to renewable and environment-friendly rural energy has adverse ecological, health, educational and livelihood implications for rural poor and undermines progress towards the MDGs.

As countries strive to find the right balance between economic growth, poverty reduction and environmental sustainability, there is recognition that a central element of this is redistributive growth focused on enabling the majority rural poor to take part in this growth and escape poverty.

In the above context, each subregion, in particular countries in South Asia, South-east Asia and the Pacific island nations must assess, initiate and strengthen appropriate policy, institutional and financial support to promote sustainable rural development that ensures sustainable natural resource management and development of a vibrant rural sector.

Commitment to Sustainable Rural Development

Commitments and Stakeholders in Asia and the Pacific

Of the wide ranging global commitments to sustainable rural development, those relating to food and livelihood security, gender equity, land and support services for rural poor, sustainable natural resource use, low-cost, sustainable rural energy, farm support services, rural empowerment through participatory approaches, small-scale rural enterprise development and fair international agricultural trade terms for small farmers, are relevant mainly to South and South-east Asia. Pacific island and Central Asian countries have to focus on sustainable natural resource management and equitable terms for rural producers in international trade negotiations (Table 1). Small and marginal farmers, the landless, rural unemployed, indigenous communities and rural persons with disabilities, in particular women and children, and organizations of rural poor are key stakeholders along with governments, non-governmental organizations, UN agencies and regional institutions.

Table 1: Summary of Key Sustainable Rural Development Commitments

Promoting Rural Food and Livelihood Security

— Improve rural poor people's access to land, production resources and social services
— Transfer sustainable agricultural production technology to rural poor
— Increase food availability/affordability through equitable and efficient distribution systems
— Promote development of micro, small and medium-scale rural enterprises, improve access to credit, market information and markets for rural poor

Empowerment of Rural Poor for Sustainable Rural Development

— Build rural poor capacities for sustainable natural resource management
— Develop national programmes for participatory local development aimed at empowerment of rural poor and their organizations, particularly through increased access to productive resources, public services and institutions
— Provide affordable energy to rural communities including cleaner, efficient and renewable energy services for sustainable rural development

Enhancing Rural Women's Role at all Levels in all Aspects of Sustainable Agriculture and Rural Development

— Improve access for rural women household heads to land and basic services
— Improve participation by women in decision-making in sustainable natural resource management

Promoting a Level Playing Field in International Markets for Small Rural Producers

— Improve market access to agricultural exports of developing countries

Constraints and Opportunities

Declining Investment in Agriculture and Rural Development

Public investment in agriculture has declined, affecting rural poverty and hunger reduction. World Bank lending for agriculture fell from 30 to 6 per cent in the past two decades, reducing access of rural poor to resources and services needed for agricultural and non-farm rural livelihoods. Arresting and reversing the decline in public investment in agriculture will have a significant positive impact on rural hunger and poverty reduction in the region, especially in South Asia and FAO has made promotion of investment opportunities for rural poverty reductions, including removal of biases in public spending for small farmers, a strategic priority area of its work in the region. Priority areas for investment include sustainable fisheries and aquaculture, improved agricultural water management and adoption of good practices by crop and livestock producers, agro-industry and ecosystem managers to promote agrobiodiversity using participatory, integrated small farmer-based approaches, in particular capacity building of small farmer organizations and cooperative enterprises.

Population, Industrial Pressure on Natural Resources and Inadequate Natural Resources Management Capacities

A significantly large proportion of rural people in the region make a living in agriculturally adverse, ecologically fragile and natural disaster-prone areas. Growing population and urbanization/industrialization are adding pressure to the over-stretched natural resource base in the region while large-scale commercial agriculture has led to erosion of natural production resources. Lack of equitable access to land, water, forests and other community resources, especially in South Asia, leads to a vicious circle of poverty contributing to environmental degradation and vice-versa. Natural resource systems in the Pacific island countries are being degraded by unsustainable livelihoods, poverty and social inequity. FAO provides technical assistance on integrated approaches to sustainable agriculture and food production incorporating good practices enhancing biodiversity and food security at farmer household level.

Climate change will affect vulnerable rural people and food systems; adoption of participatory, decentralized and integrated response strategies for agriculture and food systems represents the best way forward. FAO project experience in South Asia has demonstrated the strong positive role farmers' organizations in building awareness and adaptability to the projected adverse impact of climate change on rural food and livelihood security.

Inadequate and inequitable access to energy has negative environmental, livelihood and health implications for rural poor, particularly women and children. There are new opportunities for small-scale, local, sustainable bioenergy development for rural food and livelihood security. India has made the environment-friendly and hardy *jatropha* plant the basis for a national-level, sustainable rural employment generation programme. Access to renewable and environmentally sustainable rural energy sources is crucial for improving rural livelihoods and food security through farmer-owned and controlled rural enterprises.

Lack of Support Services and Enabling Policies for Small Farmers

Rural institutions, particularly farmers' organizations and rural finance/marketing systems lack capacities for adapting to market challenges to generate sustainable rural income and livelihoods. Effective implementation of agrarian reforms, improved delivery of production and social services to farm and non-farm rural enterprises will benefit the majority of rural poor people in the region who live in South Asia. Linking organizations of rural poor, particularly agricultural cooperatives to urban markets provides opportunities for entrepreneurial capacity- building and improved rural livelihoods. In Asia and the Pacific, FAO is collaborating with government agencies and cooperative movements to enhance business skills and marketing capacities of small farmer cooperatives as social enterprises. Regional networking activities include bilateral exchanges, development of training methodologies and capacity-building projects.

Ineffective Participation of Rural Poor in Sustainable Development

Rural poor have no say in the making of agricultural and rural development policies, legislation and investment programmes which as a result, do not reflect local farmers' needs. Decentralization of the government's role in agriculture and rural development needs to be built upon effective institutional mechanisms for participation of rural poor. Local participatory planning enhances access to and sustainable use of land, water and other natural resources, providing opportunities for improvement of rural livelihoods as well as sustainable agriculture and rural development. India's *Panchayati Raj* village-level elected self-government institutions can be a model for empowerment of rural poor for sustainable natural resource management for rural food and livelihood security.

Lack of a Level Playing Field in Agricultural Trade

Rural poor in developing Asian countries, especially in low-income South Asian countries are ill-equipped to respond to changing market and trade terms resulting from the liberalization and globalization of agricultural trade which has also increased competition for natural resources. Small farmers and rural producers need policy support ensuring a fair playing field in national and local markets affected by trade liberalization and globalization, in order to improve their livelihoods and ensure environmental sustainability. Formal organizations of small-scale rural producers, such as agricultural cooperatives can use Fair Trade channels to tap into market opportunities in developed world markets. In Asia and the Pacific, FAO is collaborating with donors in promotion of pro-rural poor trade and agriculture policies.

Gender Inequity

Particularly in South Asia, rural women face discrimination in access to agricultural production resources as well as opportunities for developing livelihoods skills. The increasingly assertive civil society and political campaign for gender equity across the region together with commitments by most countries to global gender equity commitments (MDG 3) is making an impact. India's constitutional reservation of one-third of elected village council seats for women has placed over a million rural women in decision-making positions in *Panchayati Raj* institutions implementing sustainable natural resource management at local level.

Promoting Rural Food and Livelihood Security

Asia and the Pacific has 524 million of the 820.2 million undernourished people in the developing world. The prevalence of hunger has been reduced in all countries in South, South-east and East Asia with the solitary exception of the Democratic People's Republic of Korea. However, population growth means that percentage decline in hunger has not been sufficient to bring about a reduction in the actual number of undernourished people.

Significant progress has been made in reducing hunger in China and South-east Asia. India still has the largest number of hungry people in the world with population growth limiting reduction in the size of the country's undernourished population to less than 3 million from 1990-92 and the latest assessment in 2001-03, compared to a reduction of more than 40 million in China over the same period. The world's two most populous countries have more than two-thirds of food-insecure people in the region. According to FAO assessments, reduction in income-poverty has not necessarily translated into food security and an important reason for this is that hunger itself is a constraint to escaping poverty, indicating a policy priority for targeted hunger reduction.

Despite unprecedented and continuing economic growth over the past two decades, South and South-east Asia is still home for over 40 per cent of the worlds poor, the majority of them in rural areas. The average per capita rural income in Bangladesh, India, Lao PDR, Nepal, Philippines, Sri Lanka and Thailand, is less than half of urban income. Similar glaring rural-urban disparities exist in access to basic facilities in most countries. In Pakistan, rural literacy levels are half of those in urban areas.

Agriculture's share in national income is declining in South and South-east Asia. In 2005, the agriculture sector contributed only 8.4 and 9.0 per cent of GDP respectively in Malaysia and Thailand. Among low-income countries, the share of agriculture varied from 19.0 per cent in India to 50.6 per cent in Myanmar.

However, in some countries such as Nepal, Afghanistan, Philippines and Sri Lanka, the transformation of the economy from the agriculture sector to industry and services has not been as marked, perhaps because of political instability and economic uncertainty. Farm surplus can be a source of investment for processing, marketing, rural industrial development. However, profitability is declining due to rising input costs and stagnant productivity. This will adversely affect rural poor incomes and share of agriculture in GDP growth.

China and Viet Nam's success in transforming agriculture and the rural economy underpins the significant gains in food and rural livelihood security in both countries. In the case of China, strong agricultural growth following de-collectivization of holdings in the late 1970s laid the basis for the subsequent rapid growth of non-farm rural enterprises which by 2000 accounted for one-fourth of rural employment and 30 per cent of national GDP. Hunger and poverty declined dramatically in the country as a result. Viet Nam likewise lifted nearly 7 million people out of food insecurity and reduced its share of people living on less than US$1 a day from 15 to 2 per cent during the 1990s using market-oriented economic and agricultural reforms accompanied by targeted investment in rural infrastructure development.

In comparison, Cambodia and India, notwithstanding strong annual GDP growth of 4 and 3.9 per cent respectively from the early 1990s to 2003 failed to make a dent in the total number of food-insecure people. This was mainly because of a lack of sectoral balance in economic growth and marginal improvement in agricultural productivity during the same period in the two countries.

The number of undernourished people in the Democratic People's Republic of Korea has increased by more than 100 per cent between 1990-92 and 2001-03 to 8 million due to reported negative economic growth and declining agricultural productivity. FAO experience in the region shows that pro-small farmer agricultural technology improvements speed rural poverty reduction by boosting farm incomes and lowering food prices. However, in many low-income countries in the region, especially those with high levels of undernourishment, public investment in agricultural infrastructure, including research, education and extension does not reflect the important role of the sector in ensuring rural food and livelihood security.

Inequitable access to resources and opportunities across territories and communities, limited employment opportunities, coupled with poor skill and educational levels are the main reason for the persisting high levels of rural poverty in South Asia and some South-east Asian countries.

Agrarian reform ensuring wider, secure and sustainable access to land, water and other natural resources, which significantly influence rural livelihoods opportunities, is essential for eradicating hunger and poverty, equitable development and social justice in South and South-east Asia given the typically small farm sizes. In Indonesia and Bangladesh, for instance, about two-thirds of all farms cover only one-fourth of the total cultivated area and are of less than one hectare on average.

In South and South-east Asia, agrarian reforms have, in general, been centralised, government-led operations. The reform process has been largely top-down, involving government administrative machinery as against a decentralised market-friendly and strategic partnership with participation of civil society and other private stakeholders including reform beneficiaries. The Philippines appears to be the exception to this general trend with a reasonably decentralised and participatory agrarian reform programme that has achieved relatively better results and outcomes. On the other hand, in the South Asian countries, agrarian reform programmes have been slow and achieved only modest results, except in selected states of India such as Kerala, West Bengal and Karnataka.

Although agrarian reform attempts have eliminated feudal and large absentee land-owning interests in these countries, these have failed to eliminate social differentiation based on unequal land ownership and the existence of intermediaries between tenants and owners. The limited success in freeing adequate surplus land and redistributing it among the intended beneficiaries is ascribed to a complex of factors. These include lack of strong political will, weak implementation mechanisms and inadequate financial support. Additionally, weak legal systems, resistance from surplus landowners and imperfections of the land market have also been formidable institutional barriers to effective agrarian reform in the subregion.

The prevailing high rural poverty levels in South and South-east Asia mean that employment generation through rural non-farm activities (RNA) should be a key poverty reduction strategy. With a growing rural population and land-scarcity, agricultural growth alone cannot absorb the rapidly increasing rural workforce. The relatively small urban industrial sector too cannot provide sufficient employment opportunities for the labour force released from agriculture.

The rural non-farm sector accounts for between 20 to 50 per cent of total rural employment in South and South-east Asia. An important role of the rural non-farm sector is providing work opportunities during the slack agricultural season. The sector has an immense economic contribution to make in accelerating reduction of poverty and rural-urban income gaps as well as rural-urban migration. Most South and South-east Asian countries have adopted appropriate policies and are supporting development of rural non-farm and agro-based industries for creating work and income opportunities for farm households. "The Chinese experience suggests that the impact of rapid economic growth on poverty reduction tends to slacken eventually if the rural sector does not grow hand in hand. As incomes have grown, the impact and effectiveness of general economic growth on poverty reduction have weakened."

Some big South Asian countries have not given adequate attention to developing the basic physical and social infrastructure of rural development – roads, communication, power, basic health care and education, housing and sanitation. In a rapidly globalizing agricultural economy, market connectivity, information and communication technology, farm clinics, training schools, demonstration plot, farm technology incubators, privatized extension services, market yards, processing facilities for value addition are more important than ever. Modern banking systems are not ready to venture in the agriculture sector and cooperative banking systems and self-help micro-financing groups can play a vital rolei outh Asian Association for Regional Cooperation (SAARC) countries of the SAARC Development Goals (SDG) 2007 – 2012, aiming for a poverty-free South Asia. The 22 SDGs are divided into four categories – livelihood, health, education and environment goals.

The 22 Pacific island nations include about 30 000 islands spread over a vast area. A large majority of the about 6 million people in the subregion inhabit small and remote coastal or rural communities closely dependent on local natural resources for livelihoods. Despite the paucity of data, there is evidence of growing poverty and income inequalities in several Pacific island countries (PICs), challenging the conventional view that easy access to subsistence resources and strong social networks have cushioned their people against financial hardship. There are significantly high levels of child undernourishment and the percentage of underweight children has not changed or increased in at least four Pacific island countries.

While none of the National Statistics Offices in the PICs are currently producing official estimates of purchasing power parity (PPP) adjustment factors, assessments by the Asian Development Bank (ADB) reveal that at least one-fifth of households in 12 of 13 PICs cannot meet their basic needs. Rural households in the Pacific on average spend less on non-food needs than urban and have fewer cash income opportunities. The assessment suggests a strong positive link between a vibrant subsistence agricultural sector feeding local demand and lower levels of rural poverty.

In several instances, poverty and hunger in the PICs is related to the growing economic imbalance in favour of urban areas where over 43 per cent of the population of seven out of 15 PICs resides. Urban growth rates are typically higher than rural growth rates in most countries.

Child undernourishment assessments in PIC countries are largely based on hospital referrals. Kiribati and Marshall Islands show a significant increase in the percentage of underweight children. Samoa has made significant progress in child nutrition, with only 1.9 per cent of children being underweight in 1999. However, a 2002 survey by the World Health Organization (WHO) Regional Office for the Western Pacific covering 27 primary schools in 13 Pacific countries found the prevalence of overweight children to be higher than that of underweight children. Other surveys reveal that between 2 to 23 per of children under 5 years in some Pacific communities suffer from mild to moderate under-nutrition.

The Pacific subregion, once self-reliant in food, also needs to reduce its heavy dependence on food imports. There is a pressing need to increase employment and income opportunities for small-scale rural producers. Agriculture, fishery and forestry offer lucrative livelihood opportunities. However, a major concern is the lack of interest among youth in taking up agriculture as a livelihood, necessitating identification of profitable agriculture-based enterprises that will help to change the perception of the sector as a subsistence provider. Among other things, this requires closer linkages between small farmers and large private sector processors, exporters, etc.

Important sustainable rural development issues in the Pacific related to food and livelihood security include land tenure, subsistence activities and access to natural resources, education and economic opportunities. "The complexity of poverty in the Pacific suggests that a focus on economic growth alone will not lead to eradication of poverty and hunger, but it is crucial that economic growth be pursued in a manner that promotes sustainable development."

The Central Asian region includes Asia-Pacific's fastest growing economies: three Central Asian countries – Kazakhastan, Tajikistan and Turkmenistan are among the ten countries with highest GDP growth between 1999 and 2003. These countries depend primarily on their natural resource base for economic growth and have benefited from soaring commodity prices including oil and gas, strong exports and growing trade with the reviving Russian economy. With the exception of Kazakhstan, agriculture is the mainstay of the region's economies.

The average per income is highest in oil-rich Kazakhstan and lowest in Kyrgyzstan and Tajikistan with their difficult mountainous terrain which has created artificial ethnic enclaves that act as barriers to social and economic development. The poorer countries are also constrained by high external debt. While recent economic growth has lowered poverty in Kazakhstan and Turkmenistan, poverty levels have still not declined significantly in Kyrgyzstan, Tajikistan and Uzbekistan. Deteriorating natural resources and environmental pressure – pollution, land degradation – are blamed for the growing vulnerability of the subregion to natural disasters.

Central Asian countries face the challenge of acting urgently in support of sustainable economic growth though deep-rooted cultural factors and institutional shortcomings are major hurdles to this.

Empowerment of Rural Poor for Sustainable Rural Development

Ineffective agrarian reform together with population growth, especially in South Asia, has led to land fragmentation and declining agricultural productivity, in turn contributing to widespread food insecurity and large-scale distress migrations from rural to urban areas. In South-east Asia, the Philippines and Thailand are implementing major agrarian reform. However, in Myanmar, Laos and Cambodia, equitable and sustainable natural resource management is constrained by lack of good governance in land issues. In most countries, inadequacies in public investment in agriculture and legislation responsive to the need for land reform and land use administration is a constraint to sustainable land and natural resource management.

Rapid economic growth, particularly in South and South-east Asia has over-strained the natural resource base with adverse implications for rural livelihoods. Urbanization and industrialization has reduced availability of fertile agricultural land for small rural producers, South and South-east and China.

Some 28 per cent of the land area in the region is degraded. Deforestation, unsustainable agricultural activities, overgrazing have degraded increasingly large areas of arable land on which tens of millions of rural people depend for food and income security in South and South-east Asia. Particularly in India and Pakistan, land degradation worsens the adverse livelihood effects of recurrent droughts that lead to temporary large-scale rural distress migrations. Forest cover has declined rapidly in Cambodia, Indonesia, Myanmar and the Philippines, though reforestation in some Central Asian countries, Viet Nam and China has resulted in a slight net increase in the overall green cover in Asia and the Pacific.

More and more countries in Asia and the Pacific are devising innovative approaches for participatory management of natural resources. Involving local communities in joint forest management strategies, especially in India, has demonstrated the effectiveness of local participatory approaches that inform broader sustainable development strategies in many Asian countries, notably India, Pakistan, Sri Lanka and the Philippines. India's constitutionally recognised *Panchayati Raj* elected village councils are entrusted with sustainable rural development responsibilities including poverty alleviation, land improvement, soil and water conservation, land reforms, social forestry, rural enterprise development, rural housing, rural energy, rural infrastructure and communications.

While many countries are giving a greater say to rural communities in local decision-making through some form of decentralization aimed at sustainable natural resource management for improved food and livelihood security, there is still a lack of effective participation by rural poor in decision-making. Financial resources to build institutional capacities to ensure improved access to production and social services and equitable sharing of benefits of natural resource management have still not been devolved to local levels.

The physical infrastructure for economic empowerment of rural poor is lacking in South Asia with inadequate government investment in transport, storage, power and market facilities as well as limited outreach of the formal banking sector in the rural areas. The agricultural value-addition and marketing infrastructure in South Asia is still not developed enough for effective promotion of small-scale agricultural and rural enterprises. Agricultural cooperatives, as democratic member-controlled organizations based upon social cohesion, self-help and equity, lack support for business development and in many cases lack autonomy, especially in South Asia.

Indigenous people are among the poorest rural poor in the region which is home to about 70 per cent of the world's more than 250 million indigenous peoples. The large majority of indigenous communities live in upland and forested areas relying on subsistence production systems that are being affected by deforestation and restrictive legislation (natural parks, etc) limiting their access to livelihood resources, particularly in Lao PDR, India, Myanmar and Nepal.

Sustainable natural resource management is also a major challenge in the Pacific with available data showing that in most PICs, deforestation exceeds the rate of reforestation. The Solomon Islands are projected to lose all commercial forest resources in this decade and Samoa its remaining natural forests in another five to six years. The 1995 "Code of Conduct for Logging of Indigenous Forests in Selected South Pacific Countries" and the 2003-2007 Action Strategy for Nature Conservation in the Pacific Region are addressing the concern. However, there is a scarcity of data for sustainable management decisions and PICs need capacities to monitor changes in their rich marine areas that sustain livelihoods and national economic growth but are vulnerable to overexploitation and pollution.

In Central Asia, industrial demand for this subregions abundant natural resources has led to large-scale land degradation and environmental pollution, including poorly maintained radioactive waste sites. The Aral Sea is a stark reminder for future generations of the importance of intra-regional cooperation in natural resource conservation. Water shortages, water-logging and related cross-border natural resource management problems have resulted in disputes in the past. The United Nations Environment Programme

(UNEP), United Nations Development Programme (UNDP), the Organization for Security and Cooperation in Europe (OSCE) and the Security through Science programme of the North Atlantic Treaty Organization (NATO) have conducted an in-depth assessment of the close link between environment, livelihoods and security in the highly fertile Ferghana Valley straddling Kyrgyzstan, Tajikistan and Uzbekistan. The valley is home to 10 million people with annual per capita gross national incomes of much less than US$500 and 60 per cent of the population is below the poverty line.

An estimated 1.7 billion people in developing Asian countries in 2002 relied on biomass for cooking and heating. Rural energy poverty especially affects women. "Some progress has been made in the region towards sustainable energy development taking advantage of locally available and environmentally benign renewable energy resources. It is particularly encouraging to note that many Governments are recognizing the benefits of utilizing renewable energy resources in order to provide rural energy services. Progress is however not observed across the board, and the share of modern renewable energy is marginal."

China. India, Indonesia, Malaysia, Philippines, Sri Lanka, Thailand and Viet Nam have national biomass energy programmes and projects. In India, the rural administrative sub-division of *taluka* comprising a closed biomass and rainwater basin with an average population of about 200 000, is the basis of the 1997 National *Policy on Energy Self-sufficient Talukas*. The talukas can produce an estimated 400 million tonnes of agricultural residues annually, enough for the country's rural energy, animal feed and natural fertilizer needs. India's National Biodiesel Mission is using jatropha plantations on wastelands as a mass rural income/employment-generation programme linked to commercial bio-fuel production.

"That production of biofuels are based on renewable resources, that their use reduces, or is perceived to reduce, the emission of harmful greenhouse gases, that they enhance the energy security of countries that import crude oil, and that their production may also boost domestic farm and rural incomes, are influential factors now generating substantial policy developments on a global scale."

Climate change is fast emerging as a threat to food security and rural livelihoods in the region and could reduce fresh water supply in Central, South, East and South-east Asia, affecting more than a billion people by the 2050s. Densely populated coastal regions in South, East and South-East Asia face high risk of sea and river flooding.

Crop yields could decrease by 30 per cent in Central and South Asia by the mid-21st century, increasing food insecurity. Small-scale rainfed farmers, pastoralists, fishers and forest-dependent people are most at risk.

"About half of all greenhouse gas emissions produced by developing countries (versus less than a third in developed countries) are derived from the land use, land use change and forestry (LULUCF) sectors. Globally, the main source of greenhouse gas emissions in the LULUCF sectors are deforestation (17 per cent of total), forest harvest management (2.5 per cent), agriculture and soils (6 per cent), livestock and manure (5 per cent), and rice cultivation (1.5 per cent)."

Mitigation and adaptation strategies in the marine, coastal, inland water, flood-plain, forest, dryland, island, mountain and cultivated areas of South and South-east Asia involves protecting local food supplies and livelihood resources from negative climate change effects. This requires more efficient land and water use, good forestry/fishery practices, better livestock management and more energy-efficient agro-industries.

FAO is building capacities at national, local and community levels for improved awareness and preparedness for climate change impacts. An FAO climate change adaptation project in Bangladesh has shown the vital role of local farmers organizations, cooperatives, local governments and NGOs in promoting understanding of the impacts of climate change as well as in creating "ownership of the adaptation options with the local people and institutions".

The PICs are perhaps the most sensitive to the imminent threat from climate change. Climate change-linked weather events have caused untold damage, drought, floods, volcanic eruptions in the Marshall Islands, Fiji and Vanuatu. Most PICs are implementing projects and activities in keeping with global climate change commitments and these have led to significant abatement in the levels of greenhouse gas emissions. Both the IPCC and FAO advocate sustainable development for reducing vulnerability to climate change and using adaptive strategies.

Enhancing Rural Women

Rural women need access to land, water and other natural resources, inputs and services as well as equal opportunity for skills development and use. Some countries like Indonesia, the Philippines and Thailand have made much progress in this direction through legal steps and policy measures to mainstream women's participation in development.

While gender disparities in basic education are being fast removed in South Asia, rural women lack adequate work opportunities. Rural work data from India's 2001 census shows that 30 million rural households had at least one member seeking work, the majority of them women. This is not surprising as declining rural work opportunities encourage male rural-urban migration.

Gender inequities in access to production resources are most marked in the populous South Asian countries. India's *Panchayati Raj* system of village governance has institutionalized efforts to change the equation, albeit slowly, through constitutional reservation for women of one-third of decision-making positions in village councils. More than 1 million women have been elected to the quarter of a million village councils in the country and there are several documented instances of women village council heads as successful local development mangers. Nepal's inheritance law entitles daughters to inheritance.

However, gender discrimination and inequitable social development remain serious concerns in several countries. There is also growing evidence of ethnic and indigenous communities being marginalized in the development process. Inequitable access to resources, opportunities and participation across communities and geographic regions is causing social tension and conflict in several countries.

While the PICs have made significant progress toward gender equality, women remain disadvantaged in many areas, including education, employment and political representation.

Promoting a Level Playing Field in International Markets

Most food trade in the region is to domestic markets and most consumption is from domestic food production. The Asia–Pacific region is a net importer of agricultural products. Besides world trade talks, most countries in South, South-east and East Asia are negotiating regional and bilateral trading arrangements that have a direct bearing on small agricultural and rural producers whose interests, however, have not been adequately considered, denying them opportunities in international markets.

Food procurement and distribution systems are becoming more centralized. Private and foreign investment is entering national food chains, taking away control of food production, processing and marketing from small producers.

Most Asian farms are small. In South and South-east Asia, small farmers face increasingly complex and adverse market conditions and lack competitive and organizational capacities to address the challenge. These include high food quality and safety standards and intellectual property rights introduced by trade agreements that were negotiated without the participation of small-scale rural producers.

Capacities and legislation are inadequate to ensure a fair playing field for small farmers. Legislation on agricultural cooperative enterprise development is not adapted to new market requirements for food safety and quality. Agricultural production support systems are not fully responsive to small farm producers' needs.

Globalization holds both risks and gains for PICs. The proposed Pacific Plan aims to reduce subregional vulnerabilities through enhanced regional cooperation. Failure to integrate successfully with the global economy exposes the PICs to "deepening risk of marginalization, economic decline, increased insecurity and a more impoverished region." Intraregional integration is being promoted through the Pacific island Countries Trade Agreement and the South Pacific Regional Trade and Economic Cooperation Agreement.

Policy Options

Persisting hunger in South Asia is linked to low productivity of small farmers and lack of adequate rural livelihood opportunities that limits access to food. Increasing small farm yields will boost small farmer and agricultural worker incomes which is more likely to be used for meeting food and basic non-food needs derived from rural areas.

Governments in the low-income countries in South and South-east Asia need to allocate a larger portion of government spending on agriculture and rural development for improved food security. At the same time, policies must encourage private investment in the sectors. Food insecurity affects economic productivity and income growth by itself is not always enough to reduce hunger, requiring targeted interventions to areas of high hunger.

"Agricultural growth [thus] generates a virtuous cycle in which agricultural growth and rural off-farm activities sustain each other. Such growth can make a powerful contribution towards reducing the numbers of undernourished." In order to benefit fully from agricultural growth, rural poor need support for rural enterprise development, in particular agricultural cooperatives, through provision of skills for value-added production and marketing. Especially in rainfed areas, rural employment strategies and programmes must provide additional farm and non-farm work opportunities for small farmers.

Livelihood promotion programmes are needed for other vulnerable rural poor groups – indigenous people, persons with disabilities and women. South Asia needs legislation to ensure that landless and indigenous people, in particular women, have adequate access to production resources.

Countries in the region must put small farmers at the centre of agricultural trade negotiations with a view to create a fair players' field. This must be accompanied by capacity-building for food safety and quality certification, tapping niche markets for organic produce and fair trade opportunities. The development of rural enterprises requires training capacities to equip rural poor with production/marketing skills as well as improved market information systems, provision of capital, technology, education and extension services.

Rural development approaches incorporating local governance need to integrate with policy interventions in the field of agriculture, fisheries, forestry, livestock as well as trade, finance and industry. There is need for more synergy between public and private sectors and civil society organizations (CSOs) in decentralized, participatory approaches for sustainable agriculture and rural development.

More funding support is needed from governments and donors for participatory and pro-poor sustainable rural development. India's *Panchayati Raj* institutions can be a model for strengthening self-management capacities of community-level associations of the rural poor and improving their access to livelihood resources and services. ICT facilities can promote rural enterprise development and enhance participation of rural poor in their socio-economic transformation.

The provision of renewable and environmentally sustainable rural energy can improve rural livelihoods and food security through development of farmer-owned and controlled rural enterprises.

Lessons Learned and Best Practices

Whether poverty reduction comes from agricultural or non-agricultural growth is linked to the stage of development and linkages between farm and non-farm sector. Growth in agriculture results in an almost immediate impact in terms of increased employment of rural labour in a host of non-tradable activities; most farm households supplement their income from non-farm earnings thus having an immediate impact on poverty reduction and food security.

Agricultural cooperative enterprises based upon democratic member participation, social cohesion, self-help and equity provide sustainable employment opportunities, quality production/social services and marketing networks for farm/non-farm produce. They link rural and urban areas through provision of savings and credit and social services to vulnerable rural poor.

Developing country governments need strengthened institutional capacities at decentralized level to reach out to vulnerable rural poor. There is need to strengthen inter-institutional coordination and facilitate participatory planning and devolution of financial resources.

Equitable participation by rural women in local decision-making can be improved through legislation and institutional capacity building.

External development agencies often come in with highly specialized and ad hoc, technical sector advisors while there is need for an interdisciplinary team approach based on knowledge of local rural entrepreneurial conditions and contacts with rural enterprise networks, in particular agricultural cooperatives.

Success Case Replication in South-east Asia

The Success Case Replication (SCR) methodology developed in South-east Asia by ESCAP and FAO involved multiplication of village-based, food/non-food rural enterprises in a poverty alleviation project covering 3 300 farmer households in eight countries. Involving peer training of potential rural entrepreneurs by successful ones, the project resulted in average annual income increases of US$500 for the farm families covered by the project. The successful entrepreneurs, many of them women, became SCR trainers themselves resulting in a 10 to 100-fold replication of successful rural enterprises. The strength of the methodology is the low cost of initial project preparation aimed at identification of SCR trainers in a selected geographical area. FAO Stocktaking on Good Policies and Practices on Agrarian Reform and Rural Development

Support Services for Effective Land use

In the Philippines, FAO supported the government's Comprehensive Agrarian Reform Programme (CARP) through several projects targeted at agrarian reform communities (ARCs) – a cluster of villages (barangays) where 60 per cent or more of the people have been given land under the land reform programme. The projects supported increased agricultural productivity in the ARCs through:

1. Identification by farmer-led development teams of local problems and priorities and their incorporation in community development plans.

Training in farm and non-farm productive activities including accounting, bookkeeping and gender issues.

Helping build links between agrarian reform beneficiaries and agribusinesses to provide market outlets to the farmers.

Facilitating access to credit through matching agrarian reform beneficiaries with financial institutions.

Addressing Climate Change-related Risks

FAO can support adaptation to climate change in agro-ecosystems (crops, livestock, grasslands), forests and woodlands, inland waters as well as coastal and marine ecosystems. Numerous adaptation options are available and FAO is codifying these and helping local communities understand those most suitable for them.

While IPCC advocates the integration of strategic response to climate change, resources and institutional frameworks have a sectoral focus. FAO has noted that "using food security as an entry point for evaluating priorities for food system responses to the challenge of climate change may offer an opening for developing a more integrated approach," and that adopting a participatory pro-poor integrated strategic framework which could incorporate the following strategies could represent the best way forward:

(1) Providing incentives to persuade crop and livestock producers, agro-industries and ecosystem managers to adopt good practices for mitigation and adaptation.

(2) Promoting agro-biodiversity is crucial for local adaptation and resilience.

(3) Raising productivity from improved agricultural water management will be key to ensure global food supply and security.

(4) Promoting conservation agriculture for efficient water use, promoting soil quality, withstanding extreme weather events and carbon sequestration.

(5) Capacity-building for sustainable livestock management practices for adaptation and associated mitigation should be given high priority.

(6) Promoting fishing and aquatic food production offers sustainable livelihood opportunities for people living by seacoasts, rivers and lakes.

References

ESCAP, (2005), *Energy services for sustainable development in rural areas in Asia and the Pacific: Policy and Practice,* ESCAP.

FAO, (2007), *Role of agricultural cooperatives in biofuel development at community-level for rural food and livelihood security, regional workshop*, FAO and Network for Development of Agricultural Cooperatives in Asia and the Pacific (NEDAC), 2007

FAO Regional Office for Asia and the Pacific, (2003), *A handbook for trainers on participatory local development.*

Secretariat of the Pacific Community and UNDP. (2004) *Pacific Islands Regional Millennium Development Goals Report 2004.*

2

Rural Development in South Asia: Changing Trends

For the predominantly agricultural economies of South Asia rural development is the core issue of development. Unfortunately in the rush to achieve other political and economic objectives, it has received a generally low priority in national development. As a result, South Asian rural societies have suffered a steady erosion in their living conditions and productive infrastructure, as evidenced by the high incidence of poverty. The continuing outmigration from rural areas, especially of the younger, more skilled and enterprising sections of the population is also a sign of the declining attractiveness of the rural habitat. Indeed there has been a serious and unremitting haemorrhaging of resources from the rural areas without any commensurate restitution of the damage incurred over many decades.

The *problematique* of rural development is, however, changing and has been undergoing a continuing metamorphosis in recent decades. The idyllic vision of rural areas in South Asia, as self-contained units with a progressive democratic structure and a self-sufficient, diversified and self-sustained economy, tends to be exaggerated and fantasized as a "paradise lost". Few, if any, especially among the present rural inhabitants, still hanker to bring back that vision, which has vanished from their collective memory, if, indeed, it ever existed.

The increasing contact with the outside world made possible by improved communications has considerably reduced the isolation of the rural areas. As and when transport costs fall further, imports from the urban economy (including those from abroad) will make the idyllic notion of a self-sufficient village economy even more mythical. The invasion of the electronic media and the increasing impact of urban and overseas migration and other conjunctural developments have further strengthened this trend, notwithstanding the continuing lack of development in rural areas. This has led to a corresponding change in the aspirations of the rural population, as well as public responses and the mechanisms for articulating such responses over time.

Although the rural areas in most South Asian countries are inhabited by more than two thirds of the population, national economic development efforts continue to be skewed in favour of urban areas, which tend to attract disproportionate amounts of all forms of resources other than those that are immobile, namely land and other resources. This situation is becoming untenable and political pressures are building in South Asia to redress the balance before it leads to a social explosion. The agenda of rural development itself is determined by those who do not live in the rural communities and often have little concern for the well being of those who live in them.

The decline in the importance of, and the public policy attention paid to, rural areas also stems from the rapid rise in urbanization in most developing countries of South Asia. The population in the urban centres has been doubling almost every decade, propelled both by the push of rural poverty and the elusive hope of finding a better livelihood in urban areas. The growth of urban areas during the process of industrialization has an inevitable economic logic based on economies of scale and the positive externalities generated by clusters of enterprises. However, the pattern of industrialization chosen in most South Asian countries was unbalanced and tended to exacerbate rather than bridge rural-urban disparity. As a result, in the face of a lack of progress in rural development, a negative externality manifested itself in overburdening urban services such as housing, water supply, electricity and sanitation and in the profusion of urban slums which stand out as festering sores in the landscape of urban affluence and a breeding ground for crime, hate and terror.

While it may be premature to lament that "rural development is in serious trouble" (Moreland, 1968) there is a serious need to examine what went wrong and to highlight the little that has proved right in the pursuit of rural development in South Asia in the past five decades. There is a strong need not merely to reinvent its *raison d'etre* but also to reassess its performance, reinvigorate its programmes and reconstruct its agenda.

Table 1. Urbanization trends in South Asia

	India	Pakistan	Bangladesh	Nepal	Sri Lanka
Urban population	158.8	23.2	12.5	0.9	3.2
(millions) – 1980 – 1999	280.1	49.1	30.6	2.7	4.4
Urban population	23.0	28.0	14.0	7.0	22.0
(per cent of total population) – 1980– 1999	28.0	36.0	24.0	12.0	23.0

Source: World Bank, World Development Indicators 2001.

A Brief History

The antecedents of the modern project of rural development in South Asia can be traced back several centuries. According to William Moreland, an erudite British agricultural officer the "idea of agricultural development was already present in the fourteenth century." There is considerable evidence to show that ancient and medieval rulers in South Asia invested to increase productivity, especially in organizing irrigation. By the fourteenth century, the state was engaged in expanding markets and manufacturing by building transportation infrastructure. However, as Moreland has argued, the political and social environment during the period before the British was "unfavourable to [modern goals of development]," because, military and political struggles undermined investments in farming, manufacturing, and banking, as pillage and plunder fed destructive armies and rapacious taxation fattened unproductive ruling elites.

The rural development project received further impetus under British colonial rule, although its agenda was dominated more by concerns about the maintenance of law and order and of ensuring the stability of the state and the acquiescence of the governed, as well as ensuring the supplies of cheap raw materials and cash crops for British industries.

During the colonial period the rapacious exploitation of the countryside to suit colonial economic interests resulted in the destruction of much of the rural infrastructure and institutional framework and their replacement by the modernization of the enclave economy, including railways and irrigation networks, along with the imposition of new property relations on the land, which did little to regenerate rural societies and marginalized large sections of the rural population. Unlike western Europe and the United States of America where railways played a leading role in bringing about industrial transformation, in India they were instrumental mainly in the completion of colonization. Colonial rulers attempted the commercialization of agriculture and expansion of the politico-legal system to transform the agrarian economy through new land tenures. The main objective of their rural development strategy was increasing agricultural production that could be used (as raw material) for metropolitan industrialization and by bestowing the patronage of large land ownership to those trusted for delivering both political and economic favours in return.

The commercialization of agriculture along with higher land revenue imposed by the colonial administration had a fissiparous effect on rural society and sowed the seeds of dualism in agriculture. On the one hand, it created a need for more working capital funds, which compelled the subsistence farmers to fall into debt. In consequence, widespread impoverishment and recurring famines in poorly endowed and unirrigated areas became a feature of the British period owing to increasing cultivation of cash crops in preference to food crops and the needs of the growing population.

On the other hand, those who had land and other resources became wealthier by taking advantage of the demand for cash crops. The wealthy farmers and traders encouraged poor peasants to incur debt both for productive and unproductive purposes, snaring them into the debt trap, from which they could save themselves only by selling their land to the lenders. The usurers had an eye on the debtors' lands. When the debts reached breaking point they insisted that the debtors dispose of their lands. This was facilitated by legalizing the sale of land to pay off the debt, a practice which was prohibited before the colonial rule.

On the whole, the cumulative impact of British imperial rule, while providing the basic appurtenances for the modernization of the rural economy, widened social disparities, without bringing any real improvement in rural livelihoods. The imposition of capitalism and the development of the modern state under colonialism had a profound effect on Indian agriculture. The first disrupted the agrarian order by transforming land and labour into commodities for sale; the second did so by enforcing the imposition of a market economy and by creating a new environment for the generation of peasant income. The privileged and the affluent remained in an advantageous position to consolidate their socio-economic position, and the lower rungs of the peasantry led miserable lives.

The post-independence Governments tried to reverse the collateral damage on the rural economy and society caused by colonial exploitation but continued to pursue the objective of higher growth, albeit tempered by concern for social justice through state-led planned development. Although many nationalist Governments in South Asia tried to undo the iniquitous agrarian structure introduced during the colonial period through land reforms, their efforts were largely thwarted by feudal and semi-feudal elements that became influential in national politics. Their role was further enhanced by the need to accelerate the rate of growth in the agriculture sector and to convert the marketable surplus of large farmers into exports to finance the industrial development programmes.

The role of the rural sector in the initial stages of development in most South Asian countries was seen largely as one of generating surpluses of physical (including human) and financial resources to step up the industrialization process, concentrated in a few urban centres, which was adopted as the chief means of promoting economic growth and development. But nationalist leaders in South Asia were cognizant of the need to eradicate widespread poverty in the rural areas and to undertake comprehensive plans for removing it. Pandit Nehru, the first Prime Minister of India, articulated this in one of his first speeches to the ruling Congress party soon after independence:

"Though poverty is widespread in India, it is essentially a rural problem, caused chiefly by overpressure on land and a lack of other wealth-producing occupations. India, under British rule, has been progressively ruralised, many of her avenues of work and employment closed, a vast mass of the population thrown on the land, which has undergone continuous fragmentation, till a large number of holdings have become uneconomic. It is essential, therefore, that the problem of land should be dealt with in all its aspects. Agriculture has to be improved on scientific lines and industry has to be established in its various forms ... so as not only to produce wealth but also to absorb people from the land ... Planning must lead to maximum employment, indeed to the employment of every able-bodied person".

The post-colonial regimes in South Asia – often with assistance from foreign aid agencies – launched ambitious programmes of rural development to rebuild the physical and institutional infrastructure in the countryside. However, these programmes often came to grief as a result of the multiple, often contradictory, goals they tried to achieve. The domestic and external policy milieu that emerged after the independence of these countries concentrated political and economic power in the hands of elites that were alienated from or had little empathy with the rural population. These factors contributed to an inordinate urban bias in the post-independence pattern of development and the consequent neglect of the rural sector.

The Post-independence Scenario

In the half century or so of independent existence, South Asian states have given varying degrees of attention and priority to rural development. Moreover, the motivations and objectives of public policies have varied over time and among countries owing to a complex combination of political, economic and social factors as well as opportunities for development provided by foreign assistance and global economic trends. Nevertheless, there have been some uniformities in the rural development policies of South Asian countries because of the similarities in their social and cultural milieu and a shared legacy of their colonial past which included institutions of governance and an agrarian structure suited to the needs of the colonial rulers.

The objectives of rural development followed and implemented by the various Governments have also been influenced by the overall plans for development and the performance of the economy in its global setting during this period. In particular, they have been conditioned by the international economic environment, especially for foreign assistance. Although rural development has been a priority area for external donors its importance has increased in the second half of the last 50 years as concerns about food security, the population explosion, environment and climatic changes, as well as poverty, equality and social justice have come to be increasingly perceived as being in the purview of global, rather than national policy agendas. Rural development stood at the cross-cutting path of these concerns. However, the multiplicity of the objectives which rural development was expected to achieve often deprived it of a central focus and often contributed to its failure.

The South Asian countries have, in recent years, tried to achieve some combination of the following major objectives, whose importance has differed both over time and among countries.

Raising Agricultural Productivity

This has been – and to a large extent continues to be – the primary objective of and the principal motivation for most rural development programmes, which were undertaken in the wake of rising population pressure on the land and the need for transferring resources for the pursuit of economic diversification. Before the advent of the green revolution in the 1960s most South Asian countries faced chronic food shortages, in some cases actual famine, and had to import substantial amounts of foodgrains, often financed from PL 480 imports from the United States of America and assistance from other countries.

It needs to be recognized that while raising agricultural productivity is an essential goal, it is a means for achieving larger development goals, such as increased welfare and the alleviation of poverty of the population. While increased agricultural productivity may ensure abundance of food availability for a given population, it may well not provide an adequate nutritional food intake for the majority of the population or, much more important, it may not provide sufficient access to those who need food, despite large surpluses of foodgrains. A striking example of this paradox is Brazil, which despite being one of the leading exporters (especially of soybeans and orange concentrate) is one of the most ill-fed nations in the world.

The paradox is no less evident in India, where as a result of the Government's successful drive to raise food production and stocks about 70 million tonnes of wheat and rice lie in Government godowns while over 200 million children, women and men remain chronically undernourished. Pregnant women are the worst affected, since maternal and foetal undernutrition results in the birth of children with low weight (less than 2.5 kg). Such children are handicapped at birth in mental development.

Also, as pointed out by Rao in the context of India, foodgrain security, though essential, cannot be equated with food security. The share of consumer expenditure on cereals now accounts for a little less than 40 per cent of total consumer expenditure on food in the country, the remaining 60 per cent being incurred on items such as edible oils, sugar, milk, eggs, meat, fish, vegetables and fruits. Even for the poor these non-foodgrain items account for as much as half the total expenditure on food but in order to bring the intake of these items to adequate levels their consumption by the poor has to increase at least threefold. The demand for these items of food will therefore rise at a high rate due to population growth as well as the rise in per capita income. The goal of food security, therefore, goes far beyond attaining self-sufficiency in foodgrains and should aim at attaining physical as well as economic access to a balanced food basket, especially for the poor. However, achieving economic access to non-foodgrain items would require a much stronger effort to raise the purchasing power of the poor than ensuring the necessary supplies.

There is an urgent need for diversification of South Asian agriculture from its current focus on foodgrain and cash crop production to the production of non-cereal products, which will also serve to raise employment and increase the purchasing power of the poor, to a considerable extent. This is because the potential for employment generation in dairying, horticulture, etc. is much greater than in cereals. These activities also have the potential for greater human resource development which would in turn result in higher wage rates and provide the necessary purchasing power for both foodgrains and non-foodgrain consumption of the poor.

The objective of raising agricultural productivity in the context of rural development programmes is often postulated without any reference to the agrarian structure prevailing in a country. However, there seems to be a persistent bias in such programmes towards the larger farmers. As pointed out by Banerjee, few historical phenomena share this remarkable tendency in the history of agrarian relations. "The state, it appears, has intervened always and everywhere in the markets for land, agricultural labour and other inputs into and outputs from agriculture to make life easier for larger farmers".

Such a bias could be defended as a means of achieving food security if it could be demonstrated that large farmers were in fact more efficient than small farmers. On the contrary, however, there exists a large body of evidence to show that small farms in developing countries, including South Asia, tend to be more productive than larger farms. The logic of the argument about the higher productivity of smaller farms is quite simple and is based on the higher costs of supervision of hired labour in larger farms and the relative scarcity of land in relation to the availability of family labour virtually at zero opportunity cost. The smaller farms are also able to grow additional crops and engage in subsidiary activities to supplement their incomes and for the survival of their family while the larger farms concentrate on only one major crop.

.Alleviating Poverty and Providing Employment Opportunities

At the beginning of the twenty-first century there is general agreement, at the global as well as national level, that poverty is unacceptable as part of the human condition. The global family has come to recognize that the coexistence of pervasive poverty, with the affluence of a much smaller segment of the population, is ethically unacceptable, economically inefficient and politically unsustainable. Most developing countries put poverty alleviation as their primary development goal, at least in their official plans and pronouncements.

The various global commitments to eradicate poverty have been endorsed, first at the World Summit for Social Development in Copenhagen in 1995 and then at the Millennium Summit in New York in June 2000, where the international community committed itself to halve extreme poverty by 2015. Such commitments to alleviate poverty are not new and have been reiterated in various forums for at least a quarter of a century, if not longer.

However, until recently, poverty alleviation was part of a broader agenda for development and viewed as a by-product of rapid growth. But now poverty has been prioritized as the primary objective of the global development agencies and many Governments. The international donor agencies, in particular, appear quite categorical in defining poverty reduction as the immediate priority of their various aid programmes.

The eradication of poverty, notwithstanding its prioritization in the global development agenda, however still remains a subsidiary concern of domestic development policy of most South Asian Governments whose focus is limited, at best, to alleviate poverty to a given target level.

For South Asia, which is home to about half of the 900 million poor people in Asia (with 450 million in India alone), along with high rates of unemployment, this is undoubtedly an overarching objective for rural development programmes, especially since the bulk of poverty is in the rural areas. However, until recently rural development programmes did not pay much direct attention to the task of poverty alleviation. Most of the programmes, which were statist in character and were run by the Government adopted a top down approach.

Table 2. Poverty in South Asia

	1990 Based on less than US $ 1 a day incidence (percentage)	US $1 a day Millions of poor	*Latest year* Based on less than US $1 a day incidence (percentage)	US $1 a day Millions of poor
Bangladesh	35.9 (1992)	—	29.1	37.9
India	52.5	438.4	44.2	442.9
Nepal	—	—	37.7	8.6
Pakistan	11.6	12.5	31	42.6
Sri Lanka	3.8	0.7	6.6	1.3

Source: ADB, Growth and Change in Asia and the Pacific (2001).

Promoting a Suitable Environment for the Rural Community

Among the most fundamental changes in the evolution of rural development programmes is the continuing debate about the need for a change in their ethos and the way the protagonists of these programmes (who are often outsiders) relate to their beneficiaries. Most of the earlier programmes were either paternalistic in nature or were run by self-serving bureaucrats who were often closely allied to elite groups. There are still very few programmes of rural development which live up to the motto of being of the poor, by the poor or for the poor. The induction of NGOs in poverty alleviation and rural development programmes has to some extent brought them closer to the ideal but the empowerment of the poor is still more rhetoric than reality in the South Asian context.

In order to empower rural communities, the rural development programmes along with the Governments and institutions of civil society need to focus on a number of interrelated areas, particularly on human capital development. Most South Asian countries are already committed to goals such as education or health for all, which should remain on every agenda. What is needed is not only the speeding up of the implementation of these goals, but also of moving beyond them in the direction of ensuring some affirmative action in favour of the poor. The priority should be to move towards substantially enhancing investment for the purpose of upgrading the quality and governance of rural schools and health care facilities to a level where the rural poor do not feel disadvantaged compared to the urban middle class.

Such a goal carries formidable implications as to costs and governance and may need some deployment of resources from non-priority projects. However, the resultant effect of such a process of quality enhancement efforts could enable the younger generation of poor households to compete on the basis of equality with the children of the elite for places in the universities and in employment. This would transform the competition between the children from poor and elite households into a more level playing field and would have "an empowering effect" on the poor to demand more rapid democratization of opportunities for human capacity development.

Management of the Rural Commons

A common critique of most rural development programmes is that they fail to cater to the needs of the more vulnerable groups such as women, the landless, minorities and other deprived groups of South Asia. To reach and include them requires a deeper understanding of poverty and its underlying causes; an emphasis on building critical human, social and physical assets; and more effective delivery of basic services. For example, despite improvements, access to education and health care remain, along with other social indicators, below desired levels, especially in rural areas and among women and female children. Such poor delivery of basic services works to limit progress in human development.

Besides rural-urban differences in the availability of services, the country averages also disguise variations based on caste and geography. In Nepal, for example, "untouchables" have a life expectancy of 45 years, 15 years less than upper-caste Brahmins. In India adult literacy rates among women of schedule tribes, most of whom live in rural areas, was 29 per cent compared to 39 per cent for all Indian women.

Country averages further mask the wide geographic diversity in these indicators within the country. In nutrition surveys by the National Nutrition Monitoring Bureau (NNMB) of rural areas in India, the percentage of children underweight in nine large Indian states varies from 50 per cent to almost 80 per cent and severely underweight from 15 per cent to 35 per cent. Recognizing the persistence of rural vs. urban, gender, caste or ethnic and geographic biases may help in the design and targeting of development programmes.

These imbalances can be reduced by interventions through rural development programmes that focus on increasing the access of the poor and vulnerable groups to essential services that are presently available only to the privileged and elite groups. In order to respond effectively to the needs of these vulnerable sections of the population, rural development programmes must have the following features:

(a) The adoption of decentralized, participatory and beneficiary-driven approaches designed to improve the delivery of such rural services as drinking water and rural sanitation, irrigation, extension, microcredit, education and health to the poorest sections of the population;

(b) Community management for the sustainable use of natural resources, such as joint forest management and watershed management programmes;

(c) Fiscal and administrative decentralization to local governments for enabling them to undertake the programmes identified above;

(d) Measures to improve governance and social inclusiveness of public sector institutions across income, gender and ethnic groups;

(e) Measures to reduce the vulnerability and risks faced by the rural poor and measures to help them recover from natural catastrophes such as floods, droughts and hurricanes (e.g. disaster and coastal management) and to improve the effectiveness of existing government safety nets.

These measures will require the combined efforts of the Government (at the national, subnational and local levels) as well as foreign and private donors and non-governmental organizations, including the rural support programmes.

Bridging the Rural-urban Gap

Rural-urban disparities have been an endemic problem of most developing countries and a major source of the continuing increase in their urban population. Although the main reason for the rural-urban population drift is the push of rural unemployment and underemployment, a contributing factor is also the lure of greater access to the amenities of life which is in inverse proportion to the distance from urban metropolitan centres.

The rural-urban divide is not a discrete attribute but is a continuum, ranging from the urban suburb or periphery to the most isolated or distant rural communities. Rural development programmes need to be fine-tuned to take account of the specificity of the problems that are faced by communities lying between the two ends of the rural-urban spectrum. At least four major divisions of this spread with their own distinctive rural strategies can be distinguished.

Peri-urban Areas

The main issues arising in the urban periphery are not dissimilar to those in urban squatter settlements: creation of jobs in industrial and service sectors in neighbouring urban centres, provision of adequate transport facilities and housing. Many of these areas have been reduced to dormitories of adult residents who commute daily on bicycles or animal-driven vehicles to the urban centre. To the extent there still exists some scope for farming in these areas, the rural development programmes can help promote micro-scale, high-value-added farming, such as vegetables and dairying which would provide fresh produce, create jobs and avoid pollution. There also exists considerable scope for rural industrialization in these areas which could take advantage of backward linkages with agriculture and forward linkages with urban industry. For this there will be need for credit and new credit institutions which could provide venture capital for the establishment of small-scale industries and services to enterprising individuals or groups.

Accessible Rural Areas with Good Natural Resources

These areas are good candidates for agricultural development with the help of market incentives and institutional development. They have potential for higher absorption of both labour and capital and of producing market surpluses. With investment in human development and technology, these areas could become highly productive and their products could compete in world markets. These areas could provide employment to people of other less well-endowed areas, especially during seasonal peaks.

Accessible Rural Areas with Poor Natural Resources

The possibilities of productive employment are likely to be low in these areas and migration may be the only alternative for most people. However, possibilities of livestock farming could be considerable and may provide opportunities for employment in dairying and related activities, along with handicrafts for women. The main handicap is likely to be access to water and capital investment in tubewells and small irrigation projects are likely to yield beneficial results, as land itself is unlikely to be scarce. Since these areas are not remote it may not be difficult to access services from Government and non-Government organizations engaged in rural development activities. In particular, they could receive the services of teachers and health workers for training people and providing basic education.

Remote or Isolated Rural Areas

These are the most difficult areas to deal with as the costs of construction of infrastruc-ture to reduce their remoteness are generally high. Nonetheless, measures to improve their productivity and incomes can be undertaken by subsidizing certain economic activi-ties such as poultry farming and livestock. They could also be assisted in launching public works programmes to help build the needed infrastructure. Some remote areas have the advantage of being yet unspoilt by excessive human habitation and still preserve their pristine beauty. They could become attractive destinations for eco-tourism. Inhabitants of the area could be encouraged to preserve and protect wildlife and biodiversity and to guard against poaching by illegal hunters and fortune seekers.

Disparities between Rural and Urban Areas

The disparity in the social indicators between rural and urban areas is widespread in South Asia. Literacy rates are less in rural than in urban areas and among women than in men. In Nepal, the rural literacy rate (33 per cent) in 1995/96 is more than 50 per cent lower than in urban areas. In India, the adult literacy rate in rural areas (54 per cent) in 1995/96 is significantly below that in urban areas (77 per cent), with rural female literacy rates (31 per cent) only about half of rural male literary rates. Even in Sri Lanka where literacy rates are higher than most other South Asian countries, it is estimated that only about 26 per cent of all primary students master basic literacy skills and only 18 per cent master basic numerical skills. Although infant and child mortality and malnutrition rates have improved considerably, the bias against rural areas means that other regions have made stronger progress in health. For example, in India the child mortality rate is 33 per thousand live births in rural areas compared to 17 per thousand in urban areas; while the malnutrition rate among children under three years old in rural areas is 50 per cent compared to 38 per cent for urban areas. A major objective of the rural development programmes should be to overcome the health services gap between urban and rural areas.

Enhancing the Role of Technology

Facing the increasing scarcity of arable land, South Asia must apply technological innovations to improve efficiency and sustain productivity growth. If the region's population nearly doubles, as projected from 1.4 billion in 2000 to 2.2 billion in 2045, the challenge of keeping agricultural growth rates at par with population growth will require putting available technology to better use and, through energetic research, developing new and more efficient growing methods. The average rate of agricultural growth per annum during the period 1990-98 was 1.5 per cent in Sri Lanka, about 2 per cent in Nepal and Bangladesh, 3.8 per cent in India and 4.5 per cent in Pakistan. This pace is particularly worrying as there are indications that the rate of growth of total factor productivity, despite considerable potential, is slowing down in many areas. In Pakistan, for example, it is estimated that large, existing productivity gaps in major crops indicate an opportunity to boost productivity by as much as 30-40 per cent over the short to medium term. This projection is based on wider diffusion of available, improved crop production technologies, more efficient use of land, water, and other inputs and better post-harvest handling of produce. Other South Asian countries can score similar advances.

While the benefits of the green revolution are generally recognized to be scale-neutral and did benefit the poor in South Asia to a considerable extent, the gains from technological innovation remain unequally distributed between those with access to land, water and inputs, and those without. There is broad consensus that the main causes of rural poverty lie in low rates of agricultural growth and factor productivity and that the key to raising productivity in agriculture lies largely in measures to broaden access to land and complementary inputs, along with a more favourable policy environment towards agriculture.

More equitable distribution of operational land holdings would create more equitable patterns of demand, which in turn would enhance growth in the rural non-farm sector and remove some of the biases in credit, marketing and research institutions that arise from the unequal distribution of assets and power. This is supported by recent evidence which suggests that countries with a more equal land distribution experience higher rates of economic growth.

The knowledge and information revolution is now being brought within the reach of the remotest areas by advances in telecommunications and information technology and needs to be harnessed not only for the rural elite but also for the rural poor. Formidable opportunities are being opened up in the area of distance learning and medicare, for urban standards of education, medical diagnosis and prescription to be delivered to the most remote villages. Here major investments to build the infrastructure to take the IT revolution to the villages, remains an important goal of public and global development policy. It also provides an opportunity for collaborative arrangements between the public and private sectors, as well as the NGOs. The example of *Grameenphone* in Bangladesh enabling poor, rural women to be brought into the communications revolution, as both providers as well as users of IT services, needs to be emulated elsewhere in South Asia.

A Survey of Rural Development Programmes

In the following paragraphs a survey of past and current rural development programmes in South Asia, focusing on the extent to which they have fulfilled the above objectives, is presented.

The survey attempts to highlight the successes and limitations of these programmes and the contextual conditions which accounted for their success or otherwise and the extent to which they made efficient use of available human resources, especially women, and paid full attention to the development of human resources. In a separate section the extent to which programmes can be replicated more widely both within a country as well as within other South Asian countries and how the regional countries can benefit from an exchange of experience on the overall strategy, as well as the design and implementation of various rural development programmes is examined.

The survey tries to capture the main characteristics of the rural development programmes as they have evolved during the last five decades. Information on all seven of the South Asian countries for all the parameters and time periods is not easily available. In particular, information on two of the smaller countries, Bhutan and the Maldives is sparse. In the following, we discuss the evolution of the various rural development initiatives in the five larger South Asian countries.

It is difficult to categorize the various rural development initiatives (RDI) undertaken in the South Asian region over the last half century as they have differed in terms of their approaches, objectives, motivating impulses, impacts, *modus operandi* and several other parameters. Although most rural development initiatives have emerged from a national development strategy adopted by each country at different phases of its development, each country has acquired a certain degree of autonomy nationally as well as a certain degree of uniformity over the region because of interaction with foreign donors along with global and regional think tanks and action programmes.

Although it is difficult to neatly separate rural development in South Asia chronologically, two broad periods in the evolution of two distinct paradigms of rural development can be identified: the first from 1950-1975 and the second from 1985 to the present. While the first generation programmes had a definite focus on community development, the second generation programmes have a more diverse agenda, such as the empowerment of the poor, especially women and other vulnerable groups, the protection of the environment and natural resources and enhancement of the capabilities of the poor through greater access to education, health and credit, which have been monopolized by the rich.

The decade intervening between the two broad periods can be considered to be a period of flux during which the new paradigm – though never unambiguously defined or discernible – was taking shape. It was partly built on the organizational structure and formal methodology of the projects inherited from the first period/paradigm and partly on the basis of the lessons learnt from the latter's failures. The inadequacies and failures of the first generation rural development programmes or RDPs helped not only formulate the ideas and the agendas for the new generation of RDPs but also helped provide experienced cadres who became the leaders and activists of the next generation of RDPs.

Evolution of Rural Development Programmes: 1950-1975

Concern for the poor and the pitiably neglected conditions of the countryside had often aroused benevolent and public-spirited civil servants, affluent individuals and social workers even in the pre-independence days to launch schemes which would bring about a rural renaissance. These consisted of attempts to improve not only the economic well-being, but also the socio-economic conditions, including agriculture, education, health and sanitation, as well as the enrichment of their culture. But these efforts, though well-intentioned and often beneficial, were generally sporadic and did not have a lasting impact, although they continue to be reincarnated (or recycled, to use a more modern metaphor) in various ways. Others, such as F. L. Brayne, promoted the idea of self-help and model villages, where villagers were urged to expend their time and labour, without remuneration, for improving rural life. These nascent ideas of rural development did not crystallize into structured programmes for extensive application until they were backed with the needed resources and official support. In the first quarter century after independence, the focus of these programmes, which were generally administered by a centralized bureaucracy, with some degree of local participation, was put on community development and its variants. Among these, the most prominent were:

1. Community development programmes
2. Integrated rural development programmes
2. Infrastructure development programmes

Community Development Programmes

After achieving independence, the national Governments in South Asia found it necessary to launch more systematic rural development programmes, for the benefit of their rural constituencies, often with substantial foreign assistance from Governments eager to woo them in the emerging race of post-World War II economic diplomacy, with the cold war playing its due share. The success of the communist-led peasant revolution in China just over two years after the independence of India and Pakistan led the western Governments to see rural development programmes as an effective way of combating the communist danger in South Asia. The peasants' struggle in South India and Bengal was also seen as posing a threat to both the Indian and Pakistani Governments. The United States Government and private foundations, such as the Ford Foundation, sponsored the idea of village level rural development which was embraced enthusiastically by both India and Pakistan.

The community development programmes were largely concentrated in the three major countries of the Indian subcontinent. Other countries, including Nepal and Sri Lanka, were preoccupied with other nation-building activities and major infrastructure projects to pay much attention to rural development activities during the 1950s and 1960s. In Nepal, for instance, it was not until the Fifth Plan in 1975 that "physical infrastructure was de-emphasized for the first time, with the agricultural and social sectors receiving the first and second priority". Similarly, in Sri Lanka, the major funding in development plans was allocated to such capital-intensive projects as the Mahaveli river basin project, the Million Houses programme and the free trade zone development programme. Rural development programmes served the role of "consolation prizes" and were located in areas not served by these mega projects.

India

India inherited a rich legacy of experimentation with rural development programmes, which drew inspiration not only from the Gandhian vision of a rural commune, but also from various philanthropic and missionary movements from the United States and the United Kingdom of Great Britain and Northern Ireland, as well as the late colonialist attempts to revive the stagnating Indian agriculture by drawing on the lessons of various foreign experiments, such as the Raifeissen rural credit schemes in Germany and the agricultural extension services of the United States. However, it was Nehru's statist and centralized planning policies which not only established the community as a 'site for the privileged agency of the rural poor', but also provided the full backing (including domestic and foreign funding) of the Community Development Programmes (CDP), which were launched in 1952 on the fourth anniversary of Gandhi's death, partly in deference to the Gandhian vision, which was considerably at variance with the modernist aims of these programmes.

The Community Development Programme encountered a number of problems in its implementation, not the least of which was the proper definition of a community and the degree of its social inclusiveness. There was a reluctance not to get bogged down in the argument about what is or is not a community. However, the ideal of spreading the benefits of the programme even-handedly to all members of the community conflicted with the social reality of a caste- and class-ridden society in which the poor had very little say and were bound to be discriminated against. The bureaucratic solution was to define the programme unit in technical terms. A 'project unit' of the programme included approximately 300 villages, covering about 500 square miles and a population of about 200,000 people. Each unit was divided into three blocks each containing 100 villages. These villages were further split into 'development blocks' of five villages, each served by a village level worker (VLW).

The CDP projects aimed explicitly to increase access to education, health, housing and social welfare as a means of institutionalizing the legitimacy and acceptance of the developmental state in the rural areas, but the most pressing objective of the programme was to increase agricultural production. To that end project units were located near irrigation facilities or in areas of assured rainfall. The multiplicity of the goals in the Programme, however, often led to their adverse selection of projects in terms of poverty alleviation. In all, the Programme had identified as many as 41 objectives to be achieved at the village level, but less than 1 per cent of the villages covered more than 25 of these. The main focus was on the adoption of improved agricultural practices, which had been undertaken in 95 per cent of the villages.

Cottage industries, which were the main vehicle of employment and income generation for the poor, were undertaken in only 17.5 per cent of the project villages.

All of the "social development" projects stayed at the bottom of the ranking in terms of coverage, as did co-operatives and primary education and adult literacy programmes. The distribution of benefits of the CD projects was also skewed, favouring those who were located in villages where the VLW could be easily influenced and manipulated by village elites who captured most of the benefits.

The orientation of the CD programmes gradually moved further away from a multi-faceted programme touching all aspects of rural life to one focused on increasing agricultural production. The CD projects had in effect become agencies for providing agricultural extension services and their main objective was redefined as "achieving the targets of agricultural production, on the basis of the widest possible participation by local communities". This change in emphasis led to a reorganization of the CD programme in which the number of VLWs was halved and the number of villages under their charge doubled, while the funding of the programme was greatly reduced because of budgetary constraints. These measures further eroded the programme's ability to address the problems of poverty and social development and increased the leakage of its benefits to rich farmers.

Bangladesh and Pakistan

The centrepiece of community development in Pakistan (which then included areas that are now in Bangladesh), the Village-Aid Programme, lasted for a decade (1952-1961). The programme reached its zenith during the period from October 1955 to October 1958, becoming the showpiece of Pakistan's rural development efforts. The success of the programme, however, provoked jealousy and sometimes outright hostility from two major sections of the bureaucracy, viz. the local administration, traditionally the source of all power and prestige in rural areas and the line departments which were called upon to collaborate with the programme. While the former disdained the programme's underlying democratic ethos, the latter were apprehensive of its challenge to their turf, authority and even existence.

After the take-over by the first military regime in 1958 and the establishment of basic democracies at the village level, the Programme lost favour with the Government and lost its political utility for the new regime. As a result, the Village Aid programme was wound up in 1961 and many of its functions were assigned to the Agricultural Development Corporation, which itself was dissolved a decade later.

The Village Aid Programme was by far the most extensive rural development programme undertaken in Pakistan. It cost approximately US$ 100 million, the bulk of which was spent on projects in the then East Pakistan (now Bangladesh) and the remainder was allocated to the central Government and West Pakistan. Among the more impressive achievements of the Village Aid Programme was its extensive coverage. The Programme covered 176 development areas covering a total of 24.64 million people. The Programme's physical achievements included the laying out of 150,000 agricultural demonstration blocks, digging of 1000 miles of canals, construction of 3000 miles of unmetalled roads and repair of 4000 miles of old roads. The Programme also assisted in the adaptation of improved farm practices in the development areas. The village communities contributed Rs. 12 million, or about 6 per cent of total expenditure, for social sector development through self-help activities.

Integrated Rural Development Programmes (IRDP)

A major critique of the community development programmes in South Asia was their inability to address the problems of those without land or those with small farms which were incapable of producing marketable surpluses.

The community development programmes were designed mainly to improve the efficiency in agriculture and therefore focused on larger and middle farmers. The de facto exclusion of the landless and marginal farmers from the ambit of benefits of the land-centred community development programmes gave rise to the need for programmes which would engage in a multiplicity of activities which affected the poor.

The point of departure of IRDPs was the recognition that with declining access to the land the rural poor derived a decreasing portion of their incomes from working on the farm which needed to be made up from other activities. It was, therefore, essential to develop programmes which would result in the creation of non-farm activities and provide some opportunities for non-agricultural employment. Unlike community development programmes, IRDPs were not based on the assumed commonality of interest of the entire community, but were based on a pragmatic assessment of the needs of poor households in various situations.

IRDPs were largely a response to the failure of the trickle down theory of development and the productivity-oriented community development programmes which failed to reduce – and often exacerbated – rural poverty. While the detailed specifications of IRDPs in different countries have differed a great deal, they have relied on three common elements:

(a) Some form of local participation in the identification of the needs of the people and even in the planning of the projects to fulfil them;

(b) A multisectoral delivery system, including agricultural infrastructure and inputs, and access to credit, health, education and other social services;

(c) An organizational mechanism ensuring the delivery of the services to the needy households.

Almost all countries of the region experimented with the IRDP model with varying degree of success. In most countries the programmes have been run by the same centralized bureaucratic structure, such as the ministries of rural development and local self-government, that supervised the community development programmes earlier. The required changes in style and attitudes, however, did not match the vocabulary and the jargon associated with the new programme. However, there were some successful models of IRDP, such as the Comilla model established by its legendary pioneer, the late Akhtar Hameed Khan in East Pakistan in the 1960s, which became a basis for a number of similar innovative experiments in South Asia, especially in Bangladesh and Pakistan.

Infrastructure Development Programmes

Among the most prominent issues in the rural development programmes of the first quarter century of independence of most South Asian states was the development of rural infrastructure. It was considered as a prerequisite for accelerated economic development in the rural areas, especially of agriculture. In most South Asian countries, infrastructural facilities were generally weak and inadequate at the time of independence. Since independence, although there has been considerable improvement in the availability of basic infrastructural services in the rural areas, such as roads, irrigation, electricity, transport and communications, many people, especially the rural poor and those living in underdeveloped areas, do not have access to even minimal infrastructure services.

India

Inadequate development of infrastructure, forward and backward linkages and market facilities has been another area of concern under IRDP. In an attempt to fill critical infrastructural gaps and strengthen linkages and marketing facilities, the allocation under IRDP for the development of programme infrastructure was increased from 10 to 20 per cent in all states, and to 25 per cent in the north-eastern states.

In its initial years, IRDP was implemented along similar lines as the Marginal Farmers and Agricultural Labourers Agency, under which enhanced productivity of small and marginal farmers was sought through crop loans for the promotion of high yielding varities (HYV), multiple cropping, horticulture, soil conservation, land development, minor irrigation, use of improved seeds; it was instrumental in spreading new technology in agriculture to small and marginal farms through the provision of credit at subsidized rates.

The major achievement of IRDP was the promotion of on-farm activities in the animal husbandry sector, such as dairy, poultry, fisheries, etc. for the benefit of small and marginal farmers. Land assets being limited, provision of non-land assets to the poor was an alternative way of achieving income generation. Given their labour-intensive and land-saving nature, the poorer households were better suited for those activities.

The growth of the dairy sector during the 1980s was much helped by Operation Flood Project, an integrated dairy development programme started in 1970. Wherever dairy projects were promoted under IRDP along milk routes, small and marginal farmers making use of infrastructural facilities were able to bring about a sustained increase in their income levels.

Recognizing the importance of rural roads to rural development India's Fifth Five-year Plan included them as a part of the Minimum Needs Programme (MNP). The Programme envisaged the connection, via all-weather roads, of those villages with a population of 1500 and above. In hilly, tribal, desert and coastal areas, the objective was to connect a cluster of villages of matching populations. India has about 600,000 villages of various population sizes. The improvement of the economic conditions among the rural population, a high percentage of which is below the poverty line, hinges crucially on the provision of accessibility by means of such roads. In addition, the construction of rural roads is highly labour-intensive, generating gainful employment for millions of unemployed and underemployed rural people.

Pakistan and Bangladesh (1962-1972)

After the disbandment of the Village Aid programme, the Rural Works Programme was initiated in Pakistan with its primary focus on East Pakistan. It was initially started in Comilla as a small project but culminated as a major experiment in rural development under the charismatic leadership of the late Akhtar Hameed Khan. The choice of Comilla was particularly appropriate for undertaking self help projects of rural infrastructure, such as the construction of protective walls and tube wells, since Comilla was subject to flooding in summer and water shortage in winter, allowing the growing of only one crop which was inadequate for subsistence. The close association of the rural community with the staff of the Comilla Academy also provided the opportunity for mutually beneficial interaction between the staff of the Academy and the local farmers.

On the basis of the highly successful Comilla experiment, the Rural Works Programme was extended to West Pakistan from 1963 to 1984. From 1963 to 1968, the Programme enjoyed the support of the President, but thereafter it suffered from the change in leadership and other adverse political developments. The Programme was organized under the auspices of the central Ministry of Finance and Planning, with each provincial government being responsible for project organization and execution. The Programme was directed to undertake labour-intensive projects, create and improve rural infrastructure and mobilize local resources, manpower and leadership. It was nowhere as successful as Comilla.

Although the Rural Works Programme in the then West Pakistan was much less successful than in East Pakistan, as both its conceptualization and implementation were highly flawed, it made an impressive contribution to the development of local infrastructure. About 60,000 projects at an average cost of Rs. 5,700 each were constructed with the communication sector receiving the largest share of about 38 per cent, education 21 per cent and health and sanitation 16 per cent. About 700 miles of metalled roads were constructed, 2000 miles of roads repaired and 6000 miles of unmetalled roads were constructed under the Programme. Roads under the Programme were constructed at approximately half the cost of standard highways. The provision of *mandi* (market) to village road was made for 92 per cent of the wheat crop and 23 per cent of the cotton crop. However, lack of planning created a paucity of funds for repair. Mobilization of local resources was not adequate and measures to levy taxes in times of economic prosperity were not undertaken.

The Rural Works Programme was, however, largely motivated by political considerations. It provided legitimacy to the military government of Ayub Khan by giving the impression of reducing interregional disparities between East and West Pakistan, through somewhat larger expenditures in East Pakistan. On the other hand, its programmes in West Pakistan were biased in favour of elements providing political support to the regime. The strong emphasis on road construction through capital-intensive methods apparently benefited large farmers producing a marketable surplus and led to a further increase in the inequality of rural income.

Despite these limitations, the Rural Works Programme did succeed in opening up vast areas of rural Pakistan to larger markets and linked the villages directly with the mainstream of development activity. It also opened up opportunities for the rural poor to seek employment in neighbouring urban industrial centres. It also helped in the raising of social consciousness and the spirit of self-help among rural communities and in promoting a more egalitarian social structure. The latter was done through the formation of local level committees that encouraged popular participation and fostered confidence among the people in the successful completion of the project.

Peoples Works Programme

Pakistan: (1972-1983)

With the separation of East Pakistan and the coming into power of the Pakistan Peoples Party (PPP) in West Pakistan, the role of the Rural Works Programme had to be transformed to take into account the changed political situation. However, in terms of formal structure, there was very little change except that the Programme was renamed the Peoples Works Programme and placed under the Federal Ministry of Finance and Planning.

The projects under the Peoples Works Programme covered road construction, school buildings, small irrigation dams, drinking water facilities, dispensaries, industrial schools for women, tree planting, adult education centres and cottage industries, etc. The emphasis was on the provision of physical infrastructure without organizing an appropriate machinery for their proper utilization through the active participation of the community. The hardware/software linkage was again missing as in the case of the Rural Works and Village-Aid programmes. The story of tube wells without electricity, schools without teachers and dispensaries without staff and medicines was repeated all over again.

As a result, the Programme was riddled with irregularities in the choice of projects, determination of priorities and locations by politically influential people with little regard for the needs of the community, overwhelming reliance on contractors rather than on project committees, and preference for large projects as well as widespread corruption and misuse of public funds. The impact of the People Works Programme on the alleviation of poverty and in addressing the problems of the poor were, as in the previous rural development programmes, minimal. As in the previous cases, the thrust of the Programme was least on projects such as the development of land, irrigation facilities, veterinary facilities, which would have benefited the small farmers and the landless.

New Generation of Rural Development Programmes

The Decline of the Old and the Rise of the New RDPs

Public policy enthusiasm for rural development programmes began to wane towards the end of the 1960s as planners became enamoured with the green revolution, which combined irrigation, pesticides and high-yielding hybrid wheat and rice seeds. Plans concentrated on extending the green revolution by investing in sites of intensive cultivation where well-endowed landowners controlled local labour, finance, and political institutions. The green revolution had both ardent supporters and strong critics. The latter called this strategy "betting on the rich", while supporters considered it the foundation of national food security.

During the 1970s, state planning began to lose its grip on development and contributed to the decline in state support for rural development programmes. Policy makers in Pakistan, Sri Lanka, Bangladesh and Nepal were first to shift priorities away from national autonomy as they sought to meet demands from urban middle classes and rural landowners by using massive external assistance for large development projects, such as the Mahaveli scheme in Sri Lanka and the Tarbela dam in Pakistan, one of the largest irrigation projects in the world.

By the mid-1980s most Governments in South Asia, faced increasing domestic and external debts as a consequence of the impact of misguided domestic economic policies and external economic shocks experienced in earlier years. The strategies of capital-intensive, import substituting industrialization adopted in the 1960s could no longer be pursued owing to the fall in the flows of official development assistance and increase in high interest-bearing commercial loans.

The deteriorating macroeconomic management arising from the increasing burden of subsidies for energy, irrigation, fertilizer and food, reduced the delivery of essential rural services and maintenance of existing rural infra-structure. Many governments were forced to undertake serious adjustments in their fiscal, monetary and trade policy approaches. These adjustments, often under the pressure and prodding from lenders and the international financial institutions, were undertaken in the hope of halting the flagging growth rates of the region's economies.

The changes in these policies were also prompted by the success of export-oriented East and South-East Asian economies in achieving high rates of economic growth. At the same time, the emergence of the Washington Consensus, forced South Asian countries to give up many of the interventionist programmes of development initiated in the 1960s as a result of the need to adjust their macroeconomic balances. The introduction of structural adjustment reforms in general increased the incidence of poverty, without having any significantly beneficial effect on the rates of economic growth.

These domestic and international developments impacted on rural development programmes in several ways. While the fiscal requirements for development programmes to eliminate rural poverty in each of the South Asia countries are enormous, the resources available for them diminished as a result of structural adjustment. This made improvements in the already weak social and human development indicators in the countries of the region even more difficult. Furthermore, since the main vehicle for the reduction in poverty – economic growth – itself suffered a setback in most countries during this period, there was a need to devise programmes which would specially address concerns relating to poverty and social development.

From State-led to Community-led Rural Development Programmes

The Genesis of the New Programmes

In the wake of the disenchantment with the state-led rural development programmes discussed earlier, there was a quest for alternative paradigms of rural development in the 1980s. It was becoming obvious that in order to be really effective, these programmes had to find out what the needs of the rural poor were in different localities. This could not be done by officials sitting in the federal or provincial capitals and making an occasional tour of selected rural areas and having pre-orchestrated meetings with villagers, which were often dominated by local influentials who claimed to represent the whole community. It required a high degree of commitment to understand the problems and identify the needs of the people in a particular area, not to speak of mobilizing them around a particular problem.

Fortunately, in South Asia, there has been no dearth of people, mainly from the educated middle classes, to come forward and live with and learn from the rural poor and give them hope for improving their lot. Indeed, they often joined hands with them in their struggles against the local and foreign rulers and powerful economic interests, such as landlords, intermediaries and money lenders. Nationalist leaders such as Gandhi, A.K. Fazlul Haq and Ghaffar Khan began their careers by spending a considerable part of their lives doing social work in rural areas and in organizing the rural poor.

In the first quarter century of independence many highly motivated individuals, inspired by and believing in the vision of their national leaders to build a prosperous and equitable society, chose to join the civil service, which gave them a chance to serve the people. However, many of them were disappointed by the snatch and grab politics in South Asia which betrayed the pledges of the founding fathers of their nations. Some of them later spearheaded the newly emerging NGO movement in South Asia, which took up the cause of the poor and deprived in rural as well as urban areas.

Many of the new initiatives in rural development in the post-1980 period were undertaken by similar individuals or groups who perceived the opportunity of mobilizing the poor and marginal households to engage in programmes largely through their own efforts, with the catalytic help of well-conceived and persistent efforts of outsiders, whether individual experts or social mobilizers, government agencies, universities, NGOs or donor agencies. Generally, these programmes were started on a relatively modest scale in a small locality or village, but were later expanded to cover larger geographical units, often to the entire country and in some cases were replicated in other countries, with help and assistance from the originating unit.

The Prototype of the New Programmes

Prominent among these programmes are the Grameen Bank and BRAC in Bangladesh, Aga Khan Rural Support Program (AKRSP) and National Rural Support Programme (NRSP) in Pakistan, Amul Dairy, Self-employed Women's Association (SEWA) and the Participatory Watershed Movement in (Rajasthan) India, Thrift and Credit Cooperative Societies (SANASA) and Gal Oya Irrigation Project in Sri Lanka. Nepal, Bhutan and Maldives have also replicated some of these programmes. A major problem with such programmes has often been their replication and upscaling. The dilemma is that by themselves they have little impact and if replicated indiscriminately their effect can be significantly diluted and distort the original objectives of the programme. In many cases, the core message of such programmes has often been incorporated in Government-sponsored programmes and policies.

The distinguishing common features of these new generation programmes which set them apart from the earlier programmes are:

(a) Their participatory approach;

(b) Social mobilization;

(c) The initial project area is unpromising in terms of location, economic opportunities and has a high incidence of poverty;

(d) Minimal role of foreign assistance;

(e) Galvanizing role of the initiator/charismatic leader needs to be supplemented by a process of institution-building;

(f) A remarkable ability and desire to diversify activities, initially sectoral or parochial, become more encompassing.

An important reason for the success of these programmes is the identification and choice of their thematic content, which pertains to a specific household or social need, which was not adequately addressed in the previous RDPs. Thus, for example, Grameen Bank was based on the need for providing microcredit to the rural poor, especially women, as a means of emancipating rural women and liberating their households from poverty. BRAC's focus was on providing education and training in the rural areas. AKRSP focused on rural infrastructure in the remote hilly areas of Northern Pakistan. Amul was set up to solve the marketing problems of small livestock owners in Bombay. SEWA responded to the needs of self-employed women in Ahmedabad and neighbouring areas. The Rajasthan Watershed Movement in India and the Gal Oya irrigation project in Sri Lanka responded to the needs of small farmers in rain-fed areas whereas the first generation rural development projects had concentrated on irrigated areas of South Asia which were the main beneficiaries of the green revolution.

While most of the new generation rural development programmes have been launched by NGOs, there has also been a change in the focus of Government-led programmes. Realizing the need for providing employment and credit to the vulnerable groups in rural areas, two new genres of Government-led rural development programmes, viz. public works and microcredit programmes, have been launched in recent years. A brief discussion of these programmes is provided below. Both programmes were aimed at increasing the income and employment of the poor – the first focused on wage employment and the second on providing avenues for self-employment.

Rural Public Works Programmes

In recent years, public works programmes have been used to provide wage employment opportunities for the poor. These programmes have been used to deal with situations (such as famine and drought) marked by widespread but transitory unemployment in rural areas. South Asian countries with large populations, high rates of unemployment and poverty, such as India, Bangladesh and Pakistan, have included employment creation through rural public works (RPWs) at the core of their anti-poverty strategy. RPWs also play a significant role in reducing the poverty of the landless who are forced to rely on agricultural employment with long seasonal spells of inactivity. In contrast to other anti-poverty interventions whose benefits are often captured by the non-poor, RPWs have the advantage of being self-targeting since they usually involve hard physical labour. A more relevant rationale for RPWs can be found in the fact that they may be effective in equalizing geographical disparity by creating infrastructural assets in the particularly disadvantaged areas (if one of the reasons for poverty is lack of access to these).

RPWs have become important in alleviating poverty in a number of South Asian countries, though none are as significant as in India. The size of their programmes is rarely as large as that of the major programmes in India, such as the Employment Guarantee Scheme (EGS) in Maharashtra, and its somewhat diluted version at the national level, the Employment Assurance Scheme (ESA).

In Bangladesh, the national Food For Work (FFW) programme is designed to provide rural labourers with slack season employment and income. The programme provided 105 million days of work (earthworks, roads, canals, etc.) in 1988-89. Over half the workers were reportedly landless and only 2 per cent had more than 2.8 ha of land, which suggests good targeting, in part because of low wage rates. Despite some diversion from other work, direct transfer benefits for the workers were substantial (7-8 per cent of total annual income). It has been argued that if there had been an effective RPW programme during the 1974 famine in Bangladesh, a great many people could have been saved from starvation and impoverishment; and that the FFW programme of 1988 helped Bangladesh avoid another famine.

Unlike in other countries, public works programmes in Pakistan have failed to smooth consumption in periods of high unemployment, in part due to their capture by patronage politics. Examples of such programmes are the Rural Works Programme (1962-1972), and the Peoples Works Programmes (1972-1983) discussed earlier. In this context it is encouraging that the Government's recent Khushal Pakistan Programme incorporates active community participation in programme selection. Funds are allocated under the Programme to the districts through provincial governments, the schemes under the Programme are identified and selected at the district level through active community participation, and the projects are managed and implemented in partnership with the communities.

While systematic evaluations of the recently-launched Khushal Programme are not yet available, the programme needs some basic changes in its design and implementation in order for it to attain its poverty alleviation objectives. These include ensuring targeting efficiency, maximizing employment and stabilization benefits, and creating community infrastructure beneficial to the poor.

Microcredit Programmes

Access to credit by the poor in South Asia has been recognized as one of the main causes of rural poverty. Since formal credit institutions require tangible assets, such as land, as collateral for receiving loans, the only access to credit for the poor is the informal sector, which consists of generous relatives, friends and usurious money-lenders and avaricious landlords. To augment the supply of loanable funds at affordable rates to the poor, group-based lending programmes have recently become popular in South Asia and have taken a quantum leap since the success of the Grameen Bank in Bangladesh. These programmes seek to provide credit and other services to poor people who lack access to formal credit institutions.

In the context of rural development, their role has been mainly to alleviate poverty at the household level, rather than the development of community infrastructure or to improve access to public services. Microcredit programmes typically enable the poor to acquire income-generating assets by providing access to credit, marketing and other inputs. Many rural development programmes have tried to dovetail microcredit programmes with their other activities as an incentive to members of the village community to participate in collective programmes for rural development. Most microcredit programmes also require the borrowers to deposit a small sum of money regularly in order to become eligible for a loan.

Bangladesh, which inspired the microcredit revolution in South Asia, established the Grameen Bank in 1983 under the pioneering leadership of Dr. M. Yunus, has two other microcredit programmes: the Bangladesh Rural Advancement Committee (BRAC), and the Bangladesh Rural Development Board's Rural Development Programme, which engage in a variety of other developmental activities. A United Nations study (UNDP/UNOPS/APDC

1996) on the outreach of 39 microfinance institutions/programmes in 12 countries of Asia found that they covered a total of 5.1 million households. Of this, about 4.5 million households were in Bangladesh and only 0.6 million households in the rest of the region. However, most other countries in South Asia are also emulating the example of Bangladesh.

The area where microcredit has made the greatest impact in rural Bangladesh is on the empowerment of women. Through the provision of credit and income generating programmes many poor women have improved their economic situation and in several cases taken on work traditionally regarded as men's work. Earlier, even poor women were not supposed to appear in public and talk to male persons outside their immediate family. Now it is not uncommon to see women as owners of small restaurants established with microcredit loans. Other examples include BRAC's training programme for women to become chicken vaccinators.

In Pakistan, microfinance offers considerable promise, yet at present, the existing programmes are unable to cover a majority of the poor. Less than 5 per cent of the credit needs of the rural poor are estimated to be met by microcredit programmes. The main impetus to microfinance has so far come from NGOs, primarily the rural support programmes. In view of the heightened demand for microcredit in poor communities, the Government and donors have realized the need for ensuring the supply of sufficient funds on a sustainable and institutionalized basis.

To channel the funds, two major on-lending institutions have been set up, distanced from the official bureaucracy through the involvement of NGOs and the private sector. The first, a microfinance bank called Khushali Bank, has already been established under the joint ownership of three public sector, 11 private sector and two international banks and with the structural integration and partnership of the National Rural Support Programme (NRSP), the largest NGO in Pakistan with extensive experience in social mobilization as well as microfinance.

The second umbrella institution, created with funding from the World Bank, the Pakistan Poverty Alleviation Fund (PPAF), has adopted the method of wholesaling credit through selected NGOs. Both institutions will deliver services through NGOs using their core competency in social mobilization.

For the long-term sustainability of microcredit, as well as to create conditions conducive to scaling up these programmes, links between such institutions and formal markets must be strengthened. In keeping with this objective, the State Bank of Pakistan (SBP) has envisaged licensing three categories of microcredit institutions at the national, provincial and district levels as public or private limited companies. As an integral part of microfinance structure, two funds, namely the microfinance Social Development Fund and the Community Infrastructure Fund, have been created to ensure sustained and assured investment in building social capital and community infrastructure development. Support will be provided for community organizations, skill development and enhanced access of the poor, especially women, to enable them to fully utilize microfinance services.

In India institutional credit has been the major source for providing access to small and marginal farmers and other weaker sections to enable them to adopt modern technology and improved agricultural practices. Loans are disbursed through a multi-agency network comprising commercial banks, regional rural banks and cooperatives. Although there has been an overall increase in agricultural credit, there remains a grave problem concerning overdue payments that have inhibited credit expansion and the economic viability of lending institutions, especially cooperatives and rural banks.

The National Bank for Agriculture and Rural Development (NABARD) in India pioneered the concept of the Self-Help Group (SHG) Bank Linkage Programme way back in 1992 with active policy support from the Reserve Bank of India. Over 30,000 SHGs covering about 0.5 million rural households have been linked with the banking system in different parts of the country. The programme is doing well with almost 100 per cent repayment of loans by SHGs to the banks.

Normally, a self-help group (SHG) gets established in response to a perceived need, besides being centred around specific productive activities. SHGs provide the peer pressure needed in order to ensure that credit is utilized for the purpose for which it was taken and is repaid according to schedule. The repayment performance of members of such groups has been found to be overwhelmingly satisfactory, at around 95 per cent, compared with roughly 50 per cent in the case of normal bank lending. Apart from helping to improve levels of income and savings, SHGs have also been able to bring about positive improvement in a number of social indicators such as literacy and health.

The main advantage to banks of their link with SHGs and voluntary organizations (VOs) is the externalization of a part of the work items of the credit cycle, viz., assessment of credit needs, appraisal, disbursal, supervision and repayment, reduction in the formal paper work involved and a consequent reduction in the transaction cost. Improvement in recoveries will lead to a wider coverage. VOs have a role in organizing the rural poor into SHGs and in ensuring their proper functioning. So far, in the Indian context, most VOs have concentrated their activities in the areas of education and health, and to some extent, with other general development activities. Their role in providing an effective link between organized credit-disbursing agencies and those which have the need and are eligible to obtain credit from such institutions has been minimal.

The microcredit programmes in South Asia have fulfilled a crying need of the rural poor and have restored their self-confidence. An organization such as Grameen Bank has accumulated Tk. 10 billion (about $187 million) in savings from its 2.3 million members. All these savings remain on deposit with Grameen Bank and are used for further lending to its members. Savings mobilized by other NGOs such as BRAC, Association for Social Advancement (ASA), *Proshika*, as well as by individual households, indicate that the poor are significant savers. In India, a large number of small community organizations in Andhra Pradesh have, in aggregate, accumulated savings of around $180 million which remain on deposit with the banks. SEWA, the Indian self-employed women's NGO, also uses savings as an instrument of empowerment and helps its members in times of need. In Pakistan the rural support programmes have also accumulated large savings by the rural poor which individual savers in the rural areas could never have done by themselves.

However, microcredit programmes have only a limited role in poverty eradication. Indeed, by its very nature, microcredit only addresses one of the various factors which condition the lives of the rural poor and cannot be expected to solve the poverty problem in the larger sense. It is, therefore, not surprising that Bangladesh, which has had perhaps the highest exposure to microcredit, still remains mired in poverty.

The Unfinished Agenda of Rural Development

Rural development programmes are conceived and implemented as part of a national development strategy. There is, however, considerable debate on a number of major issues of development strategy which affect rural development. Some of these issues are broader and structural in nature on which there has been a continuing debate in South Asian countries and in the development literature in general. There is another set of issues which are largely institutional in nature and which are more in the realm of policy and practice.

Structural Issues

The Macro-micro Mismatch

Neither the statist nor the NGO programmes of rural development address the issue of poverty and regeneration of rural areas in a macroeconomic framework. While most Government programmes are formulated in a sector-centric framework, the NGO programmes are project-oriented and address the issues only at the micro level. This often accounts for the gap in micro level successes and failures at the overall level of the economy or the rural population. Thus although there are examples of remarkable successes at the level of individual projects of rural development, the overall rural picture remains bleak.

A major weakness of the architecture of rural development programmes in general and anti-poverty programmes in particular is that they are conceived as having a *ghettoized* existence in "a self-contained universe of micro-oriented programmes and projects to specific groups of the poor." Such micro-programmes, from their conception, remain incapable of generating the synergy needed to eliminate poverty and tend to degenerate into welfarism. As a result, they become unsustainable without continuing access to foreign assistance.

The project approach detracts from the task of mainstreaming rural poverty and development agendas into the overall design of development, rather than hoping that the trickle down effect will do the trick if the growth impulse is strong enough. Indeed, only by mainstreaming the poverty agenda at the macro level can one expect strong growth in the economy. It is only by reversing the roles of the elitist and the pro-poor agenda, both at the economy-wide level andin rural development, can the growth of the economy be strong as well as reduce poverty and inequality significantly.

This can be best achieved by enhancing the capacities of the poor to contribute to the process of growth by enabling them to participate, on more equitable terms, in the dynamics of the market economy. To enhance the capacity of nearly half of the population to participate in a market economy, as a deliberate measure rather than as a wishful afterthought, is likely to radically transform the process of economic growth. The need for a macro policy designed to eliminate poverty is premised on the argument that poverty originates in the structural features of society which cannot be changed by tinkering at the project, micro or sectoral levels.

The present approach in rural development programmes – both statist and participatory – suffers not only from the difficulty of upscaling them without bureaucratic or mechanical replication, but also from the lack of any coordination and consistency between the goals of the myriad projects being launched through governmental or donor support. Nor are they able to mobilize any degree of collective support for the poor against the elites which protect their interests, often by joining and pre-empting the benefits of such projects for themselves.

Access to Land and Land Reforms

An issue which is of basic significance to rural development and yet has not become a part of the architecture of rural development programmes is the access to land and the related issue of land reform. Empirical evidence has shown the incidence of poverty is highly correlated with lack of access to land, although it does not necessarily imply a causal relationship. Bina Agarwal's pioneering work on India, for instance, shows that households that depend on agricultural wage labour account for less than a third of all rural households but make up almost half of those living below the poverty line. Many of these households also own some land, but in holdings that are so small or unproductive that their owners derive a greater share of their livelihoods from their own labour than from their own land.

Land plays a strategic role in rural South Asia: aside from its value as a productive factor, land ownership confers collateral in credit markets, security in the event of natural hazards or life contingencies, social status and, in the case of those with large landholdings, considerable political and economic leverage. Those who control land tend to exert a disproportionate influence over other rural institutions, including labour and credit markets, as well as access to education and other social programmes. In a recent paper, Rosenzweig shows that "the distinction between those who own land and those who do not in ruralIndia is both important for studying distributional issues and useful for understanding the role of democratisation in aiding the poor … because the large majority of the rural poor are landless and the ownership mobility is quite limited, so that classification by land ownership is related to lifetime welfare."

The principal assets available to the rural poor tend to be land and water. The three areas of agrarian reform which could be considered politically feasible as well as economically sustainable are:

- Transforming tenancy rights into either ownership rights for the tenant or through right of permanent tenancy.
- Redistribution of ownership of uncultivated land.
- Giving title to lands and watercourses owned by the state.

Transfer of tenancy rights into permanent leaseholds has been successfully implemented in the Indian state of West Bengal under *Operation Barga*, with the active participation of peasant organizations and a pro-poor administration. The operative issue here is to give those who actually cultivate the land a direct stake in the land. Without legal title to ownership or tenancy of land, the cultivators retain little incentive to invest in the land nor are they able to use land as collateral to access the credit market.

A study based on empirical evidence of the Indian experience from 1955 to 1988 concludes: "... there is robust evidence of a link between poverty reduction and two kinds of land reform – tenancy reform and abolition of intermediaries. Another important finding is that land reform can benefit the landless by raising agricultural wages. Although the effects on poverty would probably have been greater if large-scale redistribution of land had been achieved, the results are nonetheless interesting as they suggest that partial, second best reforms which mainly affect production relations in agriculture can also play a significant role in reducing rural poverty". Considerations of both equity and efficiency would therefore suggest that some form of agrarian reform remains part of an unfinished agenda of economic reforms and as a prerequisite for rural development.

Possibilities of Rural Industrialization

The virtuous cycle between agriculture and non-agricultural enterprises plays a strategic role in providing employment opportunities in rural areas.

Mark R. Rosenzweig, "*Democratization, Decentralization and the Distribution of Local Public Goods in a Poor Rural Economy*". Mimeo. University of Pennsylvania, Philadelphia, 2002. In the sample villages used in the study, less than 10 per cent of the landless households cultivate and only 5 per cent of landed households in 1982 were landless in 1971.

The countries that made substantial progress in poverty reduction, created off-farm opportunities. There has been a spurt in the growth of non-farm enterprises in the Chinese countryside after liberalization around the late 1970s where off-farm employment grew at a rapid rate of 12 per cent per annum, currently employing 31 per cent of the rural labour force. As such, rural enterprises can become both an engine of growth as well as major contributors to the reduction of rural poverty. In most South Asian countries the potential for labour absorption is high in agro-based industries, small and medium industries and the rural services sector. Most of these activities are highly labour-intensive and provide employment opportunities for semi- and unskilled rural labour and the semi-skilled urban labour force.

The rural non-farm economy plays a significant role in providing employment and income for the poor in rural areas in most Asian countries and its importance is rising as neither agricultural production nor urban industry can absorb the increased labour force.

Non-farm sources of income for the rural poor are important for two reasons:

- The direct agricultural income of the poor is not enough to sustain their livelihood, either because of landlessness or because of insufficient owned or tenanted land.
- Wage employment in agriculture is highly seasonal and requires supplementation of income and as employment during lean periods. As most rural non-farm activities require little capital and generate more employment per unit of capital, they provide a good source of raising employment and income opportunities for the poor.

The non-farm economy accounts for 40 to 60 per cent of total national employment, and the rural non-farm economy accounts for 20 to 50 per cent of total rural employment However, the non-farm economy plays a relatively modest role in South Asia. Non-farm income shares are typically 5 to 10 per cent larger than non-farm employment shares in rural areas. The importance of non-farm employment and earnings rises as the land available to the household for cultivation diminishes.

The non-farm sector also has considerable scope to complement farming because of the strong linkages between the two sectors and because the non-farm sector forges linkages between rural and urban areas. Service activities dominate the non-farm economy in rural areas in South Asia. The non-farm sector is also an important source of income for women, small farmers, landless workers and the poor living in rural towns. Manufacturing, services and trade activities are the most important sources of employment for both male andfemale workers in rural areas, though women are relatively more concentrated in these activities than men in most countries.

The rural non-farm sector is particularly important to the rural poor. Households with less than 0.5 ha earn between 30 and 90 per cent of their income from non-farm sources. There is a strong negative relationship between non-farm shares and farm size. Low-investment manufacturing and services (including weaving, pottery, gathering, food preparation and processing, domestic and personal services and unskilled non-farm wage labour) typically account for the greater share of income for the rural poor than the wealthy. Non-farm income is also important to the poor as a means to help stabilize household income in drought years.

China provides an excellent example of how a rural development strategy focusing on the non-farm sector can bring about a significant change in the structure of the national economy. This is in addition to boosting the rural economy, increasing farmers' incomes and contributing to poverty reduction. The effects of developing rural enterprises reveal the importance of expanding non-agricultural sectors in the rural areas to generate employment for increasing surplus labour. Rural industrialization, which plays a vital role in shaping China's economic growth and economic structure, is regarded as one of the major successes of the country's reforming economy. The share of rural enterprises in GDP rose significantly, from 2 to 4 per cent in the 1970s to 28 per cent in 1997 and rural enterprises dominated the export sector by the mid-1990s. They now employ nearly 30 per cent of rural labour, and comprise a major source of new rural employment.

China's experience demonstrates the importance of institutional reform, price and market reform, rural industrialization and other policies that diversify the agriculture sector and rural economy, as ways to promote farmers' income growth. The shift from the collective to the household responsibility systems also enhanced the price-responsiveness of farm households.

The slow growth of rural industrialization in South Asia is the lack of public policies to promote the non-farm sector, both direct and indirect, such as macroeconomic and trade policies. Among the support policies directed at non-farm sector enterprises, financial assistance and credit facilities to the non-farm sector and technical services of various kinds are the most important. These policies help reduce the discrimination and disincentives suffered by small scale rural enterprises through lack of access to credit, technology and markets. Given the urban bias in policies, these enterprises also suffer from underdevelopment of social, human and physical infrastructure in the rural areas. The provision of human capital is important to give the poor the capacity toenter the rural non-farm sector. This does not necessarily include formal education, as there is scope for teaching basic literacy, numeracy and book-keeping in a non-formal, hands-on manner.

Financial assistance to medium, small-scale, and micro-level enterprises is usually channelled through Government-owned commercial banks or specialized financial institutions, or by requiring private commercial banks to allocate a certain percentage of their loans to these enterprises. In the past, small enterprises often received loans at subsidized interest rates, resulting in credit rationing. The rate of repayment was very low, resulting in losses for financial institutions burdened with a large proportion of non-performing loans. However, this practice has been largely discontinued as a result of financial liberalization introduced under structural adjustment programmes.

Increasingly, financial assistance to micro enterprises in the rural areas in South Asia has been channelled through NGOs, such as the rural support organizations (RSPs) in Pakistan, the integrated rural development programmes (IRDP) in India and the Grameen Bank and BRAC in Bangladesh and microcredit institutions. The way in which these groups are organized, how they identify those in their lending portfolio and how they monitor the projects varies widely. The lending through these institutions is usually to households and economies of scale are not taken advantage of. The rural areas are also generally excluded by institutions of financial support to small and medium industries, as they are focused mainly on urban areas.

The establishment of industrial estates fully endowed with infrastructure, roads, communications, electricity and financial services in small towns or semi-rural areas for providing services to these small micro enterprises has also had mixed and generally disappointing results. Industrial estates for rural areas are widely viewed as expensive failures. A rather different approach, relying on social networks in rural and semi-urban areas, to exploit the synergy between social and economic factors, argues for the establishment of industrial clusters which can also harness the benefits of globalization for the poor).

Another source of stimulus to the growth of the rural non-farm sector is through local Government institutions which can help facilitate the development of physical, social, and human infrastructure at the local level. Decentralization tends to shift the focus of expenditure toward small-scale infrastructure projects, encouraging the growth of small-scale private sector projects. It is also likely that there will be greater equity in the distribution of public expenditures within localities because there is greater transparency and accountability in a local setting, although the South Asian experience in this regard is mixed. On the other hand in China and Taiwan Province of China, where land reforms haveeliminated the political influence of large landowners, local Governments have played an important role in the development of infrastructure and industrialization.

Rural Governance

Five decades of rural development efforts by the state and civil society, with considerable assistance from donor agencies, have transformed the nature of governance in the rural areas in South Asian countries. The writ of the central Government through its bureaucratic apparatus from the Deputy Commissioner to the *patwari* has been considerably diluted by the revival (not necessarily revitalization) of local government institutions and the growing outreach of NGOs in the countryside. The institutions of governance in the rural areas are in a state of flux and a new governance paradigm for rural areas is yet to emerge.

The growing economic differentiation of rural society, partly a result of the gainers and losers created by rural development programmes, the rapid diversification of activity and its commercialization have loosened traditional social structures. The process will if anything intensify and lead to a significant realignment of the power structure in substantial parts of rural India favouring the disadvantaged groups. Such realignments will not of course occur in all cases spontaneously and in a manner which gives an effective voice to the poor and promotes their interests. The process unleashed and the potential for change created by them must therefore focus on creating conditions which will facilitate a favourable outcome. In this context three aspects deserve special attention.

First, the state will have to continue to play a supportive role in rural development. A great deal of knowledge and expertise is needed to assess local resources and their potential, different ways of exploiting the potential, the costs involved and raising resources. This knowledge, much of it technical in nature, is often not available locally. Strong support from state agencies and/or NGOs (including educational institutions) is necessary to make it accessible to the communities and their leaders. Along with this support, the role of Government agencies also needs to change. Instead of planning, deciding and implementing schemes on their own, as they now do, the agencies will have to play a less intrusive role by facilitating coordination between the related schemes of different communities and providing a broader perspective.

Second, the creation of democratic institutions of local Government and assured representation for disadvantaged groups are necessary but not sufficient conditions to ensure that the latters' interests are safeguarded. The determination of priorities, in the context of limited resources, inevitably involves a process of bargaining between different groups. In order for this to work in favour of the poor/vulnerable, the latter have to articulate their needs andactively persuade and/or pressure the relevant forums to take necessary action to meet their needs. None of these occur easily or automatically. Conscious measures to encourage and strengthen institutions of civil society at the local level are essential. Moreover the elected local institutions cannot merely generate demands for a larger devolution of resources from the state and central Governments should be required to mobilize their own resources to meet a significant part of the costs of their programmes.

Third, non-governmental and voluntary organizations have a particularly key role in obtaining and disseminating information on the working of Government (including local Government), making people aware of their entitlements and obligations and enabling them to vent their grievances and seek redress. Besides interceding with the concerned authorities to secure benefits for the eligible and minimise leakages, they have a role in motivating and organizing local communities to take active interest in the working of specific programmes and persuading bureaucracy to work with the community for improving the effectiveness of programmes. Over time, they can help promote a process of more broad-based changes in institutional mechanisms for funding/ managing local development activities to meet the specific local conditions. Active encouragement of NGOs and giving them ample public space is therefore highly desirable for the healthy evolution of local Government.

All this implies a basic change in the relations between the state and local governments, the role of the bureaucracy and the attitudes of local governments. There are no standard blueprints for accomplishing the change. A great deal of experimentation and learning from experience is inevitable. The upsetting of existing power balances between the various groups involved creates an opportunity for engineering desirable changes through a combination of sustained pressures on the system as a whole via the general political process along with grass-roots efforts to initiate and sustain a discussion of the problem of restructuring among the concerned groups (namely the local and state level politicians, the bureaucracy and its trade unions and NGOs).

Decentralization and Local Government Structures

The system of local Government inherited by most countries in South Asia dates back to 1885 when the Local Self Government Act was passed by the British colonial administration. Local Government institutions were introduced mainly for administrative convenience and only partly to satisfy the democratic urge and placate the demand for independence. In the post-independence period, the control of the local bodies by colonial officials has been replaced by close supervision and often direct interference of central or provincial/state Governments.All South Asian countries are giving increased attention to the concept of devolving Government responsibilities downward. In India and Nepal, following the adoption of decentralization legislation, local Governments are being given greater priority, recognition, and authority. A local Government plan being prepared in Pakistan proposes devolution of political power, decentralization of administrative authority and distribution of resources to district levels. Most rural local Governments, however, are still weak, and sometimes non-functioning, non-responsive or non-accountable.

In Pakistan and Bangladesh, where military regimes have often been in power almost as often as civilian regimes, the former have shown a greater predilection for local Government, partly to avoid countrywide general elections where the established political parties have a much better chance of success. Ayub Khan's system of basic democracy was an attempt to secure political legitimacy in the 1960s. Subsequent military-led regimes in both Bangladesh and Pakistan have relied on local Government structures, suitably modified, to obtain political legitimacy and to use them to administer the rural development programmes as a means of distributing their patronage.

In India, the passage of the 73rd and 74th Constitutional Amendments which provides for a three tier system of local Government, mandatory elections every five years and devolution development functions with authority and resources from the state to these bodies, has created a space and opportunity for decentralized participatory local development effort with in-built pressures for accountability. Implementation of these provisions is far from complete.

Several states have not held local body elections as required by the Constitution. *Panchayats* are being formed in all states and powers are being delegated to them. These institutions will now have control of all rural development programmes, with the active involvement of the NGOs. However, serious problems remain in enabling local level organizations to genuinely articulate and implement the aspirations of the poor and to remain insulated from bureaucratic interference and elite manipulation and capture. Within India there is a wide variation in the degree of success of local governments among different states. To some extent the success has been correlated with the level of literacy and political consciousness of the electorate and the activism of civil society in the state. To ensure successful decentralization, two issues deserve top priority: one, support for developing an effective framework for and management of the decentralization process; and two, capacity-building of local Governments to meet the demands of their new roles.

References

Andre Beteille, (1999). "Empowerment" in *Economic and Political Weekly*, Perspectives, 6-12 March and 13-19 March.

Berry, R. A. and W. R. Cline, (1979). *Agrarian Structure and Productivity in Developing Countries*, Baltimore : Johns Hopkins University Press.

Rosenzweig, M. R. and H. P. Binswanger (1993), "Wealth, weather risk and the composition and profitability of agricultural investments", *Economic Journal, vol. 103*, pp. 56-78

Wiggins, Steve and Sharon Proctor, (2001). "How special are rural areas? Implications of location for rural development", in *Development Policy Review*, December, 19(4), pp. 427-436.

World Bank, (2001). *South Asia: A Strategy and Action Plan for Rural Development*, Rural Development Sector Unit, South Asia Region.

3

Community E-centres and Rural Development

The vision of the Information Society identified at the First Phase of the World Summit on Information Society (WSIS) is one which is people-centred, inclusive and development-oriented and where everyone can create, access, utilize and share information and knowledge. To achieve this vision of the Information Society, the WSIS Plan of Action recommended to:

- Establish rural information, communication and technology (ICT) access points
- Empower communities, especially those in rural and underserved areas, through the use of ICTs
- Promote distance learning, training and other forms of educa-tion as part of capacity building programmes
- Promote international and regional cooperation for capacity building

Access to appropriate information and knowledge contributes significantly to economic development and to ensure access to information, ICT is a key enabler. ICT provides an economic and efficient means to acquire information and knowledge.

In recognition of this need for information, the WSIS Plan of Action states:

> ICTs allow people, anywhere in the world, to access infor-mation and knowledge almost instantaneously. Individuals, organizations and communities should benefit from access to knowledge and information."

Between 1992 and 2002, ICT penetration increased significantly in developing countries. While the gap is narrowing across all types of ICT indicators, the gap still exists between developed and developing countries. The digital divide within countries and between different commu-nities must also be addressed before ICTs can deliver on their promise.

The Digital Divide

Rural and remote communities have less access to ICTs compared to their urban counterparts. In Asia, the majority of population do not live in urban areas, but are farmers, often living in under-developed and isolated areas. Rural areas are characterized by the following challenges:

- Low infrastructure for ICT usage
- Long distance to maintain and repair ICTs
- Small market size
- Low affordability, literacy and ICT literacy
- Low awareness of opportunities and benefits of ICT

To provide equitable access to ICTs to rural communities, Govern-ments and civil society organizations have set up community e-centres (CeCs) in rural areas.

A CeC is a facility that provides public access to ICT-based services and applications for education, personal, social and economic development. The concept originated in Sweden around 1985. It has now expanded to include telecentres, telecottages, community technology centres, community communication shops, village knowledge centres, networked learning cen-tres, multipurpose community telecentres (MCT), community access centres, and digital club houses.

CeCs provide ICT-based services in rural and remote areas. They provide opportunities for development through ICT; extend the reach of public services such as education, health and social services; provide information of interest to the local community including farmers, local businesses and NGOs; and create new enterprises and jobs opportunities.

The key is providing public access. The typical facilities of CeC include:

- Telecommunications facilities (telephones, faxes)
- Office equipment (computers, CD-ROMs, printers, photocopiers)

- Multimedia hardware and software (radio, TV, video)
- Location for meetings and training

Services provided by CeCs include:

- Communication (telephone, fax, e-mail, Internet and radio)
- ICT training
- Agricultural information dissemination
- E-learning
- Distance health care
- E-government services
- Small and micro-enterprise support

There is no universally accepted model or optimal size for CeCs. Every CeC operates with different objectives, services and ICT applications under different conditions. There are four different models – the adoption model, the government model, the commercial model and the school model.

CeCs are now being seen as a viable method for bridging the digital divide and means to providing access to ICTs to communities, which have been left behind in the shift to an Information Society. In light of this, Governments in the region have developed national policies including the development of CeCs that aim to bridge knowledge, social and economic gaps.

Development of CeCs

For developing CeCs, communities or organizations must first:

- *Assess the needs of the community* – Needs assessment should identify information needs, identify stakeholders and their role, and help to create a sense of ownership
- *Select the service and application* – Services and applications vary according to community. The types of services include basic telecommunication service, information services, e-learning, e-business, e-government and training
- *Develop content and applications* – Perhaps the most valuable function of CeCs is the dissemination of information and knowledge for development. CeC content can include: information on farm product prices and input prices (quality seeds/fertilisers); a directory of general and crop insurance schemes; bus/train time-tables; information on sea

conditions; enabling online registration of applications for all sorts of revenue related transactions; online public grievance systems; expert consultations; village newsletters, employment news and so on. To reach the rural poor, the content should be relevant to the local situation – if it's not relevant it will not be used. Therefore, it must be written in local language, supported by multi-media, such as voice and image for illiterate people

- *Select technologies* – Satellite technology provides a rapid and increasingly cost-effective method of achieving connectivity in remote rural areas. Very small aperture terminal (VSAT) is a particularly good option for rural communities that are too distant from fibre backbones or terrains too rough for the line of sight required between terrestrial microwave antennas. Another alternative is the Wireless Local Loop (WLL) for rural areas within microwave radio reach of existing fibre optic cable links. The use of wireless networks, and in particular WiFi, has drawn a lot of attention as a relatively low-cost way of getting fast network access to rural areas. WiFi is not the only wireless networking technology – packet radio, microware links and even 3G phone networks could all do a similar job
- Provide training
- Operate and manage
- Conduct monitoring and evaluation

To capitalize on the potential of this technology, low cost PCs (e.g. simputers, Pengachu (Thailand's low cost computers) and PDAs) need to be developed. An innovative mix of technology to maximize connectivity and to minimize the costs is also needed, and to overcome low literacy rates, CeCs need to employ technologies for easy interaction (e.g. voice recogni-tion, oral or audiovisual output).

Problems Identified

There are many challenges to overcome in setting up CeCs, including the high costs involved in the establishment (initial investment and recurrent costs) of the centres. The most significant capital costs in offering community ICT services are for hardware and network access equipment. Business plans should factor in the depreciation of equipment; slow service take-up; the high cost of repair and maintenance in remote settings; and potential power, security and technical problems. The possibility of deploying low-cost PCs need to be examined. To reduce the recurrent costs (rent, electricity, salary of staff), many telecentres hire secondary and tertiary students at low wages to serve as facilitators and perform other tasks such as repair and research, and setup the centre within an existing business (e.g. telephone call centres, temples, school, post office, government offices).

Another obstacle is the limitation of ICT skilled people. Training in operation and maintenance needs to be provided for the CeCs operator. Awareness of the benefits of ICT also needs to be raised and policy and regulatory issues which impact on ICT usage need to be addressed.

Access issues also need to be considered, such as giving careful thought to physical placement, design and staffing to serve men and women and different social groups.

When sustainability of a CeC is discussed, it is often interpreted as meaning self-financing and is equated with success. However, sustainability has many other dimensions, such as social and cultural, political, techno-logical, and financial. Social and culture sustainability is measured by whether it empowers people in the community, meets the needs of various groups (men, women, young, old), and allows for community ownership and engagement. Political sustainability is measured in terms of whether a stable regulatory framework to promote and support CeCs has been secured. While technological sustainability is measured whether appropriate technol-ogy options were chosen for the community.

Financial sustainability reflects whether a CeC has full financial viability. The centre should be able to recover its capital investment, operational expenses, and replace equipment as needed. A centre could also be partially financially sustainable only recovering operational expenses but not the initial and future capital investment. Most successful projects are those which are either private sector driven or community driven with an emphasis on viability and responsive-ness. Furthermore experiences show that rural communities can pay for the services and services that are charged for are usually more valued than those that are free.

BRIDGING THE DIGITAL DIVIDE

One of the main contributing factors to the digital divide is the poor terrestrial network infrastructure. For instance, in China, over 400 million kilometres of fibre optic cable has been laid, yet there still remain many unreachable areas, such as remote or mountainous areas. It is not commercially viable to build a fibre optic service which is able to cover all of the country.

The solution then is to build a better infrastructure. Satellite technol-ogy is the key for this, combined with more training (hardware – computer operations, and software – Internet-related) along with community and government support.

Satellites allow for fast infrastructure build-up, in terms of fast implementation, and it is scalable, in such that infrastructure can be built as networks grow. Unfortunately, satellite equipment is not as affordable as a telephone set. It is however, easy to install, taking less than two weeks to install – which is one of its main advantages. With satellites, there is also the ability to increase the capacity as needed, making it good for upscaling, enabling users to start with their minimum requirement and scale up as needed.

The challenge to satellite technology application in the Asia-Pacific region is collaboration. Though there are major advancements in informa-tion technology (IT) development taking place in many countries in the region, when it comes to satellite technology, few are willing to collaborate with each other, and every country wants to have its own satellite service rather than sharing resources, creating a problem in terms of overcapacity.

Despite this, satellite remains perhaps the most promising potential solution to the digital divide. It can reach almost anywhere in the region, making global coverage a possibility. Furthermore, broadband can also become more available through satellite and is easier to install.

One of the obstacles to satellite is the cost of bandwidth but as the technology develops the cost of bandwidth is going down, as are equipment costs.

Asia-Pacific Satellite Communications Council (APSCC)

The Asia-Pacific Satellite Communications Council (APSCC) was founded to promote satellite communications and broadcasting in the Asia-Pacific region under the auspices of the United Nations Office for Outer Space Affairs and supported by ITU. It has 100 members from Asia, Europe, and North America including satellite manufacturers, satellite operators, launch vehicle service providers, equipment vendors, consultants, and gov-ernment organizations. Membership is open to anyone who is interested in satellite communications, and is free to government organizations.

The APSCC mission is to promote satellite communications in Asia-Pacific, provide a forum for discussion and interchange of information, ideas and new technologies in satellite communications, and coordinate the International Satcom standard.

Asian Satellite Market Overview

Satellite technology is well suited to the Asia-Pacific region. Its utilization is expanding, particularly its use in emergency situations. Many regional and global satellite operators have satellites over the Asia-Pacific region, but as a result, overcapacity remains an issue in the region. Despite this, revenue is continuing to grow due to the development and availability of technology. If this is to continue, however, government regulatory issues will have to be addressed, and some of the regulatory barriers eased.

Regional/domestic Satellite Operators

In the past, having a satellite was, for many countries in Asia-Pacific, akin to having a national airline carrier. It was important for every country to have one airline carrier, and demonstrate that it was not dependent on other nations to fly its nationals. The need for each country to have their own satellite resulted in C-Band over-capacity, which is endemic across the region, and which must now be addressed through consolidation. C-Band is largely used in heavy rain areas. Ku-Band which also suffers from over-capacity, is beginning to address this problem. Capacity is currently around 60 per cent for Ku-Band, but with good government and donor support and with collaboration with other countries it could go up to 75 per cent.

There is a global average of 60 satellite deployments a year, and recently, North America has seen a surge in satellite usage, partly as a result of homeland security issues. The Asia-Pacific region is third in overall satellite deployments, and third in revenues for manufacturers as well. Throughout all regions, leasing revenues are also increasing, on average by 4.4 per cent per year.

Satellite Service Demand in Asia-Pacific

Every country in Asia-Pacific has its own domestic satellite broad-casting service. Therefore, a broadcasting and video service is what is most required in the region. Even though almost all content broadcasted on satellite is in English, there is still a need for some local content. The demand is also driven by high definition television (HDTV) and broadcast-ing which requires such large bandwidth only satellite can deliver.

Broadband services can also provide Internet Trunking Services (ITS) and direct Internet Access Services (IAS) such as enterprise network services, and remote area direct access. It is the utilization of satellite for these Internet access services, which is expected to become the fastest growing section of the satellite market in the coming five to six years.

Asia-Pacific Broadband Satellite Markets

Satellite revenue in Asia-Pacific still continues to come largely from the business sector. China and South Asia dominate the revenue streams in this area, and the industry growth is expected from there.

The key to bridging the digital gap is to enable access to the Internet for remote and under-served areas. Through the application of satellite technology, this can be achieved. For community e-centres (CeCs), sustainability is important. With government support and subsidies, this is possible.

Satellite services that can be appliced to CeCs include:

- Intranet/LAN/WAN connectivity – this allows connectivity be-tween enterprise sites, with either one-way or two-way services
- Enterprise Video distribution – such as business T V, videocasting, Web Conferencing. For this application, training of local staff is important. Using this application, distance learning can be done by uplinking via satellite to a centralized classroom
- VoIP via satellite – the cost of "voice over IP" has greatly fallen in recent years, and it can now be provided at affordable prices through CeCs

Broadband Interactive Bidirectional Data

Interactive data communications are the foundation of most corporate and government uses of telecommunications. These needs can be addressed by properly engineered bidirectional satellite links that involve multiple transmitting earth stations. The Very Small Aperture Terminals (VSATs) used by fuelling stations and discount department store chains in the Americas, Europe and parts of Asia demonstrate that such networks are practical (easy to install and centrally manage), reliable (99.9 per cent availability) and cost effective (saving users as much as 20 per cent over what an equivalent terrestrial network would cost).

VSATs are becoming attractive to smaller enterprises and for big organizations that wish to push the use of satellite communication down further in their operation. The cost of equipment per site has dropped from over US$ 10,000 in 1998 to around US$ 2,000 in 2002. Consumer versions that provide high-speed access to the Internet are offered in the United States for under US$ 500.

VSAT is able to be shared across countries, and can uplink from anywhere. Hopefully, VSAT will promote collaboration, and will enable an education network, which will be helpful for developing countries in Asia, as it will allow the information to be gathered and shared, providing a very rich resource of information available across the region.

Review of Vsat Ip Application Services

E-government:

- *Citizen Verification* – RFID (Radio Frequency Identification) is developing as a new industry
- *Law Enforcement* – for example, for customs and shipping. Post 9/11, the US Coast Guard is requesting that each container entering or passing through the United States have an electronic ID on it. It is also helpful in increasing transparency

E-education:

- Development of state-run enterprises
- Rural development of the work force

E-business:

- *Strategic* – can utilize e-business technology for satellite uses to help reduce the digital divide
- *Global* – can encourage collaboration, regionally

Broadband is an "advanced telecommunication capability". A high-speed, switched, broadband capability allows users to originate and receive high quality voice, data, graphics, and video telecommunications using various technologies on a single converged network. Satellite broadband means connectivity anywhere and at anytime.

A broadband data communications service is one that requires a transfer rate greater than that afforded by a dial-up telephone line using a V.92 modem. This places the minimum data transfer rate at about 100 kbps, which is typical of current high-speed access services from a Digital Subscriber Line (DSL) in its many forms, cable modems, and comparable fixed wireless and satellite high-speed access services. There is also the question of whether the two directions of transmission are of equal speed (i.e. symmetrical) or asymmetrical, such that the inbound speed from server to user is greater than the outbound speed from user to server.

From an IT perspective, broadband services support standard office applications includ-ing e-mail and file transfer, and major software systems such as Enterprise Resource Planning (ERP) and distance education. Organizations are structur-ing many of their IT applications for use within a standard Web browser, allowing employees and partners to access services within the Intranet and from the external Internet as well. This makes applications seem relatively similar to the network, but the detailed structure cannot be ascertained in general. High-speed access can provide video distribution, telephony and video conferencing, although these may not be deliverable through a browser since they require specialized user terminal devices or other appliances.

Without access to information, it is difficult to develop good education or infrastructure, and it is difficult to reduce poverty. Yet, without affordable communications infrastructure, access to information is extremely difficult. The key challenge is to increase access to information in order to reduce poverty.

Once affordable communication infrastructure is available, other benefits will flow. In social development, it can benefit the sectors such as education, gover-nance and health care while in economic development, it can create jobs, bring savings in time and expenses, and creat more transparent markets.

The role of government in increasing access to information is crucial. E-government can play an important role. In e-government interac-tions, the government creates the e-government platform in partnership with central government ministries, legislative and judicial authorities and local government and administration.

The simplest method to develop this platform is through Satellite Broadband Terminal Solutions (SBTS). This solution allows subscribers to receive multiple channels, even on small terminals, by bundling services together. VSAT technology can provide this.

VSAT demand is market and technology-driven. Fortunately, innova-tion of satellite broadband technologies means they are getting better and cheaper. Satellites also do not have many of the limitations of terrestrial networks and other wireless networks. For example, PSTN/ISDN/xDSL/ cable modems have bandwidth limitations, limited reach and are difficult to extend. On the other hand, VSAT enables globalization of businesses, with companies able to establish corporate intranets worldwide. VSAT also provides delivery of value-added services, such as broadband Internet access, multimedia entertainment and distance learning. Satellite is also more able to respond to the convergence of voice and data, which has been largely consumer-driven, and which became widely possible through mobile phones. Consumers want even more access, resulting more and more bandwidth.

Broadband Applications and Services

Broadband Internet access provides high-speed Internet for Web browsing, e-mail, news, downloads, video online, as well as distance learning solutions such as e-learning solutions based on satellite broadcast, which enable greater interactivity. Together with cost-effective terminal equipment, e-learning solutions provide a rich and colourful educational resource. It is also useful for distance medicine solutions such as tele-diagnostics, remote consultations, remote training and certification.

Recommendation of Satellite Solution

Currently, there is a great deal of unused satellite capacity in Asia that could be used for CeCs and other development projects if satellite companies could be found that were prepared to donate their spare capac-ity. In-kind donations of equipment are also needed, in addition to finding a flag carrier who could provide system integration and management. Lastly, assurance of government support is needed.

The Grameen Telecom Experience

In Bangladesh at present there are around one million landlines operated by the state-owned Bangladesh Telephone and Telegraph Board (BTTB). There are four mobile phone operators with a subscription base in excess of 3.25 million mobile phones. Mobile phones now out-number the number of landlines by 3.25:1. Eighty per cent of the population live in villages never used a phone previously.

Rural Communication Through Innovation

Grameen Telecom (GTC), through its Village Phone programme, has brought the latest communication technologies to rural villages, helping to connect them to the rest of the world. GTC has made mobile telephony services available to over 35,000 of Bangladesh's 68,000 villages. Previ-ously detached communities are now connected to the rest of the country and the world. Urban mobile phones have been made accessible to the rural poor, with mobile public call offices managed by "Village Phone Operators", generating income and employment in Bangladesh's villages.

Village Phones

Village Phones (VP) works as an owner-operated pay phone. It allows the rural poor who cannot afford to become regular subscribers, to make use of the service with loans from Grameen Bank.

The project aims to bring the full potential of the information technology revolution to villagers and the poor. The village phone is owner operated, with village phone operators being the main entrepreneurs. Most often, the operator takes a loan from GTC to purchase the phone. The project is focused primarily on bringing telecommunications services to the poor. From this project, it can be seen that telephones can play an important role in reducing poverty. Telephones have become an instrument against poverty by connecting rural areas to the rest of the world and bringing new opportunities to the rural populations.

The project is a collaboration between four business entities – Grameen Bank, Grameen Phone, Grameen Telecom and the village phone operators (VPO). The aim of the project is to have a telephone in every village in the country.

Grameen Bank

Grameen Bank (GB) is a pioneering micro credit organization. It provides small loans to bank members to enable them to earn a living through self employment. It is a pioneer in this area, by taking risks and believing that poor people are bankable.

Grameen Bank now has 3.7 million borrowers under 1,267 branches, and provides financial services in 46,000 villages, covering more than 68 per cent of all villages in Bangladesh. Customer repayment rates are very high, with 98 per cent of disbursed loans repaid.

Grameen Phone

Grameen Phone (GP) is the largest mobile phone company in Bangladesh with 2.2 million subscribers and 75 per cent coverage. GP has the widest GSM network coverage in Bangladesh, covering 61 out of 64 districts. Coverage in rural areas was extended after consultations with Grameen Telecom, taking into account areas which have high telephony demand. Coverage is increasing every day.

GP offers subsidized call rates for VPO's which are around 50 per cent lower than normal subscribers.

Grameen Telecom

Grameen Telecom (GTC) is a not-for-profit rural telecommunication company. Its mandate is to bring ICT services closer to the rural popula-tion. It is responsible for marketing, distribution and administration of village phones through 18 unit offices. GTC unit officers visit the Grameen Bank branches in areas where network coverage is satisfactory to provide VP service and prepare a list of villages.

Village Phone Operators

Grameen Bank (GB) chooses village phone operators (VPO) from among bank borrowers who reside in those villages and have good repay-ment records. Village phone operators are the most important component in the programme. They, most often female, are Grameen Bank members. They purchase a phone under the lease-financing programme of the Bank and provide telephone service to people in their village.

Each VPO is responsible for providing services to customers for both incoming and outgoing calls, collecting call charges, remitting pay-ments to Grameen Telecom, and ensuring proper maintenance of the telephone set. The operator's income consists of the difference between the charges paid by customers and the airtime charges billed to the operator by Grameen Telecom. Repayment of the loan for the phone set is processed through the existing loan granting and collection procedures of the Grameen Bank.

Grameen Bank managers at the community level collect monthly payments from operators, in person, at the village level.

Village Phone Operation

The village phone operation is a tripartite, coordinated service which brings communication technologies to rural areas. GB selects potential village phone operators and provides financial assistance for purchasing the handset and connection. It also collects bills on behalf of GTC.

- GP provides network support and subsidised call tariffs
- GTC provides handsets, manages distribution and billing, and oversees bill collection
- GP avoids costs of billing and bill collection from rural villag-ers, but has a steady stream of revenue from the VP service

The phones are distributed through 18 unit offices in each GB zone. In terms of billing, GP provides raw bill data while GTC processes individual bills adding both GB and GTC service charges and value added tax. GTC provides a dedicated VP call centre that provides information to village phone operators on bill status, call charges and connection status.

For after sales service, GTC has 18 mobile phone service centres that provide the necessary maintenance and technical support to village phone operators in rural locations. Without these service centres, rural people would have to go to larger towns to get their phones fixed.

Through VP connection and tariffs the project provides a steady stream of revenue for GTC. Village phone connection and handset costs are Takas 8,000 (US$ 135), and the fixed line rent is Takas 40 per month. Call charges per minute are Takas 2.24 at peak hours (US$ 3.7) and Takas 1.24 at off peak hours for local and nationwide calls.

VP operators charge around Takas 4 to Takas 6 per customer, depending on the availability of phones in the locality. The average monthly VP bill is Takas 5,200 (US$ 87.5). The average net income of a VP operator is Tk. 4,000 (US$ 68) per month.

VP operators account for 3.85 per cent of all GP subscribers, but VP revenues account for 15.5 per cent of all GP airtime time revenues.

VP Subscriber Growth

Since 1997, VP subscriptions have grown tremendously, and they have now penetrated into the most rural, remote parts of Bangladesh. It is expected that subscriptions will reach 100,000 by the end of 2004.

Social Impact of Village Phones

The phones provide village operators with a regular and good earning, averaging US$ 68 per month. This enables many operators to improve their economic circumstances, and often results in a change in their social status.

It also creates new business opportunities for villagers, leading to economic and community empowerment, and increased knowledge and confidence amongst villagers.

A study by the TeleCommons Development Group (TDG) of Canada for the Canadian International Development Agency (CIDA) concluded, "The Village Phone Programme yields significant positive social and eco-nomic impacts, including a relatively large consumer surplus and immeasur-able quality of life benefits".

A further indication of the programme's success is its successful replication in Uganda, where there are currently 1,000 village phone operators.

Pioneering Rural ICT Services

The VP programme contains many rural development "firsts". It is the first rural development micro-credit facility in a developing country to target the creation of micro-enterprises based on information and communication technology (ICT) services. It is the first rural development micro-credit facility in a developing country to assist in the creation of village telephone service businesses using digital, wireless telephony. It is the first private sector rural telecom initiative that specifically targets poor village women for establishing micro-enterprise (targeted, micro-level programme), and it is the first private sector telecom initiative with the explicit goal of rural poverty reduction.

However, despite its success, it would have been reckless for a GSM company to solely focus on rural Bangladesh because of the small market and minimal purchasing power. But by combining the skills and expertise of GB, GP and GTC, it has been possible to profitably serve the telecom-munications needs of the underserved rural poor.

Developing a Business Plan for Community E-centres

Despite outstanding achievements in the areas of ICT and high technology, two state governments belonging to two different parties in the general election of India early this year have failed to return to power, largely because the rural poor felt that the benefits of these technologies did not reach them. Community e-centres (CeCs) may be one way to improve the life of the rural community and ensure that the benefits of technology are reaching all, including those in rural areas, who need them.

Poverty is not only an absence of money. Often communities who have lived for generations in poverty develop a sense of utter hopelessness and lose their sense of self-respect and dignity. They become increasingly marginalized and excluded. They lose their voice. What can ICT do to help the poor? The last few years have seen many initiatives that deploy ICTs in rural communities in many developing countries, but are they working?

Alfonso Gumucio Dagron, development communication specialist with the Rockfeller Foundation, has written:

> "Only one out of every one hundred telecentres are really useful for the local community where they have been set-up, in terms of supporting development and social change. This may shock many of those that see ICTs as the ultimate magic solution for poverty, but I challenge anyone to show me that I'm wrong. Thousands of telecentres have been planted during the past five years and millions of dollars have been invested in buying computers and ensuring Internet connectivity; how-ever, every time we are to mention the successful experiences, the same five or six places come to mind. In other words: something smells very bad in cyberland."

A few successful examples according to Dagron are the Village Knowledge Centres established by the Swaminathan Research Foundation in Chennai, India. Dagron believes this project is a good example of CeC that really care about providing appropriate information to their constitu-ency. The concept is articulated around community needs, not the opposite. "Information shops" have been placed in various villages, and a "value addition centre" is in charge of building web pages with information that is relevant to local needs, such as market prices or local weather reports. The core concept is to build a "local web" that specifically caters to the needs of local communities, in terms of contents, culture and language.

Mr. Dagron says, "There are too many examples of projects that are only bombarding the Third World with computers, in the most irresponsible manner and for the benefit only of hardware and software companies. On the other hand, there are very few, I insist, very few experiences of use of new information and communication technologies that are paradigmatic in the way they contribute to development… this is why the Village Knowledge Centres in Pondicherry are such an important and coherent experience."

The Swaminathan Research Foundation Business, Operation and Management Plan for Community E-centres

Before setting up CeCs, the Foundation conducted a large-scale consultation with the local communities. Participatory rural appraisal (PRA) was used as a method to identify the information needs of the community. Information on district and village profiles, household details, economic activity of the village, maps, information needs, existing infrastructure such as government institutions, primary health centre, education institution, was collected. As was information on how many people are living below the poverty line.

Information was also collected on weak and strong linkages between the information disseminators and rural community, profiles of underprivi-leged communities, market information, details of artisans and small mer-chants, problems of landless labourers and local interaction patterns. This helped to create a micro-plan for the village.

The PRA was also used to assess how far the community was willing to go in operationalizing the local centre, by way of making in-kind or cash contributions. This was also used in the identification of a group of individuals who would be consensually chosen by the community for managing the local centre. Field experience indicated that three factors are very important in initiating village knowledge centres, the first of which is community ownership; the community as a whole must endorse the centre. Second, it must be useful; usefulness is more important than the use of latest technology. Lastly, it should not be associated with one group or caste.

Community participation is vital in all rural, community-based ICT projects. Having the right community champions is critical to ensuring project success. Community participation should be broad-based and representative, regardless of social and economic status and local community participation should start from the conceptualization stage and be sustained throughout.

The community will need to play a major rôle in determining the key resources, such as the project champion, and the right local institution to partner with. Multi-stakeholder partnerships can be useful for communi-ties, but care needs to be taken in selecting the partners to engage with.

New technologies, especially wireless, are increasingly important because they are easier to deploy and may cost less than conventional technologies. What already exists often determines and can limit future options. For that reason, telephony is still very relevant for rural access. Adequate technical skills are required for ensuring/maintaining a robust connectivity infrastructure. Internet technologies offer new options to pro-vide cheaper and more flexible services (e.g. VoIP).

Constraints must be removed on the basis of a malady-remedy analysis. For example, wired and wireless technologies could be used where telephone connections are not adequate or satisfactory. Similarly, solar power can be harnessed where the regular supply of power is irregular. The approach should be based on the principle that there is a solution for every problem. Connectivity must be able to address the content requirement to be adequate. Economics of scale matters – connectivity is very expensive but can be cheaper if shared. However, emerging technologies (such as VSAT and direct TV) are changing many of these assumptions. Rural communities are typically not attractive for profit-oriented telecommunications companies, and are a result the last mile solution must be self-financed in many cases. Therefore, it is important to assess the various available technology options for the last mile and the first mile (wireless, satellite, VoIP, fibre, etc.), and implement those that are cost-effective and reliable. Building a resource for the technical know-how will be useful.

Creation and updating of relevant content to suit local needs is a key factor in the e-community programme. The information provided should be demand-driven and should be relevant to the day-to-day life and work of rural women and men. Also, semi-literate women should be accorded priority for trainings to operate the centre, since this is an effective method of enhancing the self-esteem and social prestige of women living in poverty. Another important technique is the packaging of appropriate content (e.g. in local languages) for specific community needs and choices.

Content should be delivered in both conventional and electronic means (use not only web sites, but also community newspapers or radio). Knowledge dissemination should be linked to access to the inputs needed to apply the knowledge for economic activities. It is important to be strategic in generating or procuring content in view of the potentially high cost involved. Equally important as understanding the content is to take the appropriate action based on the information provided.

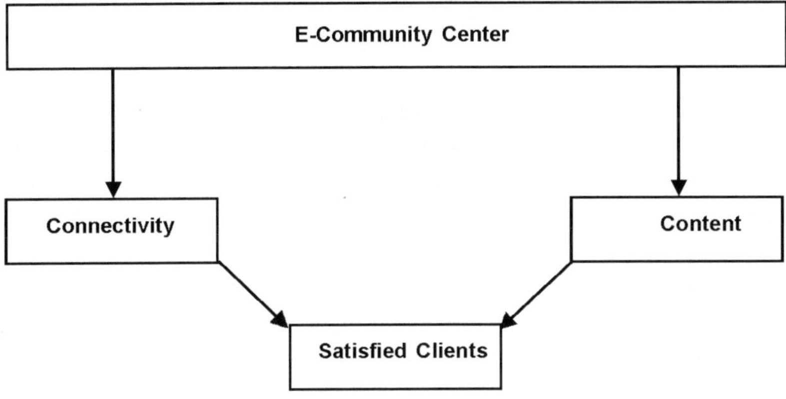

Figure 1. Connectivity and content in a community e-centre

Using the hub and spokes model, CeCs have both connectivity and content. This model is designed to empower rural families with new knowledge and skills and should be designed on the *antyodaya* (unto the last) model, where the empowerment starts with the poorest and most underprivileged women and men.

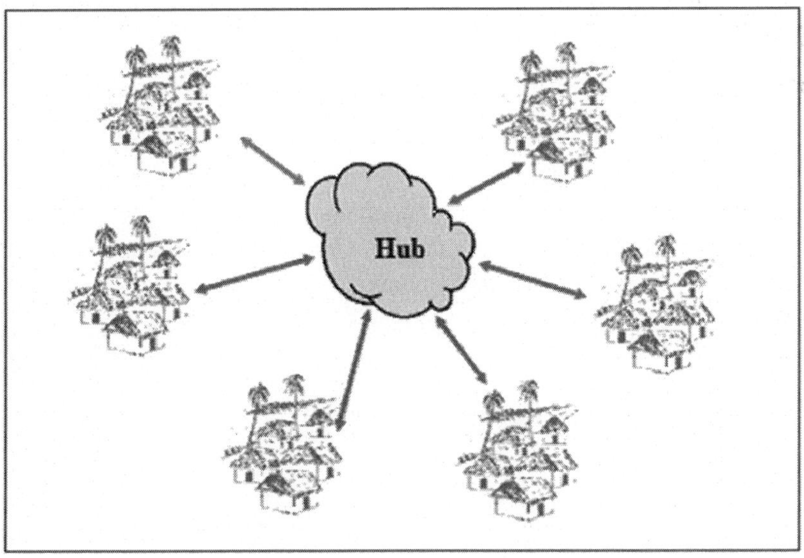

Figure 2. The hub and spoke model

In this model, the local population has a sense of ownership of the CeC. It is client managed and controlled, and information provided is demand- and user-driven. The local population should be willing to make contributions towards the expenses of the CeC, so that the long-term economic sustainability of the programme is ensured. Contributions in cash or in-kind generate a sense of ownership and pride and create an economic stake in the operation of the centre.

Of next importance is management. Involving youth in the management and decision-making aspect of CeCs is very important. Managers should be familiar with the technology, willing to learn, and have an interest in the needs of the community. The management processes should be flexible, collective and where necessary hierarchical with individual accountability. The community's role in management should typically be advisory; functional management by the community is not necessary. It is important to find a strong leader with good communication skills who enjoys the confidence of the community.

How to Convert the CeC into a Business Model

CeCs can create long-term, self-sustaining solutions which reflect local needs, but they require local entrepreneurship, which in turn, can fuel the creation of additional local business community enterprises. The CeCs need to be made available in larger numbers and information exchange must be available at lower costs if recent ICT advances are to have a significant impact on development for the world's poorest people.

The business of CeCs can be increased through several value-added services, for example by providing access to telephone, fax, voice mail, email, SMS and the web. This will increase demand for further IT training and access to computers and applications and information about distance learning programmes and information (weather, government services, news, entertainment), electronic libraries and publications, databases on appropriate technologies as well as connectivity and web space for local institutions (schools, health units, local government, NGOs, SMEs, farmers' and producers' associations).

CeCs can also provide administrative, accountancy and bookkeeping services; resources for offices, such as business development, marketing and technical support; telehealth, telemedicine and continued education to local health care workers; as well as e-banking, micro-finance and e-commerce facilities; tools and resources for community organization and participation in decision-making; digital recording of multimedia products for local business and culture promotion – examples might include pictures of arts, crafts, tourist accommodation; and local business facilities. Other services include providing ICT tools (portable computers, wireless telephones, and audio equipments) for rental, and providing facilities such as printers, photocopying, scanners, digital cameras, conference rooms, library and TV/VCR equipment; and locally relevant services such as birth and death registration, land registry, primary produce processing information and detailed market prices.

People in poorer communities could gain through increased knowledge of everything from food prices to new business ideas. By providing such services, CeCs could also become more financially self-sustaining by taking a percentage of payments made for non-free information, such as horoscopes or business courses.

In every programme, harnessing the power of partnerships is very important. It is only through partnerships that the gap between "scientific know-how" and "field-level do-how" can be bridged. Therefore, for CeC programmes to succeed they need to ensure they bring in partners from sectors relevant to their users, for example in agriculture, education, weather, health and business.

The Rice Knowledge Bank

Farmers regularly identify access to credit, good prices and knowledge as major limitations to improving their livelihoods. Although information and communication technology (ICT) is recognized as holding great promise to help meet information and knowledge needs, there have been few examples of success. To capture the promise of ICT, the International Rice Research Institute (IRRI) developed the Rice Knowledge Bank (RKB) – the world's leading ICT repository of rice-based training and technology information. Since its launch in September 2002, it has received over four million hits. This presentation outlines how the RKB is designed to deliver focused, credible, value-added and demand-driven information. The presentation also highlights the role of partnerships in ensuring that the information available on the RKB reaches those who can benefit from it. Highly focused, accurate information combined with a set of committed partners makes ICT successful – it is ICT structured for success.

Knowledge

The major limitations farmers feel they face, almost universally – irrespective of the country they are in – are credit, price and access to knowledge.

While recognizing the need to work with a range of players to address the credit and price gaps, IRRI saw a tremendous opportunity to have direct impact on addressing farmers' knowledge gap. In particular, IRRI saw the potential of harnessing the power and promise of ICT to address the knowledge access problem.

Can ICT Really Help Farmers?

The major question for IRRI was, "if we develop an ICT-based resource, will farmers really be able to access such knowledge and truly benefit?" While the statistics for personal computer access across most of Asia suggest that presently there is little hope, the future may be more promising. Farmers themselves may lack direct access, but IRRI targets many research and delivery partners, such as scientists and agricultural extension workers (who educate farmers to produce better crops at a lower cost), who do have access. ICT tools are, therefore, available to the people who work with and train the farmers. Further, the proliferation and increasing use of Internet cafés suggests that ICT does have potential as a tool to reach farmers directly.

Unfortunately, potential alone is of little use. What is the reality? There is cause for optimism in recent informal studies that indicate that every single major NGO and government research and extension partner has in its offices personal computers with CD drives, and most offices have at least some machines with Internet connectivity. ICT tools *are* available to the people who work with the farmers.

IRRI's Response to Knowledge Needs and the Potential of ICT

Seeing the potential and promise of ICT, IRRI developed the Rice Knowledge Bank (RKB), which contains a wealth of information for rice related training and extension, and is the world's first digital extension service. The RKB has received critical acclaim as a tool to distil, store and provide access to the vast array of IRRI's training and support knowledge for rice science and extension. This success was not accidental: IRRI devised a clear strategy for the development of the RKB. IRRI staff recognized that creating a digital repository was only a start. There were plenty of other projects that also had large "shovel-ware" repositories – sites where anything and everything related to an area were placed. IRRI saw that, in developing countries, major issues needed to be addressed if the RKB were to serve its ultimate purpose of helping rice farmers improve their rice-based livelihoods while protecting the environment. In particular, if the RKB was to be used effectively by farmers and their intermediaries, it was critical that its content be focused, credible, demand-driven and value-added.

Focused

A great temptation when using the immense power of ICT is to include as much information as possible – the principle that, "if a little is good, then more is better." Given more than 40 years of science and research, IRRI was well equipped to pursue this strategy. However, the RKB developers recognized early the importance of ensuring that the site remain focused, containing only knowledge that is relevant to extension and research training and support. This way, the target audience can quickly identify knowledge that is directly relevant to it without having to search through large amounts of irrelevant information.

Another aspect of focus relates to the target audience – the rice farmers of Asia are unlikely to gain regular, reliable access to ICT in the immediate- or medium-term future. The RKB was, therefore, designed to target the farmer intermediaries – research and development workers who already have access to ICT and need access to information to help farmers. Targeting these people is especially effective because many are already educated and experienced in training farmers.

Credible

A search of the Internet using the keyword "rice" results in some 12.8 million "hits" – but which of these can you believe? To address this problem, IRRI ensures that the RKB content is credible and accurate. To achieve this, IRRI instituted and maintains a rigorous quality-control process, which involves sign-off on content by the relevant IRRI scientists and review by RKB staff. With these mechanisms in place, combined with IRRI's 40 years of proven research results, users can be confident about the quality and relevance of the knowledge in the RKB.

Value Added

The RKB is value-added because it is available in a range of forms suitable to the needs and circumstances of the target users. All the knowledge is assembled and then made available either online, on CD-ROM or in print. The RKB's structure makes it a single-source publishing resource.

It was felt strongly from the beginning that RKB content should not just be a series of computer files online. Rather, the RKB presents information in forms that make the knowledge more accessible and more directly usable. Examples of this include:

- *Decision Support Tools* (*TropRice* and *Rice Doctor*), which are computer programmes that lead users easily through a process to solve their particular problem and find possible solutions
- *Fact sheets* that present the distilled essence of topics in one or two pages, these "how to" sheets allow practitioners to actually implement practices
- *Reference guides* on field-related information that are concise and easy-to-read, the RKB does not include the original scientific papers but rather draws on best practices in the private sector to present information in an easy-to-use, fully indexed, book form
- *E-learning courses* that have been created to capture and present a selection of key training topics in a form that users can access when and where they want and at a time of their own choosing

Demand Driven

The RKB team recognized that long-term success depended on access methods and content that is driven by user needs. This is ensured through IRRI's extensive in-country networks, which continually identify country needs and provide feedback on the relevance and ease of use of the RKB. In addition, the RKB site has extensive, up-to-date usage statistics – providing information on the most searched-for topics and key words – that help refine analysis of needs. One particular demand-driven innovation is the development of country-specific sites. These sites, the links to which sit under national flag icons on the RKB homepage, contain the best and most relevant local knowledge provided by users in each country. Much of this information is in the local language.

Utilised – the Ultimate Definition of Success?

The ultimate success of the RKB is defined by more than just the amount of access to the information. It is also dependent on how successfully the knowledge is applied to farm practices.

One heartening example highlights this process in action. Upon walking into one of the cramped Internet cafés that dot the roadside in the impoverished rice-growing areas of north-eastern Thailand, Mr. Ragat Nag, Director General of the Mekong Department of the Asian Development Bank, noticed an enthusiastic group of youngsters taking delight in showing their parents how to use a computer. What intrigued Mr. Nag most was what the children were showing their parents. Choosing to ignore the latest computer games, they were viewing pages from Rice Doctor, a diagnostic programme developed by IRRI to help rice farmers manage rice pests and diseases, and translating the relevant pages into Thai for their parents.

Although encouraged by this type of story, IRRI knows that rice knowledge rarely flows this directly from IRRI, through the Internet, to farmers. As a result, IRRI focuses its ICT and knowledge-dissemination efforts on the intermediaries – those staff members of national agricultural research and extension systems (NARES) and other partners such as NGOs who run extension services. These are the real target users of the RKB. In other words, IRRI trains trainers, who then adapt IRRI research methods and recommendations to local conditions and relay them to farmers.

There is little doubt about the success of access to the RKB. The site has registered over five million hits since its inauguration in September 2002 and the number of users continues to grow. At present, the RKB averages just over 1,000 visits per day at an average of 12.40 minutes per visit. This equates to almost 10,000 person-days of "training" per year delivered to people where they want it, when they want it. Some argue that this form of training is even more effective than traditional face-to-face methods, as the participants get information on exactly what they want. The access statistics do not include internal IRRI traffic or use of the many thousands of RKB CDs already distributed. While the RKB team is happy with these numbers, it aims to turn access into application. Thus, the RKB project continues to look for better ways to ensure application in both the classroom and the field. User feedback tells us that such application is happening, and it is in field application that we hope to see continued growth.

Future of the RKB

This presentation has so far established what the RKB is and that it is being widely accessed, but what of the second question in this presenta tion – "Can e-communities benefit?" The authors feel that e-communities can and are accessing the RKB, but for real success the RKB must be more cohesively linked to field activities. The RKB team is encouraging effective application by developing relevant content that grows along with in-country partnerships. The RKB will continue to develop: 1) targeted content with the addition of more locally-sourced and validated content, and 2) extension of RKB application and use in countries across the region by government organizations, NGOs, universities and training partners, particularly in linking access to field-oriented activities.

All future development will continue to ensure that the RKB's focus remains strong, its content always targeted, up-to-date and accurate, and that effective in-country use of this content meets the demands of farmer intermediaries and farmers.

Plans are in place to further improve content and to link the RKB to a participatory approach in field delivery, ensuring that knowledge not only becomes more widely available, but also more widely applied to help farmers. Success depends on changing old linear delivery modes to participatory models that bring together partners skilled in technology (the researchers), delivery (the extension experts) and relevance (inclusion of farmers as key partners). While such efforts are easy in concept, there is no doubt that ultimate success relies on the hard work of the many field workers who make science a reality by turning ideas into practice and by supporting the old saying that "seeing is believing" or the old Chinese proverb: "When I hear, I forget; when I see, I remember; when I do, I understand."

The RKB team will improve participation by:

1. Working with selected partners who have ICT access and skills, and who are also committed to training and field delivery. IRRI will help make the knowledge and skills gained through the RKB more accessible to other in-country partners (extension workers, for example) at a time and place of their own choosing.
2. Expanding the quality and scope of the country-specific information by capturing the best local knowledge available, thus ensuring that RKB material remains demand-driven and easy to use.
3. Transferring to national systems the considerable knowledge of how to develop, maintain and use ICT-based knowledge banks in agriculture. This will help national systems develop their own rice knowledge banks with whatever information they decide meets their

farmers' needs. They will also be able to transfer this knowledge to the field and to other crops. IRRI will help national systems develop their own knowledge banks.

The RKB Vision

The vision that IRRI has for the RKB remains essentially unchanged since its conception – the RKB aims to provide necessary, accurate information in the most appropriate form for the target audience. The current vision states:

> "IRRI's Rice Knowledge Bank is the world's leading provider of rice-related training and technology information, used by farmers and people who help them to improve the livelihoods of rice-dependent communities".

Stakeholder Partnerships for ICT in Rural Communities

In recent years, the term "multi-stakeholder partnership" (MSP) has gained much currency in development circles. However, there are few documented examples of truly effective MSPs in the realm of Information and Communication Technologies for Development (ICT4D).

MSPs are about partnerships that are greater than the sum of their parts and about creating lasting and meaningful impact at all levels of action. They are meant to promote a more holistic approach to development and better governance. Principles governing the management of multi-stakeholder ICT4D partnerships for sustainable development include:

1. Know when to apply a multi-sector ICT partnership
2. Before agreeing to enter into partnership, weigh its merits against the alternatives and risks
3. The interests of all partners should be mutually reinforced
4. Successful partnerships are built on complementary competencies and resources that, in combination, meet the parameters of some strategic design
5. The resources and competencies contributed to the partnership should be drawn from as close as possible to the core business of the partner organizations
6. Consensus should be sought for a written document identifying: the shared vision of the partnership; the objectives of each partner; and the division of roles and responsibilities

7. When evaluating the outcomes of multi-stakeholder ICT partnerships, care should be taken to identify the incremental contribution of the partnership activities over and above external factors and the next most likely alternative

Stakeholder Perspectives

Different types of organizations in society view multi-stakeholder partnerships in different ways.

Business Perspective

From a business perspective, no single company can deliver on the myriad of expectations surrounding sustainable development articulated by all its stakeholders: staff, shareholders, customers, suppliers, regulators and local communities. The reputation of the business, its ability to manage non-commercial risks, its capabilities to meet both internal and external requirements for corporate social responsibility, and its ability to realize opportunities for growth that benefits those socially excluded, will all depend on a business model that fully exploits its core competencies, whilst

concurrently partnering with other organizations who can bring the necessary complementarities to form more complete solutions. From this perspective, multi-stakeholder partnerships for sustainable development are thus no different in many of their principles from conventional business-to-business strategic alliances.

Public Sector Perspective

In the context of the dual forces of economic liberalization and the proliferation of (or demand for) democratic decision-making, both central government and municipal authorities find it increasingly challenging to achieve the right balance between their wide range of civic duties relating to sustainable development. Regulation of the free market is needed to ensure corporate responsibility, the promotion of foreign investment to stimulate employment opportunities, social inclusion, environmental protection, the provision of affordable public services, and responsive governance. In this context, it is not surprising that there are increasing numbers of examples of government departments and agencies seeking partnering opportunities with business and civil society organizations in order to enhance their capacity to administer the challenges of sustainable development.

Civil society perspective

The size and influence of this "third sector" has been increasing in the last two decades. Recent international studies of its economic contribution have shown it to be significant and growing – particularly in developed countries where a substantial proportion of social services are delivered through civil society organizations (CSOs). Likewise, in developing countries, an increasing proportion of development aid is being delivered through CSOs. Civil society groups can either play an advocacy or campaigning role, or they can become part of the solution, drawing on their local knowledge, capacity for innovation and trust of the general public to contribute in partnership to sustainable solutions.

Multi-stakeholder Partnerships

A set of principles for multi-stakeholder partnerships was drawn up in a preparatory conference in Bali, Indonesia in 2002 as input to the World Summit on Sustainable Development. Designed for so-called "Type II" partnerships, the principles are as follows:

Partnerships should:

- Help achieve the further implementation of Agenda 21 and the Millennium Development Goals, consistent, where applicable, with sustainable development strategies and poverty reduction strategies
- Be voluntary and self-organizing
- Be based on mutual respect and shared responsibility of the partners involved
- Have a multi-stakeholder approach, arranged among any combination of partner
- Be international in their impact, beyond the national level

One of the dangers of the current "partnership" movement is that the idea is fast becoming an 'end in itself', rather than a "means to an end." The conclusions of the Digital Opportunities Initiative (DOI) suggest that since ICTs are in practice "enablers" of sustainable social and economic development, multi-stakeholder ICT partnerships (i.e. strategic compacts between different ICT players) are likewise enablers and not ends in themselves. The DOI concluded further that the complexity of meeting the challenge of ICT as an enabler of sustainable development requires a holistic approach. The first stage of any multi-stakeholder partnering process is therefore to identify the "design parameters" of the desired solution. Only then can one scan society to find partners with the right suite of competencies, resources and incentives to collaborate in successful implementation. Drawing on these ideas, and the language of the DOI, a new definition for multi-stakeholder partnerships in the field of ICT sector is proposed:

Multi-stakeholder ICT partnerships are alliances between parties drawn from government, business and civil society that strategically aggregate the resources and competencies of each to resolve the key challenges of ICT as an enabler of sustainable development.

The Partnering Process

Multi-stakeholder ICT partnerships for sustainable development will invariably involve new forms of collaboration between non-traditional parties. Partners may, therefore, have quite different organizational cultures, ways of taking decisions, perceptions of accountability, methods of working and modes of behaviour. A key principle of successful partnerships is their ability to satisfy the drivers and interests of all the partners. Effective partnerships have to manage cultural differences, build trust and satisfy underlying interests. This requires effort to be placed not only on structural components of the partnership – the objectives and division of roles within a partnership – but also on the design of the process of multi-stakeholder partnering itself. Although the "partnering process" is likely to be different for different types of partnerships, there are some common steps. These are discussed below.

Partnership Exploration

Drawing on the principal conclusion of the DOI, namely that ICTs are enablers of sustainable development rather than ends in themselves, the first task in developing a multi-stakeholder ICT partnership is to understand what the development goal is that the partnership is intended to deliver. In the first instance, this is most likely to be chosen by the organization that is self elected to convene the initial discussions, and is usually developed as a simple and consistent "theme." Over time this theme often transforms, by consensus, into the overall vision or leading objectives of the partnership.

A frequent error of any organization contemplating entering into a partnership arrangement is to launch into discussions with others before fully understanding their own needs and interests. These include:

- The organizational drivers and interests to be served by the partnership
- Which in-house activity, programme, management system or department the partnering process and resulting partnership will integrate with
- The organization's negotiating strategy during the early consultation period
- The anticipated benefits of the partnership weighed against the costs and risks

Working through these steps will enable each prospective partner to judge the merits of entering into collaboration. However, once this assessment is complete it is still not certain that a partnership will develop. Before this can happen a degree of "buy-in" has to be generated within suitable partner organizations. A targeted process of consultation is the best way to secure this. The consultation should:

- Establish channels of communication with a range of potential partners and interested parties
- Develop the strategic design parameters of the partnership dialogue or solution that will deliver the agreed sustainable development goal, i.e. "requirements modeling"
- Identify those parties best positioned to bring the right resources and competencies to meet the design parameters, and assess their likely capacity to implement the future commitments
- Agree on a process by which the partners will consult/ negotiate the terms of the partnership

Partnership Building

A partnership will not progress unless all parties are able to reach consensus over how their underlying interests will be fulfilled and who will take responsibility for what action. What should be avoided is any one partner dictating the objectives and terms of the partnership. Building agreement over the details of any collaborative arrangement requires all partners to adopt a style of negotiation that accommodates differences in both culture and interests, and still achieves consensus. Conventional "adversarial" styles of negotiation often lead to "win-lose" outcomes and are therefore, a poor basis for developing mutually reinforcing partnerships. More likely to be effective is a consensual, "win-win," style of negotiation, where mutual understanding and a "celebration of difference" are key features.

Central to the effectiveness of multi-stakeholder ICT partnerships is the quality of resources and competencies committed by each party, and the degree to which these match the required design parameters. In addition to the more obvious resources and competencies, there are also those that are "hidden" and yet which might play a key part in the success of the partnership. These include staff secondments, local knowledge, office and other standard equipment, project management skills, administrative services, mediation skills, influence over and access to key individuals, willingness to adopt a leadership role, an ability to borrow capital at low interest rates, and a capacity to leverage resources from others. Once the vision and objectives of the partnership are agreed upon, along with a work plan outlining the division of roles and resources and other required structural components, the final task is to ensure that the partners have the capacity to implement their commitments.

Partnership Maintenance

Whether in networking, dialogue, hardware or software types of partnership, as the partners begin to work together there are bound to be tensions. Over time, the partners may need to convene to re-negotiate certain aspects of their original set of agreements, including, for example, the range of resources committed, key roles of certain partners, and the addition (or deletion) of new objectives or partners. Conventional organizational management tools such as SWOT analysis and decision-trees have proven to be useful at this juncture.

The need to adapt the configuration of multi-stakeholder ICT partnership over time is likely to derive from one or more of the following causes:

- Unanticipated behaviour of, or between, the different partners
- Design parameters that lack the strategic complexity to deliver the intended sustainable development outcome
- Insufficient capacity of a partner organization to implement its resource commitments or roles
- Changes in the external business or political environment

- Completion of agreed "milestones" in the work plan (e.g. the end of the design or construction phase, or the planned review of a "pilot" or beta site)

In addition to occasional re-negotiations, the partners need to be in regular communication with each other, to prevent differences from escalating into disputes, and to solve problems jointly and creatively. The more the partners interact, the more likely it is that the partnership will be successful.

Multi-stakeholder ICT Partnerships in International Development

The Global Knowledge Partnership (GKP), founded in 1997, is a worldwide network committed to harnessing the potential of ICTs for sustainable and equitable development. Within the GKP framework, governments, civil society groups, donor agencies, private sector companies and inter-governmental organizations come together as equals to apply ICTs for development (ICT4D). GKP recognizes that "access to information and knowledge is essential if the disadvantaged, the marginalized, and the poor are to improve their lives and lives of their children." In the context of international development, the GKP views multi-stakeholder ICT partnerships as the combined efforts of the public and private sectors and civil society stakeholders to:

- Better inform policy and decision-making on development
- Encourage shared commitment to common development goals
- Increase the impact and extend the reach of ICT development initiatives
- Leverage human and financial resources
- Maximize the outcomes of applying ICT

At the second GKP conference in March 2000, delegates highlighted the importance of multi-stakeholder ICT4D partnerships, recommending that, "the GKP promote the creation of multi-stakeholder partnerships to increase access to ICTs." In response to this, in January 2003, GKP led a workshop on the theme, "ICT at the service of development – multi-stakeholder initiatives and lessons learned". As part of the challenge to "create" multi-stakeholder ICT4D partnerships, the GKP has agreed to organize the ICT4D Platform of the World Summit on the Information Society (WSIS). The Platform will showcase a number of multi-sector ICT4D partnerships and, it is hoped, begin the task of developing a strategy for formulating pioneer partnerships integrated with the dual-summit format of the WSIS process.

The Persistent Challenges of ICT4D

ICT can make a significant contribution to poverty reduction and development in the developing world. ICTs can improve the effectiveness of disaster relief, for example, through speeding procurement of the more urgent types of humanitarian assistance; enhance the efficiency of health services, in the form of improved record keeping, more accurate diagnosis and information exchange on prevention; and provide access to educational services, for example through distance learning.

ICTs are also a means of improving the responsiveness of government to local priorities, disseminating information and opportunities for rural producers and poor urban dwellers to tap into new markets or find employment, and for engaging civil society and business in the reform of public sector institutions.

Beyond these more obvious applications, there is growing interest in the value of ICT in international development for two further reasons. The range of communication types available should mean that different technologies can be strategically selected to offer the closest fit with the needs of poor communities. For example, communities within microwave radio reach of fibre optic cable links can make use of a range of Wireless Local Loop (WLL) technologies such as the corDECT system. For those more distant from the countries' infrastructure backbones, or in hilly terrain, Very Small Aperture Terminal (VSAT) satellites are now available and actively promoted by some international development agencies. Connectivity based on VHF or UHF wireless technology is another, narrowband, option.

The second is concern over the low level penetration of ICT in the poorer regions of the world. Some interpret this as a future opportunity for business, namely that the mass of rural populations offers an as yet untapped market. Others view the lack of ICT penetration less as a business opportunity and more as a moral imperative for poverty reduction. Either way, as Chapman and Slaymaker argue, "The contradiction between the potential for ICTs to address the challenges faced by rural and urban development, and the current failure to harness them for this purpose, is striking."

The challenges to achieving greater ICT access for poor communities and the subsequent utilization of this access to reduce poverty are many. They include the ineffectiveness of the regulatory regime to attract new investment; the design of ICT transactions with the private sector that fail to deliver affordable ICT solutions; unprofitable business models for rural ICT access; ICT strategies that fail to exploit the diversity of technologies; and content that is irrelevant to the poor communities.

Models of Community E-centres for the Poor

In the Information Age where information is considered to be a vital resource for achieving our missions and needs, both individually and collectively. Information and communication technologies (ICT) can provide a wide array of information, accurately and quickly, to meet people's requirements, facilitating the building of constructive social capital from the point of view of the rural poor. ICT can strongly contribute to poverty reduction by enhancing income generating opportunities including employment for people with a low income. Information plays a crucial role in the livelihood of people, while integrating them into communities, nations and global economies.

In Sri Lanka, like in most of the developing countries, the use of ICT has been limited to a small segment of the population, which is considered to be the privileged group. The community at large and especially people with low incomes in Sri Lanka have not benefited from ICT due to the high costs of service providers coupled with the lack of suitable and accessible facilities.

Recently, there have been some attempts to introduce ICT to the poor, especially those living in rural areas. One such attempt, under the auspices of the Asian Development Bank and the Ministry of Education, was the Community Information Project for the Poor (CIPP) of Sri Lanka which was commenced in September 2003. The project involves the transfer of ICT to members of low-income communities.

The main purpose of the CIPP project is to create opportunities for people with low incomes to participate in economic growth by providing them with vital information. This is a pilot project, in the form of a Technical Assistance (TA) grant given by the Asian Development Bank. The project is implemented by TEAMS Consultants. The Government of Sri Lanka has developed a vision statement "e-Sri Lanka: An ICT Development Roadmap," with the goal of taking ICT to every village, business and citizen. In these terms, the CIPP could be seen as a way of assessing the feasibility of achieving this goal.

Organization of Community Information Centres and Models Used

CIPP involves three major components: (1) Establishment of community information networks (CINs) in each selected district for the provision of information services for the poor; (2) capacity building and skills development among local stakeholders for managing CINs and for the poor to use information services; and (3) social preparation for sustainability of the ICT services by local stakeholders beyond the project period.

The project has established community information networks in three selected districts of Sri Lanka – the Gampaha, Ratnapura and Kalutara Districts. Each network has one district community information centre (CIC) and ten village information centres (VICs). These three networks are coordinated by a project implementation unit (PIU) operating from the Ministry of Education. The project period is 15 months from September 2003.

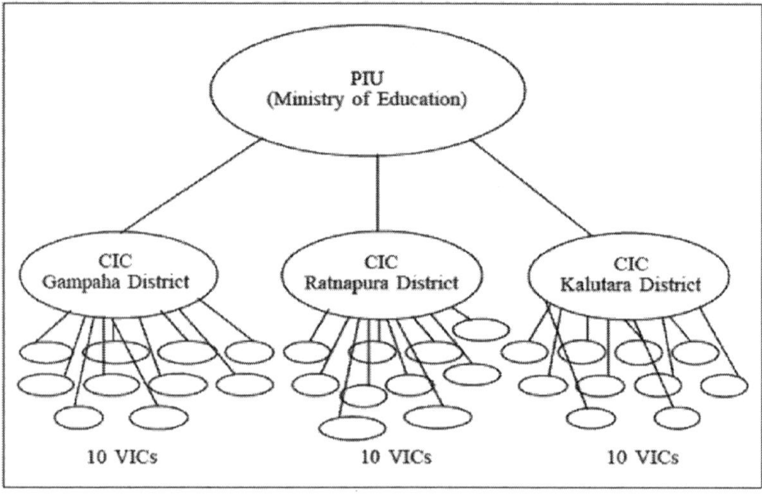

Figure 3. Structure of community information centres

The target group of the project are those who receive a monthly income of less than Rs. 3,000 (US$ 30) and low income groups such as farmers, labourers, plantation workers and fishermen. The aim of CIPP is the provision of vital information to the poor for their livelihood improvement, not simply providing ICT skills training for the people. However, the project involves providing basic computer literacy for the beneficiaries to access information. Extensive training is also provided to the operators of CICs and VICs and members of stakeholder groups on the use of computer hardware and software and the Internet. This is to ensure that the local operators can handle the operation and maintenance of the networks by the end of the project. The project also explores ways in which people of low income can access public and private sector services at a minimum cost. The maximum contribution from the communities of the relevant districts is tapped to ensure their ownership and active participation.

At the inception, the three CINs were established with three different service provision models in mind. The network of the Gampaha district was initiated as a model of e-governance linking public entities such as divisional offices, public extensions service centres, government training/ skills development centres, public health centres and state enterprises. The network of the Ratnapura district started as a model of e-commerce linking private entities such as private clinics, private schools, businesses, etc. The model used for establishing the Kalutara district network was a combination of both e-governance and e-commerce. The project anticipated to learn for future projects from these three networks by taking these as case studies. In other words, as a secondary project objective, it was envisaged to learn lessons on how e-commerce and e-governance could effectively reach the low income people.

The CICs and VICs were established in locations that could be served by various agencies without charging a rent. In choosing the locations the following criteria were taken into account:

- Readiness of the agency to provide a suitable area
- Degree of accessibility to members of poor communities and degree of centrality of the location
- Provision of appropriate space and infrastructure by the relevant agency to establish the CIC or VIC
- Safety and security aspects of the location
- Geographical location
- Distribution of VICs to represent different rural communities and/or different community cross-sections, economic activities and resources in the district

- Likely contribution to future sustainability

All three CICs are situated in locations provided by Local Authorities (Town Councils) in those districts. The VICs are situated in a wide range of locations such as divisional secretariats, local authorities, public libraries, market complexes, cooperatives, NGOs, Buddhist learning centres and divisional education offices. There is one VIC focusing specifically on soldiers with disabilities which is located at an Army Rehabilitation Centre.

The PIU, CICs and VICs were structured with the relevant technical expertise. In addition to the project staff, the Government of Sri Lanka appointed a counterpart staff for the project (a manager at the PIU level and coordinator for each district). With ADB funding, each CIC has been equipped with 18 computers including a local server, fax machine, scanner, photocopier, digital video camera, multimedia projector, printers, PDAs, mobile phones, telephone, Internet connection etc. The transport requirements of CICs were facilitated by providing them with a vehicle and five motorcycles. Each VIC has been provided with a computer, fax machine, telephone and Internet connection.

Operational Details of Community Information Centres

In accordance with the vision of the Project, the exact profile of information services to be provided by each CIN was fully tailored to meet the priorities of the community and to be continuously updated. For this purpose, an information needs assessment survey was undertaken at an early stage of the project to understand and prioritize the community information needs of each project district.

From the inception, it was recognized that in order to attract the target group (those with a monthly income of less that Rs. 3,000) there was a need firstly to attract certain "opinion leaders" who could act as catalysts within the rural community to make use of the services provided by the CIPP. These opinion leaders included teachers, Grama Niladharis (village level officials) Samurdhi officials, agriculture extension officials, members of the clergy, officials of people's organizations (such as farmers' organizations, rural development societies and women's groups). Action was taken to attract these village opinion leaders and then in turn to attract the target group with their assistance. The information needs assessment survey conducted in the three districts included a sample encompassing the target group as well as the opinion leaders mentioned above.

The information needs assessment survey provided some insights into the status of accessibility of ICT services for the poor in rural communities in the Gampaha, Ratnapura and Kalutara districts. The availability of and access to ICT for members of rural and poor communities was found to be very limited in all the three project districts. The survey revealed that for the Gampaha district, only five per cent of the respondents had access to computers and only seven per cent considered themselves computer literate; for the Ratnapura district only three per cent of the respondents had access to computers and only six per cent considered themselves computer literate; for the Kalutara district only four per cent of the respondents had access to computers and only five per cent considered themselves computer literate. The survey also revealed that very few of the respondents in the three districts had access to the Internet, e-mail, or facsimile. For example, in Gampaha only two per cent of the respondents had access to the Internet and e-mail; only three per cent had access to a fax; while 47 per cent had access to telephone facilities. A large percentage of the respondents had access to radio, television and newspaper modes of communication.

The number one priority category of information required for each project district differed, but overall the ten most sought-after information categories in these districts were: (i) education; (ii) employment; (iii) agriculture; (iv) business; (v) banking; (vi) industry; (vii) health; (viii) prices of commodities;(ix) public services; and (x) subsidies.

At the very early stage it was recognized that a reasonable quantum of information desired by the poor was not available in electronic form in the Web sites operated by different institutions and departments. Such information was available only in "hard form" as leaflets, booklets, manuals and brochures. The CICs were instructed to collect these sources of information. It was decided to serve the poor with information available in both electronic and hard form to meet all their needs.

The survey clearly indicated that the great majority of people required information from both the private and public sectors. As the main purpose of the project was to serve the poor with the information required for livelihood improvement based on their needs, the views of the benefi ciary groups were given prominence over the second objective of the project which was to learn lessons by trialling the CINs using three different service models. As a result, all three CINs have been serving the poor with both public and private sector information, a combination of e- governance and e-commerce models. In other words the project recognized that community information services for the poor should be based on the model of the people's needs rather than being limited to preconceived models such as e-governance and e-commerce.

The Community Information Networks (CINs) in the project districts have linked district offices, schools, training institutes, job placement centres, hospitals, markets, private companies and villages, in order to share vital information with local communities, using cost-effective and feasible communication modes. The types of information provided include job opportunities, education and training opportunities, agriculture services, health and medical information, weather and disaster warnings, public announcements, commodity and crop prices, and banking.

Based on the information needs assessment, the project has established a national level community web site as well as three district level community web sites to collect and disseminate information required by the low-income groups. In each district, important information is collected daily by the information collectors at the CIC, utilizing motorcycles. Similarly, the information collectors attached to the PIU are responsible for collecting important information at the national level. These project web sites are continuously updated by obtaining the views of the district level steering committees. However, there are limitations as many departments and institutes with vital information have no Web sites that could network to the project Web sites.

Important information is collected daily by information collectors, based on an analysis of the demand for information by the target group. The collected information is analyzed, verified and uploaded to the web sites of the project districts immediately. Newsflashes are prepared daily in each district to highlight news and important information in the district. This news is disseminated daily to VICs through electronic mail (e-mail) or facsimile, to ensure that key information reaches target beneficiaries without delay. Monthly newsletters are also published in three languages providing further information services to the target groups. Information collectors continually feed back information from community groups in terms of their information requirements.

Several activities were undertaken to attract target groups to the centres and to assist capacity building and skills development for managing CICs and VICs. The main activities undertaken were: (i) Setting-up and activating steering committees in all the CICs and VICs; (ii) conducting community awareness and promotional programmes; (iii) conducting training programmes for CIC operators and VIC operators; (iv) conducting basic training programmes for improving the computer literacy of members of local communities; and (v) developing strategies for the future sustainability of the project.

Awareness raising strategies have been developed and implemented in order to create community awareness and promote community participa tion in the project. The community awareness strategies that have been adopted so far include creating awareness through: (a) the media; (b) ceremonial inaugurations at the CICs and VICs; (c) special workshops; (d) project leaflets, posters, banners; and (e) training programmes.

Achievements and Future Sustainability

Over the past year, CIPP has served a significant number of rural people in the districts of Gampaha, Kalutara and Ratnapura. According to the records maintained in the CICs and VICs, approximately 31,000 members of the rural community in the Gampaha district have used the services provided by the Gampaha CIN. Among these users about 41 per cent belong to Samurdhi recipient families (Samurdhi recipients are people with a monthly income of less than Rs. 1,500, who are given special government assistance for poverty alleviation). These families live below the poverty threshold and are thus classified as the poorest of the poor. Also, according to the records, over 75 per cent of the users of the CIN are classified as poor (i.e. have an income of less than Rs. 3000) and the most sought-after information categories/types by the information seekers using the Gampaha CIN were information on employment opportunities; information related to education; and information related to industries. Although the majority of the users (about 58 per cent) were served with electronic information, about 42 per cent were served with information available at the centre in "hard form".

The CIN of the Ratnapura district has been patronized by over 17,000 rural poor of whom about 36 per cent are Samurdhi recipients. Here again, the majority of the users obtained their specific information requirements via the Web/Internet, while the others were served with information available in the centres in hard form. According to the records maintained, the most sought-after information categories by the information seekers using the Ratnapura CIN were information on employment opportunities; information related to education; and information related to agriculture.

About 18,500 rural poor have visited the CIN of the Kalutara district of which about 32 per cent are Samurdhi recipients. Once again the majority of the users visiting the centres obtained specific information using Web/ Internet sources. According to the records maintained, the most sought-after information categories by the information seekers using the Kalutara CIN were information on employment opportunities; information related to education; and information related to agriculture.

The performance of the CICs and VICs and the overall progress of the project was monitored continuously. A mid-term project review was conducted by the ADB and the Ministry of Education together with the project consultants. While progress in general was acceptable, project achievements in terms of providing important information to the project target group was found to be inadequate. Consequently, the organizational structure of the project and the implementation strategies were re-structured. In this process, the terms of reference of the consultants (the project team) and the required qualifications of the consultants were re-formulated focusing on "social mobilization", "outreach to the poor" and "social preparation at the community level for sustainability of CINs". With these changes, social mobilization and associated work became the main focus of the project. The project period was extended by four months, until the end of April 2005.

It is anticipated that gradually, the community operators will take over information collection, analysis and verification, information uploading to the Web site, publication of news and services to the rural poor so that by the conclusion of the pilot project, the information network can be sustained by the community. Cost recovery measures will also be explored extensively by introducing user fees, paid advertisements, soliciting donations. These measures will be determined by the steering committee of each district. This process is currently taking place.

At present, ICT services are provided to the community via CICs and VICs at no charge. Although the main focus is to serve the target group mentioned earlier, any rural Sri Lankan can visit the CICs and VICs and use the computers if they are unoccupied. The project team recognized that a charge levying system needs to be implemented on a cost recovery basis for the CICs and VICs. In order to formulate the rates of the charging system, a rate survey was carried out in the three project districts. The rates are based on the lowest commercial rates for communication services. The main aim of the fee levying system is cost recovery, with no profits anticipated. Further, following the objectives of the project, subsidised rates are proposed for the target group members. It is proposed that the money collected by this charge levying scheme should be deposited in a separate account for each CIN and that proper accounting procedures should be maintained.

The analysis of the results of the rate survey revealed that 80 per cent of the survey respondents were willing to pay for the services provided at the Gampaha district CIN, while 67 per cent were willing to pay for the services provided at the Ratnapura district CIN and 62 per cent of the survey respondents were willing to pay for the services provided at the Kalutara district CIN. This is an important factor when considering the design of strategies for the future sustainability of the project.

From the very inception of the project, it was recognized that sustainability measures are important to guaranteeing the continuity of community ICT services to the poor. The following sustainability strategies were identified by the project team:

1. Ensure the active involvement and participation of relevant stakeholder organizations, institutions and the community in operating CINs;
2. Promote among the stakeholder organizations and the beneficiary groups the value of the services provided by the project and enhance community participation to improve the utilization of ICT services via community awareness programmes and computer literacy training programmes;
3. Establish and activate steering-committees of the CICs and VICs to improve the functioning of CICs and VICs and to facilitate the future sustainability of the CICs and VICs;
4. Develop workable and efficient cost-recovery measures for the sustainability of the CICs and VICs;
5. Encourage commitment by stakeholder organizations to take over the operation and running of the CICs and VICs; and
6. Undertake capacity building measures for CICs and VICs to operate by themselves and minimize the "dependency syndrome" on the TA team, towards the end of the TA.

Currently, these strategies are being developed into an action plan with the help of the steering committees of the CICs and VICs.

Issues Faced and Lessons Learned

There are many socio-economic and cultural barriers that need to be overcome to ensure that members of poor local communities freely adopt information and communication technology. Some of the main barriers that have been encountered by the project team during the course of the project include: (a) a general lack of computer literacy; (b) a fear of modern technology and a natural reluctance to use new technology; (c) language barriers; (d) access problems in very remote rural areas; (e) frequent power outages, especially in the remote rural areas; (f) the costs involved in adopting information and communication technology; and (g) natural disasters including floods, landslides, etc. which cut off entire villages from the rest of the world. These socio-economic and cultural barriers that need to be overcome to ensure that members of poor local communities freely adopt ICT, narrow the existing digital divide and empower poor rural communities to seek and achieve a better quality of life.

One of the main difficulties faced during the project was the selection of appropriate locations for setting up the district CICs and VICs. This has been difficult because the sites had to meet certain minimum project criteria or requirements. Locating and acquiring sites that meet these requirements or criteria has been difficult. Thus, a number of site evaluations, reviews and changes had to undertaken in order to set-up the CICs and VICs.

Another important constraint, especially in establishing the VICs, has been the technology scarcity in some areas in the project districts. Because the aim of the project is to reach poor people, there has been a need to establish the VICs in very rural areas, where services such as telephone connections, Internet connections. are scarce or even non-existent. This technology barrier has delayed the setting up and operation of the VICs in all three districts. Also, undertaking activities such as building renovation and repairs and the provision of services such as electricity, telephone connections, Internet connections is quite a time consuming process. This has also delayed the setting up and operation of the VICs.

The computer literacy of members of poor communities is very low. Hence, the need for more effective computer literacy training programmes and community awareness programmes has been identified. Several computer literacy training programmes and awareness strategies were implemented and are continuing to be implemented for communities of the project districts.

A reasonable volume of information desired by the rural poor was not available in electronic form due to limitations of web sites maintained by various institutes and departments. Therefore, the users visiting the centres were served with information both in "electronic form" and in "hard form". In setting up the project web sites, some technical difficulties were encountered. This was mainly in relation to establishing the Web sites in the national languages of Sinhala and Tamil, where the consultants experienced some technical difficulties in adopting existing computer software to construct the Web sites. However, these problems were resolved subsequently.

As mentioned earlier, each of the CINs was established with a predetermined model in mind, models on e-governance, e-commerce and a combination of the two. However, the need as expressed by the CIN users, i.e. the rural poor, was to receive information covering aspects of both e-governance and e-commerce. Thus, perhaps the most important lesson from the project so far is that in a community information system such as the one explored in this project, the service model should be demand driven and user centred rather than predetermined. This is important in order to achieve its mission and to ensure user support for sustainability.

Economic Analysis of Community E-centres

Most rural people have much lower levels of economic development and health, education, and general well being than their urban counterparts because of lack of access to universal services and markets. This is due to poor infrastructure provision such as transport and communication networks and deficient institutional systems for financial operations. The ultimate objective of rural development is improvement in the quality of life for rural people by removing the impediments of developing rural economies and providing basic infrastructure in rural areas. Information and communications technology (ICT) is one of the most effective tools for assisting rural communities to leapfrog over such hurdles to development.

ICT is defined as a set of activities that facilitate the processing, transmission, and display of information by electronic means. Generally, ICT has made a great impact on economic growth and social development by:

(1) enhancing the productivity and efficiency of existing sectors and industries;

(2) creating new business and/or development opportunities, which would not be possible without ICT;

(3) facilitating an open economy and promoting a competitive market environment through enhanced information accessibility; and

(4) improving quality of life and human well-being through accessibility to various new e-services.

However, in order to fully exploit those benefits from applying ICT to the existing economy, it is important to strengthen a set of complementary factors that assist the necessary socio-economic transforma tion of the economy. These include the mind-sets of people, ways of communicating, the structure of the economy, and the level of literacy.

To provide public access to ICT-based services and applications, community e-centres (CeC) have been recognized as a cost-effective facility, especially in rural areas, given the limited resources and number of people who can afford ICT-based services. However, previous experience gained in establishing CeCs raises the issue of CeC sustainability as the most critical issue. Experiences show that although CeC is seen as sustainable in the long-term once its socio-economic impact is realized, surviving up until that point is difficult due to the lack of a self-sustainability mechanisms and its inevitable reliance on public support. Therefore, due consideration should be given in the beginning, when designing and establishing CeCs, to the long-term sustainability of the operation. In view of this, this presentation emphasizes the importance of flexible investment planning and decision-making processes.

As an effective economic analysis tool to analyze flexible decision-making processes, the "real option" approach is introduced and explored in this presentation. Real option is defined as the right, but not the obligation, of investment to get the payoff from the investment decision in real assets and thus, it is a contingent claim on its value, which is dependent on uncertain future demand. The establishment of CeCs can be viewed as an initial investment for increasing e-awareness among local communities that creates a variety of follow-on commercial and social development opportunities. In this sense, investment in CeC can be regarded as a real option on future development and commercial impact. The real options valuation approach is useful, especially in situations where a high degree of uncertainty exists and large up-front investment is needed that will be followed by several subsequent investment opportunities like investment in CeC.

The Role of ICT for Development

In the shift from the Industrial Age of the 20th Century to the Information Age of the 21st Century, there has been a convergence ICT with the market and government. The result is that the commerce sector, through the impact of a number of interlinked forces, has become e-commerce, and at the same time has become globalized and more value oriented. The same is true of sectors such as manufacturing, agriculture, finance, education, health and even governance. The result of this convergence has been the facilitating of an open economy and promotion of a competitive market environment; the creation of new businesses and/or development opportunities; and the enhancement of productivity and efficiency in existing sectors and industries.

Along with the traditional economy, there is now the ICT (Network) Economy. Keywords for this new economy include network externality, path-dependency (lock-in), increasing returns (positive feedback) and critical mass. These keywords both characterize and dictate the success of ICT.

In terms of rural development ICT can play an important role in improving the quality of life for rural people. However, that promise has yet to be realized due to the lack of connectivity and accessibility to universal services and markets among rural communities. Therefore, it is necessary to remove the impediments faced by the developing rural economy and provide basic infrastructure in rural areas to enable the spread of ICT. This would enable ICT to be part of a comprehensive socio-economic development strategy for rural development as a means, not an end.

In rural areas, CeC's are a crucial element and key instrument in efforts to bridge the digital divide. CeCs can be defined as shared premises where the public can use basic telecommunications services, access the Internet and utilize ICT applications for their interests. Its functions include increasing accessibility to basic telecommunication services such as telephone, fax; expanding access to universal services such as education, health, government and social services through ICT connectivity; and providing information and services for the commercial interest of the community through ICT connectivity.

Whilst CeCs hold much potential, sustainability is a serious challenge. This is due to a lack of self-sustainability mechanisms; CeCs' inevitable reliance on the public supports; and "high uncertainty in demand and complementary factors".

Given the high uncertainty in demand, flexible investment planning and a strategic decision-making process is needed for CeC establishment and management. Further, comprehensive economic analysis is needed to increase the value of investment by increasing flexibility in the decision-making process.

Key Elements in Designing a Sustainable CeC Model

The major elements required for economic analysis of CeCs in order to design a sustainable CeC model include the analysis of local demand, the supply condition, and the demographic characteristics of the area. In addition, the economic impact of CeCs can be affected by the existence and intensity of a range of complementary factors that support the socio-economic transformation of rural communities into the one that able to meet the demands of the information age.

The supply condition refers to the potential network, terminal, and application options. A local demand analysis must be conducted first to select the optimal mix of those three options. Based on the local demand analysis, the expected impact of a CeC can be measured, including quantitative and qualitative; direct and indirect; and short-term and long-term impact.

Generally, for rural economies much higher investment and operating costs are required for utilizing broadband connection. This is caused by the difficulty of accessibility to backbone infrastructure and despite rapid developments in wireless technology and PLC technology, it still remains as one of the greatest physical hurdles in designing CeC's investment plans. One way to address this is to expand the broadband infrastructure based on the demands and readiness of rural communities.

The difficulty in using this approach is that it is much more difficult to judge what the estimated revenue from several ICT applications might be in rural communities as there is much higher uncertainty in local demand. Compared to urban communities where potential consumers can be relatively easily captured, users in rural areas have often never sat down in front of a computer before, know little about traditional information search methods (perhaps owing to a lack of rural libraries), have little schooling, and have no experience using the Internet or e-mail. To offset the risk caused by this high uncertainty, CeC investment and management planning should be more flexible.

Flexibility is the mechanism by which an alternative route to success can be obtained should the preferred route fail because of a risk. Flexibility therefore, implies the potential of bringing a benefit to a project and increasing its value. The more flexible an investment is, the more the management of a project can take advantage of a beneficial event and offset an adverse event. The value created by flexibility is turned into a real financial benefit, thus resulting in stronger sustainability.

The Real Options Valuation Approach (ROVA)

The real options valuation approach (ROVA) is an emerging economic analysis tool, which challenges traditional approaches such as discounted cash flow method and decision-tree analysis. The objective of a traditional economic analysis is to assess the impact of a project on the local, regional or national economy to see if the investment of the project can be justified in terms of economic net present value (NPV) or internal rate of return (IRR) using the discounted cash flow method. This is done by defining the project objectives and rationale; forecasting demand for the project output; choosing the least-cost design or alternative to meet project demands; quantifying economic benefits and costs by NPV or IRR; and establishing that a project will be sustainable in financial, environmental or social terms over its operating life if the economic NPV is positive or IRR exceeds the minimum hurdle rate.

These traditional methods tend to undervalue investment opportunities due to the basic assumption that the investment opportunity is not totally reversible or is a now-or-never opportunity. Therefore, one of their major limitations is that they do not consider the flexibility of the investment, such as altering the pace of investment, or stopping investment at some point if conditions are unfavourable without revisiting the issue of uncertainty and risk reduction. This kind of single-point decision process obviously raises the cost of projects that turn out to be failures. The real options approach, on the other hand, can incorporate such flexibility into its decision process as a monetary term and suggest ways to increase the value of flexibility given high uncertainty to make a strategic and forward-looking investment.

Real options can be defined as the right to get the payoff from the business or organization's investment decision on real assets. It is a contingent claim on value, which is dependent on uncertain future demand and/or uncertain output volume. It is not only a valuation tool but a way of thinking.

The real options methodology emerged from the theory of financial option pricing. Application of real options includes design, evaluation and optimal timing analysis of project or investment plans in natural resources development projects, real estate, manufacturing and infrastructure investments and R&D projects.

CeCs can be considered a real option. For example, the establishment of a CeC can be viewed as an initial investment for increasing the e-awareness of local communities, creating a variety of follow-on commercial and social development opportunities in the future. In this sense, investment in CeC can be regarded as a real growth option, call-like type, on future development and commercial impact.

How to Design a Sustainable CeC Model

The procedure for designing a sustainable CeC model is:

(1) demand analysis and impact measurement;

(2) technological feasibility study and cost estimation;

(3) complementary factor analysis;

(4) business model design; and

(5) pilot test and feedback.

In the analysis, the rural economy is divided into farming and non-farming economies, where the latter includes service, trade, and household manufacturing activities except for the farming activities. These activities depend to a large extent on local and regional demand and tend to grow rapidly in the context of agricultural growth.

The characteristics of the CeC investment process include:

1. *Staged investment*: providing telecentres and training, computer centres, network centres, e-service centres;
2. *Uncertain outcome*: Different outcomes for different regions depending on the associated idiosyncrasies; and
3. Possibility of changes in decision.

It is suitable for the ROVM framework (e.g. no further investment or change to alternative form of investment if negligible expected outcome from the earlier stage investment).

Policy Implications of Economic Analysis of CeCs Using the Real Options Valuation Approach

The key points for institutionalization of the real option model for a single project are the need to have a plan reflecting the contingent decision-making and to conduct periodic reviews to assess the strategy in the following-on stage based on the revealed information in the previous stage. For multiple projects, the key point for institutionalization is establishing the staircase for successful projects to develop further with larger investment. The SBIR (Small Business Innovation Research) Programme in the United States is a good example of this.

Sustainability is the most critical issue in establishing, managing, and operating CeCs. In this sense, a new economic analysis paradigm such as the real options valuation approach enables CeC policy makers or operators to enhance its sustainability by creating more options (or opportunities) through stage-wise investment, comprehensive periodic reviews, various e-applications provisions and strengthening of complementary factors.

Local Knowledge Management Through Community E-centres

Local knowledge is knowledge held locally, held by local people. This may appear straightforward, but it is actually more complex than it seems. The focus is on two aspects of local knowledge: "formal information" (i.e. information written following the tradition of scientific method) about a local situation and "indigenous" knowledge, or knowledge that is imbedded in local traditions, stories, and other repositories of local wisdom. This presentation explores how to combine and integrate such "local" knowledge with "global" knowledge to facilitate the actions of health workers and managers at the community level. Particular emphasis is given to the role of information and communication technologies (ICTs), specifically the Internet, in this endeavour.

Knowledge is the product of many minds, spread over generations and geographical areas, being added to or adapted as it develops over time. Many indigenous practices are spread across a number of countries, or regions, or even parts of the globe, and it is hard to tell where these practices are really local, and where they have been imported.

Equally, with the increasing travel and emergence of diasporas, the phenomenon of "globalization" has arisen, where local practices travel with the movements of the labour force or refugees to very distant places, where they may be shared by expatriate communities, modified and then re-imported to the mother country.

Beyond that is the distinction between local formal knowledge – such as locally published books and journals, locally generated epidemiological information and medical patient records – and local indigenous knowledge, which embraces local customs and practices, often in oral or other traditional forms of expression, including storytelling, song, theatre and dance..

Knowledge that is generated locally increasingly comes into contact with, and is influenced by, externally produced knowledge. Such external knowledge is provided in journals, through radio and television and, more recently, electronic media such as CD-ROMs and the Internet. This external knowledge can be either:

- Of generic relevance (clearinghouse information, standards and norms from such bodies as WHO)
- Knowledge that refers to the local health situation (papers and reports about, or directly relevant to, the local situation, but produced externally). In practice, such external knowledge can be seen as an extension of local knowledge, even though it was created outside the country or region
- Finally, there is the category of information produced by other countries and locations in the region, which is likely to be of relevance locally, given some adaptation

Local knowledge may originate locally, be recognized as relevant and collected for dissemination – written up, drawn or photographed, recorded or filmed – and then transmitted to others. Equally, knowledge can originate elsewhere and be transmitted to the local setting on paper or electronically. Once it arrives, it may be localized (adapted to make it locally appropriate).

Local Non-formal or Indigenous Knowledge

According to the World Bank, indigenous knowledge (IK) is simply, "local knowledge" which is unique to every culture or society and which serves as the basis for local-level decision-making in agriculture, health care, food preparation, education, natural resource management and a host of other activities in communities.

The World Bank believes IK is important because firstly, it provides problem-solving strategies for local communities, especially the poor. It represents an important component of global knowledge on development issues. Secondly, indigenous knowledge is an under-utilized resource in the development process.

Increasingly, local knowledge is being collected into digital repositories. The effect of such collection is both to help preserve the knowledge and to spread it more widely. By collecting indigenous knowledge in databases and applying the techniques of comparative analysis and scientific method, the value of such knowledge is coming to be appreciated more widely. This sometimes has unwelcome consequences – when, for example, a foreign company attempts to obtain a patent for an item of indigenous knowledge. For example, there have been battles fought over patents granted to some foreign companies for medicinal uses of leaves from the *neem* tree, which grows in many parts of South Asia – even though such medicinal uses have been known in the traditional culture for over a thousand years.

Examples of Western Science Methods Used to Assess IK

The following are some examples of Western science methods that could be used to assess IK. This list shows that approaches developed in different disciplines can be used. These methods should be combined with insiders' assessment.

Animal Production and Healthcare

If a community wishes to expand and improve its livestock production system, the following Western science methods could determine the efficiency of local animal production and healthcare practices and indicate which aspects of the indigenous system could be used, improved, or blended with Western practices:

- Measure productivity of animals, recording both inputs and outputs
- Observe the condition of livestock kept in the community (this could be done by visual inspection, weighing and measuring animals, etc.)
- Test for parasites by investigating faeces of randomly selected animals
- Identify medicinal plants used by the community and test their efficacy. The medicinal qualities of some plants have already been established in the scientific literature

Indigenous Paper Making

- Calculate amount of raw materials and energy used in the production process
- Test quality of paper in the laboratory (do not forget to keep the local use in mind when making any statement about the paper's quality)

Effect of IK on Environment

- Assess biodiversity in the environment of the study community (e.g. count number of species in an area of a certain size)
- Measure nutrients in soil
- Measure runoff and soil erosion from fields

Indigenous Birth Attendants

- Collect data about course and outcome of deliveries assisted by indigenous birth attendants and analyze results using statistics
- Investigate condition of instruments used by local birth attendants (e.g. whether the instruments are clean, which bacteria they contain, etc.)

Indigenous Communication

- Assess number of persons reached by messages transmitted through indigenous channels
- Measure time needed for transmission

Knowledge Management and the Field of Development

Contemporary development debate centres on the over-arching issue of "globalization" – the idea that the global economy either is, or should be, or should not be, global in scope. With the global economy comes a host of other global issues – global culture, global standards, global legislation, global development – and global knowledge. There are many aspects to this debate. Suffice it to say that many people believe that globalization can be destructive to local economies, cultures and environments.

Addressing the Global Knowledge II Conference via a video link, World Bank President James Wolfensohn said, "Knowledge is perhaps the only unquestioned value of globalization". Even that may have been over-optimistic, as the relationship between local and global information remains to be fully clarified.

To introduce this topic, the work of two key exponents of "localization" – Stiglitz and Hines – is summarized below.

The End-users

Who are the end-users of locally relevant knowledge? The categorization of target audiences for health information as an example presented below was drafted at a meeting held at WHO's Eastern Mediterranean Regional Office:

1. Policy-making levels in the Ministry of Health
2. Health professionals with university training
3. Health professionals with full, normal training but not university
4. Policy-making levels in the government
5. Professionals in health-related fields with university trainin(managers, accountants, nutritionists, etc.)
6. Technicians in various fields
7. Paramedics, health technicians
8. Health auxiliaries
9. Traditional birth attendants and traditional healers
10. Other auxiliary staff, community workers and local NGOs
11. Community leaders (religious, social leaders, teachers, etc.)
12. Public opinion leaders (including social writers)
13. The general public, educated (secondary school level and upwards)
14. The general public (including village communities, etc.)

The breadth of this classification is worth noting – from politicians and civil servants, academics and researchers, to practitioners at all levels in the public health infrastructure (from central services to community-based services) and right down to the general public.

Each group requires information and knowledge tailored to its needs. This is true throughout the world, and is a particularly significant issue in developing countries.

Knowledge Integration

The key question is how to bring together global and local knowledge, and "expert" and indigenous knowledge.

A number of initiatives are working on this, some focusing on bringing external information into the local sphere and adapting it to make it locally appropriate. Others are strengthening the capability of local information to be recognized and operate locally and to participate in the international flow of information. Still others focus on making huge collections of formal health information available. Some of these will be described below.

Information Waystations and Staging Posts: Electronic-print Chaining

The information waystations and staging posts activity provides a number of examples of how knowledge networking can be applied in formulating large collaborative projects. From 1998, INASP-Health has managed the Health Information Forum (HIF), a regular series of meetings bringing together many organizations interested in health information. Right from the start, HIF participants considered technological options for getting health information to health workers in developing countries. The challenge was to develop a coherent, cost-effective approach. An e-mail list was used to extend the discussion as widely as possible (over 2,000 messages were sent), and gradually two concepts arose:

- *Information waystations:* local points of access to health information received electronically
- *Staging posts:* "relay stations", translating and adapting information materials in order to make them locally appropriate

Thus, information waystations are concerned with bringing the technology to developing countries and training people to use it to obtain health information, while staging posts focus on adapting the information materials received in such a way as to make them more appropriate for local use.

The Open Knowledge Network: Local Content Creation and Exchange

The Open Knowledge Network (OKN) arose from work done by the G8 DOT force between 2000 and 2002. Representatives from government, civil society and the private sector in both developed and developing countries worked on a wide range of initiatives to help bring digital opportunities to the South. Among these initiatives, the creation and exchange of local content was identified as a keystone in any bridge across the digital divide. Without appropriate local content, users could arrive at community access points only to find little of relevance to their lives, almost nothing in their own language and few ways to use this new technology to increase their chance of an improved livelihood. The Genoa Plan of Action therefore called for a "national and international effort to support local content and applications creation" that would in particular:

1. Encourage networking among bodies which acquire, adapt and distribute content on a non-commercial basis;
2. Encourage governments to provide widely-available free-of-charge access to state-owned information and local content, except where it is private or classified; and
3. Encourage commercial publishers to explore possible business models to enhance greater accessibility for poor people to relevant content.

The consultation process began under the chairmanship of OneWorld International (the civil society DOT force delegate from the UK) with support from the Department of International Development (DFID) in the UK. What emerged from six months of consultation and research into existing best practice was a proposal that came to be called the "Open Knowledge Network" (OKN). The purpose of the OKN is to promote both the creation and the exchange of local content as widely as possible across the South. Local content development is closely tied to human development, and the ultimate goal of the OKN proposal is the empowerment of local communities.

The following key concepts are included in OKN:

- Connect to the Internet without going online, using local public access points/CeCs to upload or download information in short, inexpensive bursts
- Focus on content, not technology, which is always changing. The forms best adapted to one Southern context may be inappropriate in another
- Agree on using standards for exchanging digital content worldwide
- Network knowledge workers and translators across the South
- Use a network of knowledge hubs to support the local access points
- Encourage circulation of works that are affordable by Southern users, while still allowing such users to profit from their own contributions to the knowledge base. This will require an Open Knowledge License for proprietary material, which will include the rights to copy, modify and translate information, to offer it for public distribution among

members of the OKN network, and to circulate it further in non-digital formats such as hard copies, radio broadcasts and community bulletin boards

- Encourage a market for local information, while maintaining the principle that knowledge for development should, wherever possible, be free at the point of use in poor communities.

References

Chambers, R. (1997). *Whose Reality Counts?* Intermediate Technology Publications, London.

Harris, R. W.(2005). *Building telecentre services.* APEC Telecentre Training Camp. (January 24-29, Taipei, Taiwan).

Jensen, M. & Esterhuysen, A. (2001). *The community telecentre cookbook for Africa – recipes for self-sustainability – How to establish a multi-purpose community telecentre in Africa.* United Nations Educational, Scientific and Cultural Organization, Paris.

Parkinson, S. (2005). Telecentres, access and development; experience and lessons from Uganda and South Africa. IDRC. Retrieved from Web: http://www.idrc.ca/en/ev-87255-201-1-DO_TOPIC.html

Roman, R. & Colle, R. D. (2002). Themes and issues in telecenter sustainability. In *Development Informatics,* Working Paper Series no. 10. Institute for Development Policy and Management, Manchester.

Rothenberg-Aalami, J. & Pal, J. (2005). Rural telecenter impact assessments and the political economy of ICT for Development (ICT4D), Berkeley Roundtable on the International Economy (BRIE) Working Paper 164. University of California, Berkeley.

4

Infrastructural Interventions in Rural Areas

Most of the developing countries are characterized by low levels of per capita income, low resource productivity, non-availability of modern technology in the production process, lack of skills and training, and, more serious, burgeoning population. In all development literature, rapid economic growth is recognized to be the most effective instrument for raising the standard of living of the masses and eradicating poverty. Rapid economic growth, in turn, depends on the level of investment, state of technology and availability of skilled labour and entrepreneurship.

During the 1950s and 1960s, a high growth strategy was deliberately adopted by most developing countries not as an end in itself but "as an activist interventionist strategy" to eradicate poverty. Basing themselves on the experience of industrialized countries in the West, the developing countries came to the conclusion that it would not be possible for them to eradicate poverty without rapid diversification of the economy and without achieving a significant acceleration in their overall sectoral growth rates. According to this view, rapid growth would succeed in pulling up the poor through widening the production base and through the provision of productive employment to hitherto underemployed or unemployed labour force.

It was further argued that rapid growth would, in addition, also enable the government to mobilize resources out of incremental income for further investment for growth and for social expenditure on education and health. Therefore, most developing countries adopted policies that ensured rapid growth of gross domestic product (GDP) for maximizing national product. For maximization of growth, national economic planning was widely adopted.

By the 1970s, the development experience of these countries turned out to be quite mixed. While a few of them achieved high growth combined with rising per capita income and a significant decline in poverty, many others were only able to record low to moderate growth with no significant reduction in poverty. The policy of active State intervention combined with relatively open trade regime and large foreign investments resulted in high growth in many East Asian countries as also in China after it reoriented its economic policy in 1978. Notably, the growth rates recorded by these countries also resulted in perceptible decline in poverty. On the other hand, by the 1970s, it was apparent that many developing countries in South Asia and Africa were unable to achieve any significant rise in living standards or to make a visible dent on poverty. Although, generally, the incidence of poverty was slowly declining in their case also, yet rapid population growth in some of these countries resulted in a perceptible increase in the number of rural and urban poor. The only exception to this were some well-endowed subregions within these countries which experienced high growth rates in agriculture and a reduction in rural poverty as a result of successful adoption of new technology after the mid-1960s.

The failure to achieve the goals of equity and large-scale persistence of poverty and unemployment resulted in a rethinking of plan priorities in many countries. Several extreme views were expressed. According to some critics, planning with its primary concern with only growth was an inappropriate strategy for eliminating poverty because it ignored equity considerations, had an anti-agricultural bias and concentrated attention on investment in heavy industrial sector with limited linkages effects. It was argued that "development from below" strategy was more appropriate for meeting the needs of the rural poor as against the "top down" strategy pursued so far by these countries. This was because the main objective of bottom up strategy was full development of a region's resources and human skills for the satisfaction of basic needs of all strata of regional or national population.

Another variant of growth-equity strategy was to concentrate not on growth of GDP but on human development through devoting a major proportion of investment resources to education and health in rural and urban areas. The objective was better health and increased level of literacy and human welfare and increased labour productivity. It was claimed that this strategy yielded rich dividends in the case of Sri Lanka and Kerala in India where, as a result of large investments in health and education, human development indicators showed significant progress.

It is interesting to note that, during the 1980s, the indirect route of eradicating poverty through rapid growth was once again recognized as the only sustainable strategy of poverty reduction and the difficulties of traversing the direct route to eradication of poverty were being increasingly appreciated. Simultaneously, structural adjustment programmes introduced in many developing countries during the 1980s emphasized the role of the private sector, assigned a limited role to the public sector and advocated its privatization.

The growth equity debate has enriched the development literature and also influenced policy and its orientation. In response to some of these criticisms and the objective reality of the prevalence of large-scale poverty and unemployment, the policy makers in these countries gradually started changing and amending their development strategies. Thus, along with indirect growth strategy for improving the well-being of the lowest income groups, direct policies for the eradication of poverty also became an important complement in most developing countries. The general consensus was for a strategy advocating "redistribution with growth" or "growth with equity".

For example, India's Fifth Five-Year Plan included, along with growth, *Garibi Hatao* (Poverty Eradication) as one of its central objectives. Many other countries also adopted a mixed strategy and allocated large resources in schemes designed for rural development aimed at benefiting the rural poor. As a result, many anti-poverty programmes were launched by these countries. In some countries like India, these anti-poverty programmes had two essential aspects : one, raising the productivity of the self-employed through asset creation; and two, generating employment through special employment programmes and encouraging labour-intensive patterns of production in the economy.

At the same time, it was realized that besides low incomes, the poor also lacked adequate access to some public utilities like public health, safe drinking water, sanitary facilities, education, etc. that are crucial for better health and productivity. Therefore, the 1970s witnessed, in addition to promoting investments for growth, initiation of programmes for augmenting the productivity of the self-employed, generation of employment opportunities through public works, food for work programmes, public distribution of food items and various nutrition programmes, and extension and expansion of essential public services like health, water, education, electricity, roads, etc.

Over the years, many a lesson have been learnt at the practical level. Besides, the growth strategy itself has tended to become more oriented towards the welfare of the poor. The multilateral lending agencies have started giving importance to direct poverty eradication programmes. Simultaneously, in many projects, including infrastructure projects dealing with transport, irrigation, power, etc., poverty concerns have been explicitly built in. In many countries, the national governments have started introducing policy-induced pro-poor bias in the growth process through selective policies like land reforms, and reforming or building institutional mechanisms like special credit facilities for rural areas and for the poor, and special schemes for disadvantaged sections of the population.

In the direct route which consists of provision of education, health, sanitation, and other social infrastructure, there has been a deliberate pro-poor bias aimed at giving special consideration to the poor through subsidies, stipends and reservations. More importantly, in many cases there has been a deliberate attempt to build growth objectives in the direct anti-poverty programmes, and many growth oriented programmes, like rural transport, irrigation and rural electrification, have been given a pro-poor orientation and are also being frequently included in the anti-poverty programme.

One of the most important examples is the Million Wells Scheme in India which was conceived as a part of the direct poverty reduction programme called the Integrated Rural Development Programme (IRDP). Simultaneously, an attempt is also being made to focus even the indirect growth oriented programmes of infrastructure development like rural roads, irrigation, etc. primarily on poverty alleviation. Building of a rural road in a poor locality in preference to a well endowed area is an example. Thus, in many cases, the programmes are being so designed as to simultaneously fulfil the growth and equity objectives.

The decision regarding the size of allocation to growth programmes and anti-poverty programmes is a political decision that is taken during the budget-making process. In a democracy, it is expected to reflect the behaviour of the voters, both rich and poor, as interpreted by the party in power. It is sometimes suggested that quite often political decisions favour the rich as against the poor, since most of the techniques that are used for the selection of a project, like benefit-cost analysis, involve adding the gains and losses to all affected groups on the same basis and it involves a selection orientation against low income groups. Then, what is the way out. In a democracy, ultimately decisions have to be taken through a democratic process and through voting. But both the policy makers and the public could be better informed about the likely distributional implications of alternatives. The lending agencies while providing loans for projects could also contribute to project reorientation towards the poor through built-in norms or, sometimes, through explicit conditionalities favouring poverty orientation of the project. But such conditionalities could be ineffective and sometimes counterproductive because of lack of popular support. Democratic decentralization of political power and its devolution to the village level and local level participation in the decision-making process through village level elected bodies (like *Panchayats* in India and Pakistan) is one of the preferred democratic methods for selection of pro-poor projects. Decentralization has a special advantage since village-level elected functionaries are likely to be more responsive to the needs and demands of the poor. These functionaries could be helped through the dissemination of relevant information on the likely distributional implications of a given project.

On the other hand, in a traditional semi-feudal set-up, the rich may completely dominate local institutions and use them for grabbing more power and common property resources. Certain built-in mechanisms like reservations for the low castes, the poor and women could counteract these forces. Finally, and most importantly, the project selection can become pro-poor only if the poor get organized and are able to assert their rights. Howsoever benevolent a State may be, it is ultimately the prevailing power structure in the rural and urban areas that plays a decisive role in the decision-making process. It is in this context that the organizations of poor peasants, the rural workers' unions and other non-governmental organizations (NGOs) can play a useful part in organizing the poor and empowering them. To sum up, in a democracy, there are no short-cuts to decentralization and devolution of political and financial powers to local governments. Building strong movements of the poor and involving them in the decision-making process through their active participation, could contribute significantly to the objective of giving a pro-poor content to the planning process.

Given that it has been decided to launch pro-poor schemes, a further problem is to choose between various types of anti-poverty programmes, like building of rural infrastructure, namely, roads, rural electrification, irrigation; direct disbursement to the poor; public distribution system and provision of subsidized food; distribution of food stamps; provision of education and primary health; provision of subsidized inputs for increasing agricultural production; employment-generating programmes; asset creation for generating income streams over a period of time; credit for purchase of a cow or buffalo or a cycle rickshaw; repair kits for tubewells; training for self-employment, etc. The task, therefore, still remains of sub-allocating funds budgeted for social programmes and anti-poverty programmes into their various components. A further decision pertains to the distribution of different programmes among various layers of the government, that is, among the federal government, the states and local bodies after decisions regarding financial devolution have been taken. In some countries like India, Pakistan and Sri Lanka, constitutional provisions exist as to the devolution of resources and distribution of functions between the central and the state governments. Devolution to local bodies is not that common, except in some countries like Sri Lanka and now India where a beginning has been made in this direction.

Project analysis through benefit-cost method is one of the most widely used techniques for setting out decision rules for selection of one or a combination of projects given their respective benefits and costs, the overall objective being to bring about the most efficient use of given scarce resources. But this is easier said than done. In a project which produces physical goods, it is quite easy to value the produce by taking market prices. Further, in most industrial projects, it is very easy to evaluate the likely benefits, since the output is repetitive, i.e. given a certain technology, engineers will be able to tell the likely quantum of output over specified periods of time. In its conceptual frame, the conventional social benefit-cost analysis (BCA) also generally underlines the need for measuring the "secondary benefits", "externalities", "linkages" and "intangible effects". However, in practice, despite the recognition of their importance, these are seldom considered.

Generally, infrastructure or social overhead capital refers to basic public services and facilities which provide an environment for productive activities of individuals and groups in society. An infrastructure project aimed at poverty reduction in rural areas has no doubt some easily measurable direct and tangible benefits. However, the main benefits to flow from these projects are likely to be indirect and intangible. Further, their main merit is that they generate lots of externalities and also have impact through linkages. Although these benefits pose difficult measurement problems, it is these which are likely to be of paramount importance in rural infrastructure projects like building rural roads, irrigation, education, health and housing, which are aimed at overall economic development and poverty reduction in rural areas.

For example, it is not possible to directly quantify all the benefits that are likely to flow from a rural road, which is likely to foster economic activity through increased connectivity and access to other services like education and health. Again, an irrigation project besides leading to increases in output also creates many externalities in the form of raising the water table in surrounding areas and improvement or degradation of the environment. The benefits of education are not only improvement in the skills of labour and earning capacity of the labour force, but also reduction in crime and a better social life. Again, the likely benefits of poverty reduction are increase in welfare, increase in the capacity of parents to send their children to school, and increase in the efficiency and productivity of the workforce owing to better health. These benefits are also intangible and are not amenable to easy measurement. Besides, these are not repetitive since some of the programmes are completely new and some others might have different outcomes if they operate in a different socio-economic milieu. For example, in the case of rural roads, the outcome would depend on the regional pattern of development, the density of population, the nearness to a market or industrial town and the mobility of the labour force.

The measurement problems get further exacerbated because most of the infrastructural projects are lumpy in nature, have externalities and quite often produce public goods where user charges are difficult to collect because of free riding. In their case, valuation creates innumerable theoretical and practical problems. BCA is neither a foolproof recipe nor a substitute for clear thinking and explicit value judgement. It is a useful way to organize information. Uncertainty about future outcomes would remain even after benefits and costs have been estimated and compared. BCA is useful insofar as it lays down the first principles for improving public allocation of scarce resources.

To recapitulate, given limited resources, policy makers have to make decisions about choosing from among various growth and anti-poverty projects. For this, it is important to measure benefits and costs carefully and set out decision rules as clearly as possible.

Benefit-cost analysis tries to deal with measurement problems in a systematic manner. This analysis does not provide perfect answers but tries to reduce the extent of arbitrariness in the calculation of relative benefits and costs of alternative projects and, thereby, is an aid in the decision-making process. The analysis is useful as it can make the decision-making process less arbitrary and help public authorities make a choice from among numerous competing projects. But the conventional analysis also underplays, if not disregards, most of the indirect benefits like externalities, linkages and other intangibles which are characteristic of a rural (or urban) infrastructure project. An attempt is made here to first briefly describe the main contribution of rural infrastructural projects like rural roads, irrigation, rural electrification, credit, market, agricultural research and extension. This is followed by a critical examination of the conventional benefit-cost methodology and some of its limitations in terms of dealing with the measurement of benefits and costs of an infrastructure project aimed at poverty reduction in rural areas. Finally, an attempt is made to suggest some additional and supplementary methodology to deal with the specific problem of measurement of benefits from an infrastructure project aimed at poverty reduction in rural areas.

Types of Infrastructural Investment

The term "infrastructure" has been variously defined by scholars. Infrastructure development is often divided into two categories, namely, directly productive economic infrastructure and social infrastructure. The distinction between these two is often made on the basis of their differences in the production process, as discussed below.

Economic Infrastructure

Economic infrastructure produces services that directly facilitate and are basic to the carrying out of a wide variety of economic activities. These are generally priced low, are subject to public control or regulation and investment therein is characterized by lumpiness. Rural infrastructure, therefore, includes investments that directly and indirectly affect productivity in agriculture and other rural non-farm activities. The main categories of economic infrastructural activity are investments in rural electrification, rural credit institutions, scientific agricultural research and extension, flood control and drainage, irrigation works, rural roads, rural transport, markets for inputs and outputs, storage structures and warehousing facilities, common property resources, and watershed development. In addition, it includes infrastructure for developing allied and non-farm activities like dairy development (i.e. improvement of milch animals, milk collection and chilling centres) and agro-processing and other village industries and crafts. While some infrastructures like irrigation, credit and agricultural research enable the adoption of new technology, some others, like transport, provide intermediate services to facilitate interaction between productive activities.

Social Infrastructure

Social infrastructure includes activities like access to schools, primary health centres, safe piped drinking water, sanitation, pavement of streets and building of community centres. While investment in economic infrastructure primarily plays a complementary role in increasing productivity of existing assets, generating more employment for labour and providing increased access to urban markets including labour markets, investment in social infrastructure results in creating a healthy working environment as well as facilitating human capital formation in rural areas.

Objectives of Rural Infrastructural Development

In most developing countries, the main objective of planning and development policy is growth with equity. Investment in rural infrastructure constitutes an important component of national planning and thereby subserves the various objectives decided upon by the policy makers. For example, the main objectives of the Ninth Five-Year Plan of India are higher rates of growth of output and employment, human development, eradication of poverty, development of social sectors, minimizing economic disparities and correcting regional imbalances, building self-reliance, empowerment of the poor and women, food security, environmental sustainability and promoting people's participation in government.

The multinational agencies have also adopted growth, sustainability and poverty reduction as the main goals for their project assistance. For example, the UNIDO Manual states several goals like increasing aggregate consumption, income redistribution, generating employment, improving environment, rural area development and self-reliance as the main goals of development policy and project aid. Similarly, UNDP and other donors have adopted sustainable human development, including poverty alleviation, employment, environment, good governance, and women's development as their goals and objectives.

There are certain types of infrastructural investments like in rural transport, irrigation, new technology, etc. which benefit all sections of rural society with certain time lags. But there are others, like development of air transport, that are almost completely biased towards the rich. A popular view is that, in general, benefits from rural infrastructural projects accrue to all sections of the rural society, perhaps more or less in proportion to their asset base or political clout. However, most empirical studies bring out that the poor also benefit a great deal because of the availability of more employment opportunities. But, a careful targeting, like giving of subsidized credit to the poor, could result in a flow of greater benefits to the rural poor.

Various objectives of rural infrastructural development are given below.

Growth with Equity

Growth with equity has become the avowed objective of development and planning in most developing countries. The basic aim of infrastructural development is to promote growth and to the extent the infrastructure is located in rural areas, which generally have higher incidence of poverty, any gains in productivity consequent to the increased investment in infrastructure are going to benefit the poor also.

However, in the initial stages, it is the rich who are likely to benefit the most from an infrastructure project. This is because the distributional impact of infrastructural development would depend both on the prevailing institutional set-up, social relationship and political power structure and, particularly on the land distribution pattern prevalent in the rural areas. One of the most important institutional factors is land distribution. For example, the benefits of irrigation infrastructure would flow, more or less, in proportion to the distribution of land in the village. Hence, in countries and areas like China, the Republic of Korea, Taiwan Province of China and the states of Kerala and West Bengal in India, where land reforms have been implemented, the poor are also likely to benefit, unlike in areas where land is concentrated in the hands of a few landlords. In the latter case also, irrigation may benefit the poor indirectly, as the demand for labour and wages rises as a result of agricultural development. But this would also depend on the various other factors like capital intensity of the production process and the introduction of labour displacing technologies.

The development of transport infrastructure plays an important role in the growth process through increasing mobility of resources and increasing factor productivity. Transport infrastructure saves time and decreases the cost of transportation, and, thereby, helps both the rich and the poor. Transport development in rural areas strengthens linkages between towns and the countryside. Along with irrigation, it helps adoption of new technology by reducing the cost of inputs and marketing of outputs. It helps the rural poor by increasing their accessibility to schools and health centres and enables them to obtain non-farm employment in far-away places.

It is often argued that because of relatively lower valuation of time by the poor compared with the rich, the poor would benefit more from non-mechanized transport while the rich would benefit more from mechanized transport and would be willing to pay more for it for saving time. Therefore, while the poor should get non-mechanized transport, the time-saving mechanized transport should be for the rich. However, this extreme argument has serious implications. It is true that in a traditional set-up, the poor are almost entirely dependent on low level supportive mechanisms of infrastructure.

However, with economic development and the availability of regular wage employment in secondary and tertiary sectors, transport development enables the landless labour also to commute quickly to save time. Thus, even for the poor the value of time changes very quickly. This points to the need for development of public transport facilities that are made available to the poor at reasonable prices. Hence, equity considerations in the development process should not become a means for the perpetuation of technological dualism. This underlines the need for taking a more dynamic view in the valuation process.

Besides physical distance, socio-cultural and economic conditions are sometimes identified as major determinants of access to infrastructural services. Transport and communications also tend to shatter some of the social prejudices by increasing interaction with the town and also enable many so-called high caste but poor cultivators who avoid the stigma of undertaking manual work within the village to move out to obtain wage employment in other places.

The choice from among various projects with differing objectives is normally based on benefit-cost analysis. As will be discussed later, in many cases where the benefits and costs are intangible, and in some cases which involve value judgements, pure benefit-cost approach has to be tempered with decisions taken through the political process. It is sometimes suggested that the political process itself may favour the rich against the poor. So, how can equity considerations be directly built in the project selection? This issue also needs to be discussed.

Increasing Productivity

Developing countries are characterized by low levels of productivity of land, labour and capital in almost all sectors of the economy, in particular, in agriculture and allied sectors in rural areas. Infrastructural development does not directly raise productivity, but provides the necessary preconditions for increasing it. Given an appropriate institutional set-up, infrastructural investments help to shift the production frontier outwards. Infrastructural interventions like investment in rural transport, irrigation, rural electrification, rural credit, roads and communications, regulated markets, agricultural research and extension, land reforms, education and health, and investment in common property resources are universally acknowledged as the most important sources of increasing productivity of resources in both farm and non-farm sectors in rural areas.

For example, the development of transport infrastructure plays an important role in expanding the product and factor markets, in reducing the costs of marketing agricultural produce and in transmission of price thereby increasing farmers' profitability and reducing labour market imperfections by cutting down interlocking between land, labour and credit in rural markets. The expansion of product and factor markets is generally instrumental in promoting specialization in production both in agricultural and non-agricultural activities. Economically backward villages which could not interact with towns earlier had to specialize in the production of low value perishable produce or cheap foodgrains for a limited local market because of lack of transportation. With the availability of transport infrastructure, they start producing for the larger market. This gives them an incentive to increase their productivity and incomes.

Along with other infrastructure, transport development accelerates the adoption of new technology by making inputs cheaper and increasing interaction with extension agents, and also helps in marketing the surplus produce. The two rival states of Punjab and Haryana which pioneered the green revolution in India had a running competition in claiming to be first in achieving some landmarks relating to the building of rural infrastructure. While Haryana claimed to be the first to have provided electricity to each village, Punjab claimed to be the first to have connected each village with a metalled road.

In most developing countries, a majority of the rural population still depends on agriculture with low productivity. Land reforms remove the barriers to agricultural development by removing institutional constraints like outmoded land relations including large scale prevalence of tenancy and create necessary incentives for increasing productivity in agriculture.

Again, irrigation infrastructure is a prerequisite for the adoption of new seed-fertilizer technology for increasing productivity in agriculture. The experience of most of the East Asian and South Asian countries brings out that the adoption of new technology enabled the farmers to record significant increase in their productivity and income and also enabled the agricultural workers to obtain more employment at higher wages. The existence of road and transport infrastructure facilitated the farmers to sell their surplus produce in market towns without incurring exorbitant costs. Credit infrastructure entitled all categories of farmers, including the small and marginal farmers, to purchase necessary inputs. This resulted in significant increases in the income levels of all categories of cultivators and agricultural labourers. This also enabled these countries to improve their food security which had been seriously impaired during the 1960s.

Most important, in many instances, rapid agricultural development triggered growth in secondary and tertiary sectors through input, output and consumption linkages, thereby resulting in higher labour productivity and wages. The existence of other infrastructures like rural roads, transport and communications, collection centres and, above all, rural electrification provided the necessary prerequisites for growth of on-farm and non-farm activities in rural areas. There is sufficient empirical evidence that a consistently high agricultural growth and consequent higher growth in the secondary and tertiary sectors through the multiplier effect in some regions of Asia made a significant dent on rural poverty. Hence, by all accounts, rural infrastructure played a major role in increasing productivity and contributed to rural development.

Access of Women to Infrastructure

It has been found that in spite of the existence of physical and social infrastructure, certain disadvantaged groups like poor children and some women are unable to make use of infrastructural services like education and health care. For poor children, education does not become available because they have to work for a living. For women, social prejudices preclude them from making use of these services. The result of their inability to access the social services is increased morbidity, lower education, and continued ill health.

Consequently, improving the access of women to education and health infrastructure is recognized as one of the important measures to improve socio-economic conditions of women.

Market Extension

Infrastructural investment in rural roads, transport and communications has profound effect in establishing links between rural and urban areas and thereby augmenting existing production activities through input, output and consumption linkages. This takes place through diversification of economic activities, increase in mobility and accessibility of both output and factors of production. The most important impact is because of the increase in labour mobility due to increased accessibility and the establishment of road networks. This enables workers to move to higher wage occupations in non-farm urban labour markets and results in increase in rural wages.

Environmental Sustainability

Sustainable development is the development that lasts. Keeping in mind that sometimes growth can be oblivious to environmental considerations and that environmental degradation makes the future generations worse off by degrading the earth's resources and polluting the earth's environment, the objective of sustainable development has now been universally accepted. It is also increasingly appreciated that the cost of maintaining the sustainability of the environment ought to be borne by the present generation.

But there is no agreement on the major causes of non-sustainability. One point of view has put high population growth and poverty as the main cause of degradation. It is argued, for example, that the reason why the poor today degrade their environmental resource base is that their poverty forces them to discount future incomes at unusually high rates. Others have argued that it is the low rates of return on private investment in the resource base owing to institutional failures which are mainly responsible for degradation of the environment. Some others have asserted that high rate of population growth is the main cause of depletion of natural resources like land, water and other resources. On the other hand, some scholars have argued that it is the insecure property rights of peasants and persistence of semi-feudal relationships along with the decline in common land in the villages, that have gradually deprived the poor of an important source of income. The lesson is that it is only the empowerment of local governments with adequate representation of the poor which can act as an effective counterweight to forces that erode environment and reduce the availability and access to common property rights.

However, sometimes local communities are also likely to take a short-sighted view regarding environmental implications because of lack of awareness and high value accorded to present income as against future income. For example, in Rajasthan, India, village common lands were found to have declined by 25-60 per cent over a period of about three decades, ironically because of unimaginative implementation of land reforms. Again, in Orma in north-western Kenya, there took place a large-scale privatization of common grazing lands with the consent of elders. The willingness to change transaction costs was brought about by cheaper transportation and widening markets.

The environmental benefits and costs may not be measurable in all cases; therefore, it is difficult to put an economic valuation on their outcome. But the costs should be made as explicit and transparent as possible to enable the policy makers to form informed judgements. Generally, for any major project where environmental effects are likely to be large, and for specific projects designed to improve the environment, any economic valuation should include environmental BCA.

Income Redistribution and Augmentation

Historically, in almost all countries, public works programmes like the building of roads or canals have been initiated during periods of distress to provide employment to poorer people. This continues even today in the modified form of special employment programmes which are designed in many countries to help the rural poor. It is done either through the provision of assured minimum earnings like food for work or through employment-generating schemes including employment guarantee schemes.

Special anti-poverty programmes have also been designed with a view to improving the productive base of weaker sections. For small and marginal farmers, quite often, inputs like fertilizers, water for irrigation, electricity and credit are supplied at subsidized rates.

The nature and composition of the promotional efforts depend on the composition of the population of the poor in a given rural setting. For example, if the majority of the poor, such as small and marginal farmers and agricultural labour, are directly or indirectly dependent on agriculture, investment in infrastructure aimed at improving agricultural development like irrigation, electricity, credit, and transport should be assigned priority, keeping in view their demand and supply. More important, sometimes, as in India, irrigation infrastructure constitutes an in-built component of the direct anti-poverty programmes. For example, under the Million Wells Scheme in India, the government gives money for an employment programme for the purpose of digging wells or tubewells only for the poor. Similarly, the Indira Awaas Yojana is also a part of the employment programmes where houses are built for the poor and scheduled caste families.

Provision of Minimum Needs

Investment in social infrastructure aimed at providing basic minimum needs indirectly leads to poverty eradication by providing a better working and living environment, physical health and human capital formation amongst the poor. In most cases, poverty itself is manifest in inadequate social infrastructure services like safe drinking water, sanitation, housing, health, family welfare, rural electrification, rural schooling and training institutions. For example, unsafe drinking water, lack of sanitation and unhygienic housing are directly related to the prevalence of water-borne, human waste related and air-borne diseases like dysentery, cholera, diarrhoea, tuberculosis, bronchitis, influenza, malaria and measles. Therefore, investment in water supply, sanitation and housing shall considerably augment the earning capabilities and nutritional status of the population not only through reduction in the incidence of disease and morbidity but also through reduced birth rate, better physique, saving on medical costs, expanding working time, and minimizing productivity losses. Similarly, human capital formation through formal education and training is considered to be the most potent weapon against poverty.

Self-Reliance

Another important objective of investment in infrastructure aimed at poverty reduction is to make the poor self-reliant and capable of meeting their basic needs out of their own resources. There is enough empirical evidence to show that the landless labourers, small and marginal farmers and the village artisans that produce traditional goods and services constitute the hard core of rural poverty in most of the developing countries. Therefore, policies aimed at self-reliance should address specific requirements of the hard core poor. The foremost policy of self-reliance is the redistribution of existing assets (mainly land in rural areas) among the landless or near landless farmers through land reforms of the type implemented in mainland China, Taiwan Province of China, Republic of Korea and in some states of India. However, implementation of land reforms and land redistribution requires strong political will, which is not evident in most developing countries.

Alternatively, the goal of self-reliance can be accomplished by improving the productivity of the existing asset base of the rural poor. This requires, apart from supplementary policies, helping the poor to overcome the impediments of low returns from assets and increasing the productivity of their land by adopting modern technology. One of the major contributions of the new seed-fertilizer technology was that it was land augmenting and, as such, to some extent, eased the disadvantage of small and marginal holdings. Still another way to achieve the goal of self-reliance is to supplement the productive base of the poor through the provision of productive assets to the self-employed. Simultaneously, the landless poor can be provided employment through employment guarantee schemes. The asset-creating and employment generation programmes should be accompanied by development of credit infrastructure especially catering to the needs of the rural poor for supplying them adequate and subsidized credit. The creation of specialized financial institutions assumes significance in this regard because supply of credit to the poor involves high risk and carries exorbitant interest rates. The task of the special financial institutions would be to identify impediments to enhancing the productivity of existing assets and to find ways and means to overcome these and simultaneously to promote viable economic activities for the rural poor. The Gramin Bank of Bangladesh which provides credit at reasonable rates to the poor to enable them to become self-reliant by undertaking productive activities is one of the most cited success stories of the operation of a specialized agency of the type required to serve the rural poor.

Improvement in Common Property Resources

Income flows from village common property resources like village common land, woodlands and local forests, grazing lands, water resources and village ponds. Inland and coastal fisheries are an important source of supplementary income for the rural poor. In particular, common property resources constitute an important complementary source of income to the poor population in ecologically fragile, arid, mountainous and unirrigated regions. The income earned by the rural poor from the sale of fuel wood, water for irrigation, fodder and other commercial grasses, berries and nuts and gum forms a significant proportion of their earnings.

The main objective of investment in these resources is to augment the flow of benefits to the village population in general and to the poor, in particular. Most of these investments, like those in forests and common property rights, not only augment income but also help to check degradation of the environment and other natural resources. However, quite often, the fact that the poor do not possess any assets and do not have a regular source of income from wage employment often leads to excessive exploitation of these natural resources and can damage the environment. Further, in a village hierarchy, there is always the possibility of the cornering of benefit flows from more remunerative common property resources by the rural rich. Suitable measures have to be taken to counteract these negative features.

Empowerment of Local Government and Community Participation

Decentralization of power and empowerment of local government and communities are important components of democratic functioning and extension of democracy to the grass-root level. Community participation in the development process at the local level directs the bias of development towards local problems and the local poor.

There are two aspects of empowerment. One is political power delegated to local bodies through appropriate legislation. The other and an equally important aspect of empowerment is the devolution of financial resources to these bodies. Without these financial powers, their ability to initiate development projects for growth and poverty eradication remain just on paper. In India, recently, with the passing of the 73rd Constitutional Amendment Act, state governments have enacted enabling legislation providing for elected bodies at the village, intermediate and district levels, with adequate representation from the weaker sections and women. State finance commissions have also been constituted in all the states with a view to developing financial resources for the local bodies, including municipal committees.

The *Panchayats* and *Panchayat Samitis* (elected bodies at the village level and at the level of cluster of villages) have been given necessary powers and authority to enable them to function as institutions of self-government with the responsibility of preparing plans for economic development and social justice and implementing them. It is such institutions which can be expected to undertake infrastructural and other employment-generating activities for helping the rural poor.

However, adequate care must be taken to ensure that the rich, who are generally well entrenched in the rural hierarchy, do not use the local government as an instrument for grabbing more power and resources for themselves. The Indian model (73rd Constitutional Amendment) that reserves 22.5 per cent seats in the local governments for the scheduled castes and scheduled tribes and 33 per cent for women in every *Panchayat Samiti* (local government at the level of cluster of villages) can act as an important antidote to the rich power grabbers and could be emulated by other countries.

Integrating Infrastructural Investment with National Planning

Infrastructural investment constitutes the hard core of national planning and a large proportion of plan resources are generally devoted to its development. Since these projects operate at different layers of government and in different agro-climatic regions, there is need for a careful selection of projects and their proper integration with the national plan. The plan priorities ought to be worked out keeping in view the broad objectives set out in the national plan. The detailed disaggregated schemes should be formulated in the light of variations in agro-climatic conditions, occupational composition of the population, varying economic opportunities, availability and requirements of infrastructure and other constraints.

Local planning strategy has to proceed in three stages. The first stage is to take an inventory of physical endowments of the area and to identify the potential and constraints vis-a-vis optimum utilization of existing physical and human resources. Data on numerous aspects like availability of underground water, resource endowments like availability of minerals, forests and other resources and socio-economic variables may have to be collected from secondary sources and also by employing modern scientific techniques like satellite imagery and remote sensing and mapping by using geographic information systems (GIS). In the second stage, viable activities relating to agriculture and allied sectors like animal husbandry, floriculture, horticulture, fishing and agro-processing should be identified. The main objective should be to undertake those projects which lead to the welfare of the local people, in general, and the disadvantaged and the poor, in particular, keeping in view the availability of resources. Other important aspects like long-term viability, flow of benefits to the targeted population and environmental impact have also to be given due consideration in local area plan formulation.

In any multilevel planning exercise, projects at the local level have to be integrated with the plans at the district, state and national levels. At every step, the viability and availability of resources along with technical soundness has to be kept in mind. Finally, all state-level plans have to be further integrated with the national plan within the framework of available resources and national planning priorities and objectives.

Growth-Equity Trade-off

In all developing countries, there are competing demands on limited resources. In the process of planning also, resources have to be allocated to various programmes, including those designed for different types of infrastructure and direct anti-poverty programmes, and there is always a trade-off between growth and equity objectives. The choice between various competing projects becomes quite difficult. This is because the choice depends not only on the quantum of benefits and their time profile, but also on the indirect and intangible nature of benefit flows over a period of time in a dynamic context. For a policy maker, what is needed is a decision rule that enables him to make rational choice from among a whole set of programmes that range between direct anti-poverty programmes, anti-poverty cum growth programmes and indirect growth programmes. There is also a need to develop a criterion for making a choice among numerous programmes and projects that serve the given objectives. Thus, growth-equity trade-off becomes a crucial policy issue.

In classical literature, the choice between growth and equity objectives was supposed to take into consideration not only the present values of costs and benefits but also their impact in terms of future streams of income from alternative investments. It is often argued that owing to their higher marginal propensity to consume, increased distribution in favour of the poor tends to reduce the rate of savings in the economy, thereby adversely affecting investment and incentives for the future.

On the other hand, it has been argued that additional demand due to higher consumption consequent to the pro-poor distribution of income, would generate additional demand for domestic production that would lead to creation of more jobs and hence stimulate growth through the multiplier effect. Furthermore, redistribution strategy would improve the productivity of the existing labour force because of better nutrition intake, education, training, etc. made possible by higher incomes. This would augment the future productive capability of manpower. However, if the benefits accrue after a long time gap, the present value of benefits would work out to be quite small.

The choice among various infrastructural programmes is often based on benefit-cost analysis. But benefit-cost analysis of infrastructural programmes poses several difficulties because of complexities of identifying multifaceted benefits and measuring them in a dynamic world. For example, in a study of transport in Bangladesh, the benefit-cost ratio of improving a deteriorated road to paved road worked out to be 1.19 on the basis of existing traffic but as much as 3.48 when the projected increase in traffic was taken into account.

A static analysis based on user-cost saving and existing volume of traffic does not take into account the effects of changes in traffic likely to result from increased agricultural output and consequent increase in secondary and tertiary activities because of input, output and consumption linkages. Some of these concerns were sought to be taken into account by the multiple criteria appraisal method designed by some scholars for studying the aggregate benefits and costs. But this aspect will be discussed later. Although some techniques like input-ouput multiplier method may capture some of these effects, in general, their valuation is based on arbitrary value judgements of policy makers or experts.

It is often argued that infrastructural development has a built-in pro-rich bias. The argument is that any benefits of development, including those from infrastructural development, are distributed as per the distribution of assets amongst the poor and the rich. For example, it is argued that green revolution mainly benefits the rich because they have more land and have command over larger resources. However, the poor do derive benefits since they own more labour and effects on employment and wage rates must also be considered in the calculation of the relative costs and benefits. Because of growth of secondary and tertiary sectors in response to the growth in agriculture, wage incomes generally rise faster than other incomes. Wages also rise because the supply of labour from rich households is reduced as the rich withdraw their labour when their incomes increase. Further, the poor also benefit from labour intensive allied activities like animal husbandry and also from growing high-value crops on their plots. Even the direct anti-poverty programmes are more effective in areas where infrastructure is developed. Besides, certain programmes like Gramin Bank in Bangladesh by providing credit to the poor make a significant contribution in increasing their income.

Finally, a choice on grounds of equity would require assigning of distributional weights to various sections of society. But, as discussed earlier, the valuation of benefits becomes quite difficult in a dynamic setting and their use for determining distributional weights is quite complex and could pose innumerable problems. In the absence of standard methodologies, the choice of weights would ultimately depend on value judgements by the experts or policy makers. It would certainly be more helpful if the extent of arbitrariness is reduced by devising appropriate methodologies. This aspect will be discussed later.

Distributive Impacts

Some scholars have tried to build a taxonomy of scenarios regarding the distribution of gains between different sections of the people say, the rich and the poor in the village, as follows :

The Win-Win Scenario

The win-win scenario could be neutral, that is, when there is no change in income distribution and the project benefits everyone proportionately;

relatively retrogressive when all groups gain but the rich gain proportionally more than the poor; and, finally, relatively progressive when the project benefits the low income group more than the rich relatively.

The Win-Loss Scenario

The Rawlsian Progressive is a case when the project benefits the poor the most and may or may not benefit others. Should it benefit the rich also, it becomes a win-win situation, otherwise it is a win-loss situation. The absolute progressive scenario would be the one where the project benefits the poor but makes the rich worse off. On the other hand, the absolute regressive is the case where the project benefits the rich but makes the poor worse off.

Short Term Gains vs Environmental Degradation

It is widely acknowledged that during the 1950s and 1960s most investment projects in developing countries paid very little attention to environmental concerns. In quite a few cases, investment in industrial projects led to numerous negative externalities like air and water pollution. The existing laws on pollution or emission of chemical or toxic matter were not effective and their lax implementation made the environment around industrial units extremely polluted. Rapid and unplanned urbanization added to these problems through creation of large-scale slums and unhygienic living conditions because of inadequate availability and tardy development of urban infrastructure in housing, water, sewerage, transport and electrification.

The environmental concerns were also neglected in the case of rural projects. For example, investment in irrigation projects aimed at increasing agricultural productivity and income of the cultivators often led to the cutting down of forests for extension of arable land, waterlogging and salinity of soil.

Infrastructure development plays an indirect but crucial role in the development process through promotion of growth by increasing the productivity of factors employed in the production process. Infrastructural investments generally constitute the core of development planning in most developing countries and large resources are allocated to investment in infrastructure like transport, electrification, irrigation, communication, research and development and social overheads like education and health. In addition to promoting growth, infrastructural investments are quite often assigned numerous other objectives like attainment of equity, appropriate income distribution and augmentation, provision of minimum needs, market extension and improvement of common property resources.

Recently, infrastructural investments are increasingly being used by the national governments to achieve poverty reduction in rural areas. Multilateral agencies also provide various loans for projects that are specifically designed to help the rural poor. In order to make infrastructural investment more efficient and pro-poor, rural infrastructural investment needs to be integrated with the national planning and local bodies have to be strengthened with a view to decentralizing the choice and execution of these projects by local authorities. Finally, it has to be recognized that the growth objectives of infrastructural development may conflict with the equity objective. Hence, the nature of trade-off between growth and equity has to be analyzed with a view to resolving the conflict and making the interventions pro-poor without losing the important objective of faster growth of the economy. The second important trade-off is between growth and environmental degradation.

It has to be recognized that the debate on development versus environment sometimes tends to become highly emotional and quite often excessive enthusiasm for environmental protection tends to become anti-development. On the other hand, sometimes genuine environmental concerns are completely brushed aside in the name of development. Some of the environmental concerns which have now emerged as a major issue in debates on development have not received due attention in most developing countries. Even the existing laws for control of pollution are seldom applied rigorously because of lax administration, with the result that industrial growth has led to increasingly serious damage to land, water and some other natural resources. Policy makers need to appreciate the seriousness of the problem and ought to conceive and implement right and balanced policies for addressing these concerns.

Infrastructure plays a strategic but indirect role in development, and, more so, in poverty eradication. Furthermore, quite often, poverty eradication is not the sole objective of most infrastructural projects, but constitutes one among many other objectives. Associated with it is the complex process of interrelationships through which the flow of benefits from infrastructural intervention emerges and affects poverty. For example, road projects are often aimed at increasing accessibility. Since accessibility, in turn, is likely to increase labour mobility and expand the job market, the effect on poverty reduction is indirect. Problems also arise owing to joint project benefits. This is because the projects usually have numerous other objectives in addition to poverty reduction. For example, a transport project not only makes the carrying of goods and passengers much cheaper by reducing the cost of transportation, it also increases accessibility of the poor to schools and to health centres. The question is how to calculate separately the benefits and costs of each set of contributions made by the project (a case of joint products). This makes the measurement of their contribution towards poverty reduction quite difficult.

Impact of Rural Infrastructural Investment

Infrastructural investments in transport (roads, railways and civil aviation), power, irrigation, watersheds, hydroelectric works, scientific research and training, markets and warehousing, communications and informatics, education, health and family welfare play a strategic but indirect role in the development process. Unlike sectoral development, of, say, agriculture or industry, infrastructure does not directly increase output, but makes a significant contribution towards growth by increasing the factor productivity of land, labour and capital in the production process. Theoretically, economists proceed from the premise that the creation of infrastructure by generating external economies leads to widespread benefits.

The crucial role of transport in economic development has been universally accepted. For example, the rural urban linkages and the pull effects of urban growth centres have long been recognized to be essentially dependent on transport and communications linkages. Again, transportation and communications were the central foundation for the opening up of new colonies like Australia and America.

Owen used a cross-country comparison of the levels of passenger and freight with per capita income and demonstrated that the level of mobility in a country roughly reflected the level of the country's wealth. According to von Thunent, transport improvements reduce the cost of moving agricultural products to market and, therefore, extend the market, thereby encouraging cultivation, etc. Rural transport also has an important impact on the rural economy. Investment in rural roads and transportation results in reducing the cost of transportation of goods and passengers and tends to increase the share of farmers in the final realization of farm produce, thereby increasing their welfare.

Infrastructure provision and the efficiency of production extension is a precondition for the adoption and diffusion of new agricultural technology. This, in turn, increases the income of all categories of cultivators as also of landless agricultural labourers. Not only that, the existence of infrastructure like roads, communications and transportation is considered to be critical for the growth impulse generated by agricultural development through input-output linkages. The increased income of cultivators and landless labour leads to a diversification of their consumption basket, thereby giving fillip to consumer goods industries and services.

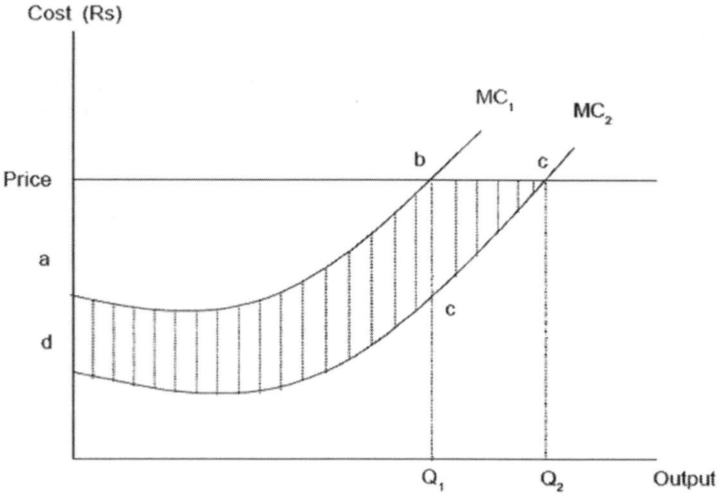

Figure 1. Infrastructure provision and the efficiency of production

The diffusion of agricultural technology is also facilitated by infrastructural development in transport and marketing. Travel by extension workers becomes much easier. Farmers can easily move to the demonstration farms and interact with the scientists. The access to modern inputs also becomes easier. Farmers can readily obtain high yield variety (HYV) seeds and fertilizers. Similarly, they can also take advantage of the repair facilities for the implements in market towns and other bigger towns.

The enhanced mobility of labour induced by infrastructural development, such as the opening up of rural roads, helps the rural poor in commuting to work and travelling to jobs where the wages are relatively higher. It also helps small and marginal farmers in moving away from their villages, where manual work is looked down upon, to far away places where they enjoy relative freedom from such inhibitions. Transport development also helps the small and marginal farmers to grow vegetables and other high value crops on their tiny plots and to find a market for these in nearby towns. Linkages also help the richer sections to divert their investment from limited credit markets to non-agricultural activities in rural areas or in towns. This also helps in providing additional employment to rural labour. The reduction of marketing margins has far-reaching consequences for the comparative advantage enjoyed by a country and for its competitive strength in the world economy.

Again, access to institutional services like health care, education and credit becomes much easier. This helps not only in increasing productivity but also in reducing credit constraints which are the main instrument of exploitation in the rural setting. Thus, by increasing the income of the rural people, infrastructural development can also be instrumental in breaking the stranglehold of moneylenders and reducing the impact of interlocking between land, labour and credit markets.

Finally, changes in prices and expansion of demand brought about through infrastructural investment have an important influence on the pattern of household consumption. This is for two reasons. First, with the price differences between local and imported goods becoming less, there is some diversification of consumption demand. Second, much of the latent demand becomes realizable with the opening up. For example, the latent demand for services, mainly by the rich, becomes effective demand with the result that the multiplier effects and linkages of household demand to the second and third round of activity becomes stronger.

The Impact of Infrastructural Intervention on Poverty Reduction

The impact of infrastructural intervention on poverty reduction takes place bothdirectly and indirectly. The indirect impact is through its contribution to the growth of the economy. The three most important infrastructural investments that go a long way towards alleviating rural poverty, namely, transport development and irrigation, credit, and scientific research are briefly discussed below.

Role of Transport in Poverty Reduction

Development of the transport sector like other infrastructure sectors leads to increase in factor productivity in various sectors by increasing accessibility and reducing transport costs. In general, transport development focuses on increasing efficiency and growth, although in some cases like connecting rural link roads to tribal or remote areas it may directly focus on poverty reduction. It is, however, notable that even growth oriented transport development projects make important contribution to poverty reduction

Transport projects can be divided into (a) those focusing on poverty; (b) those focusing on efficiency and growth; and (c) efficiency-cum-poverty projects. It is sometimes difficult to measure the impact of transport on poverty reduction since it involves many links within the general equilibrium framework.

It is recognized that sustained economic growth leads to alleviation of poverty. Transport provides intermediate services which facilitate interaction between productive activities. Transport development reduces the cost of assembling inputs, including capital and information, for production from different locations, thereby reducing the cost of production. Further, it facilitates the diffusion of technology through increased speed of dissemination of know-how. The output prices also get reduced, thereby leading to increase in demand and promotion of regional and international trade. It also enables agriculture to commercialize, industry to specialize and the economy to enjoy benefits of scale. It also promotes diversification of the economy. Thus, the crucial role of transport development in stimulating growth is universally acknowledged. There is a strong consensus that good transport is a necessary condition but not a sufficient condition for economic growth. On the other hand, economic growth increases demand for transport.

Investment in the transport sector generates income-earning opportunities for the poor by creating jobs for unskilled labour in construction and maintenance of transport infrastructure. In addition to employment, investment in rural transport results in transport induced lower prices of consumer goods that bring relief to the poor. Further, by lowering prices of agricultural inputs, it helps poor farmers to modernize their production pattern. It also leads to higher realized price for farmer's output because of reduced transportation costs. Furthermore, increased accessibility also leads to increased well-being through facilitating higher personal mobility and diversification in socio-economic activities that results from increased flow of information and increased use of transport services due to reduction in the cost of service delivery to the rural poor. Investment in transport, however, may have adverse impact on the poor through the environmental degradation that needs to be taken care of in transport investment planning. Lack of transport facilities results in low agricultural productivity, high transport costs, low profit margins, higher spoilage and loss of goods during transportation and, hence, lower levels of income and increased poverty.

Infrastructure Development, Agricultural Growth and Poverty Reduction

Rural infrastructure development, like irrigation, electrification, credit, roads and communication, regulated markets and agricultural research and extension are essential prerequisites for modernization and growth of agriculture in developing countries. The growth of agriculture, in turn, results not only in increasing the productivity and income of all categories of farmers, but also in providing greater employment to rural labour. The employment elasticity of agricultural growth was found to be positive and quite high in almost all states of India during the post-green-revolution phase. However, recently, in some highly developed agricultural states like Punjab and Haryana and also in Kerala, where wage rates are relatively high, labour is increasingly being substituted by capital and the employment elasticity of agricultural growth has become either very low or even negative. This notwithstanding, agricultural growth induces growth of labour-intensive manufacturing activities in rural areas that provide employment to the poor in allied and non-farm occupations. There is sufficient evidence to indicate that the growth of agriculture has a significant impact on reduction in poverty.

Growth of manufacturing has also a positive effect on employment and reduction in poverty, although because of the high capital intensity of modern manufacturing, the employment effect may not be very large. For example, in the case of the textile industry in India, during the rationalization period of the 1980s, the absolute employment tended to decline even when textile output was increasing. But the development of the tertiary sector in general leads to more employment.

The direct effect of infrastructural investment can be in various ways. First, during the construction phase of infrastructural projects like roads, watershed development, construction of irrigation dams or powerhouses, the poor are provided employment and income-earning opportunities. Again, the most important contribution of transport is that of improving accessibility of socio-economic activities to the rural population and the rural poor and, to that extent, they benefit. The role of road construction for disaster management is universally recognized.

The availability of health infrastructure tends to reduce infant and child mortality, as well as fertility rates and leads to eradication of certain diseases (World Bank 1993). Health infrastructure contributes to growth in several ways: (a) reducing production costs; (b) permitting the use of natural resources as accessibility increases; (c) enrolment of children in schools; (d) freeing resources that would have been spent on treatment of prevalent diseases (World Bank 1993); (e) education, health and age of women at marriage, leading to a decline in birth rates, infant and child mortality rates; and (f) enhancing women's ability to improve their own life and status as well as the lives of their children.

Infrastructure and Poverty Reduction—The Process

The process through which infrastructural investment reduces poverty is quite complex, has numerous dynamic links and operates through different income groups and affects them differently. Consequently, tracing the pattern of distribution of benefits of different types of investment projects across various income groups and geographical regions generally poses serious difficulties.

The first impact is indirect through its contribution to economic growth. The impact of growth on the rural poor would depend on several factors like the type of infrastructure, the nature of services, and the location of the project. It also depends on the operating environment, such as market structures, the degree of imperfections and government regulations.

For example, an irrigation project is likely to increase the productivity and incomes not only of the rich but also of the poor, small and marginal farmers. Thus, it has an indirect impact on poverty through growth of agriculture. In the second round, it affects the landless labour by providing more employment in agriculture and later in the allied manufacturing and services sectors. Canal irrigation leads to a rise in the water table thus bestowing a benefit on the farmers living close to the canal. It may also result in environmental damage through increased salinity and degradation of soils unless accompanied by proper drainage.

Transport project development leads to accessibility of services to all sections of population. It also creates employment both during its construction as well as for its maintenance. Poverty gets reduced if the jobs become available to the unemployed.

Empirical Evidence

Numerous measurement difficulties notwithstanding, some empirical studies have tried to calculate the impact of investment in rural infrastructure like transport, irrigation and watershed development on growth and poverty eradication.

For example, many studies have tried to bring out the historical role of transport in the process of economic development. But the calculation of its impact poses serious problems because of the difficulties in measuring the capital stock and other aggregative variables pertaining to transport. The aggregate analysis undertaken by some scholars brings out that the development of transport infrastructure has a significant positive effect on economic growth although the effect is indirect and relatively long term. The positive effect is treated as suggestive only and specific to the area from where data has been collected. Many studies find correlation of per capita gross national product (GNP) with passenger and freight transport volumes. The conclusion is that transport development plays a very important role in the growth process. In a case study of Palanpur village in Uttar Pradesh, it was shown by Longust and Stern that the availability of rail transport had helped the villagers to commute to towns of Moradabad and Chandausi for employment and thereby improved their living standards.

Several empirical studies have tried to calculate the effect of infrastructure on productivity and incomes in rural and urban areas. Some of these are described below.

Aggregate Production Studies

One of the most important aggregate studies was by Antle, who undertook a cross-sectional study of 47 less developed countries. He used the Cobb-Douglas production function and found a strong positive relationship between infrastructure and aggregate agricultural productivity. His conclusion was that transport and communication infrastructure contributed to the explanation of aggregate agricultural productivity across a sample of developed countries.

The second aggregate study was that by Binswanger et al. (1987) which involved a cross-country analysis of annual data (1969-1978) collected from

58 countries. The authors found positive and significant correlation between aggregate and crop production functions and the two road variables in the pooled country analysis. The elasticity of fertilizer demand with respect to road density was found to be quite high and roads were also found to have directly contributed to both growth of output and use of fertilizers. There is some criticism of this methodology since the shifter variables like road density and pavements seem to be capturing the other country effects also.

A recent study at the International Food Policy Research Institute (IFPRI) has undertaken a comprehensive analysis of the impact of infrastructure on poverty in rural India by looking at the relationship between government expenditure incurred on R and D, irrigation, roads, education, power, soil and water, rural development, health and family welfare, and the impact of each of these expenditures on the incidence of poverty in rural areas by employing a simultaneous equation regression model. The study is based on time series of state-wise data on poverty, rural employment, wages and government expenditure on specified infrastructures. By using a simultaneous equation regressive model, the authors bring out that government expenditure on roads had the highest impact on reduction of poverty, followed by that on welfare, health, rural development, education, and soil and water.

Country and Village Studies

Some studies have also tried to find the relationship between infrastructure development and agricultural growth by using country or village level data. The impact of infrastructural investment on increasing agricultural productivity and incomes of farmers, improving their access to market, and providing more employment thereby contributing to poverty reduction has also been brought out by some country and village level studies. Most of these concentrate on the impact of the development of rural transport (in conjunction with other rural infrastructure) on increase in agricultural and other sectoral output and incomes and consequent reduction in poverty.

Evenson used farm-level data for the Philippines from 1948 to 1984 to estimate the effect of public investment in farm level output supply and input demand. Roads were found to have a positive effect on aggregate output per farm, as well as on fertilizer use. The output elasticity with respect to roads worked out to be as high as 0.31. But strangely enough, he found negative elasticity of output with respect to rural electrification.

In their pioneering study of Bangladesh, Ahmed and Hossain chose a sample of 130 villages across all the agro-climatic zones of the country. These villages were divided into two groups according to the aggregate index of accessibility to village of various services like markets, schools, banks and administration. Villages with better access were found to be significantly better off in a number of areas including agricultural production, household incomes, wage incomes of the landless labour, health, and the participation of women in the economy. For example, they found that development of infrastructure had a positive effect on the marketing of agricultural produce. The development of infrastructure enabled cultivators to obtain a slightly higher price for their produce and to buy a larger proportion of consumption needs from the market as compared with the undeveloped villages. The land market was also found to be tighter in developed villages where small and marginal farmers were able to move to non-agricultural jobs by selling their tiny plots of land as compared with the underdeveloped villages where such farmers stuck to their land for want of alternative opportunities.

In low income villages, infrastructure development improved access to institutional credit significantly (sevenfold), shifted the allocation of credit from unproductive to productive activities, and hastened the growth of mercantile capital in rural areas. Infrastructural investment did not lead to a significant improvement in literacy rates, but it did have a significant impact on health conditions and on acceptance of family planning practices. Infrastructure development also enabled the small and marginal farmers, who could not leave cultivation, to have increased access to non-farm activities. The effect of infrastructure on diffusion of modern technology was found to be quite extensive. An indirect effect was that infrastructure also led to slightly higher savings through its income-enhancing impact.

By far the most important conclusion of their study was that contrary to the often expressed view that development of rural infrastructure is likely to aggravate rural poverty, such development helped alleviate poverty in Bangladesh by increasing agricultural and wage income of landless and small landowning households.

The study by Barner and Binswanger analysed data from 108 Indian villages for the period 1966-1980 to study the effect of rural electrification and infrastructure on agricultural productivity and input use. Population was the main deciding factor among village demographic characteristics for the location of infrastructure like banks, schools, agricultural services and transport. Rural electrification was found to lead to an increase in agricultural productivity by bringing about improvement in irrigation through the use of pump-sets. Electrification also led to improvements in processing and technology transfer.

The study by Binswanger et al. used data from 85 selected districts of 13 states of India to examine the role of rural infrastructure like rural roads, banks, and education in agricultural investment and output. The authors used a reduced form regression model with fixed-effects technique to avoid simultaneity and measured the impact of various factors on agricultural productivity and growth. Their results confirmed the conclusions arrived at by many scholars that, whereas prices did have a positive and significant impact on increase in aggregate agricultural output, the impact as measured by the elasticity was too small. On the other hand, the impact of infrastructural variables like credit, irrigation and education was much greater. Improved road investment enhanced agricultural output quite significantly (elasticity of about 0.20). Availability of education infrastructure and rural banks played an overwhelming role in determining investment. Availability of banks was found to be a more important variable that determined fertilizer demand and crop output than the interest rates. Regulated markets and primary education increased output while electricity promoted investment in irrigation infrastructure. The study also brought out that the availability of electricity along with increase in agricultural output also stimulated the growth of grain mills in the countryside. With its combination of random and fixed-effects analysis, the study has contributed to a greater understanding of the interrelationships between infrastructure and agricultural production. However, according to critics, because it is in aggregate numbers, the study is unable to shed light on individual farmer decisions.

A study by Levy examined the socio-economic impact of improvements to rural roads in Morocco. The study compared conditions in the areas of the project roads, 5 to 10 years after project completion, to the situation prior to improvements ("before-after" the project), and to the conditions in comparison to the roads that were located nearby and were not subject to improvements during the project period ("with-without" the project). The study found that the benefits of paving rural roads extended considerably beyond the improvement of road use efficiency in terms of lower cost and higher quality. The extended benefits included major changes in the agricultural economy, including higher output, transformation of the agricultural output mix from low-value cereals to high-value fruit, and increased use of modern inputs, especially fertilizers. Moreover, improved access to education and health facilities increased enrolment rates in rural schools, as well as led to higher frequency of visits to health care services, and enabled the recruitment of professional personnel to staff schools and health facilities. The impact on women was especially beneficial and girls' enrolment in primary schools more than trebled in the project zone a few years after the completion of the project. Again, positive feedback from higher rural incomes possibly contributed to reverse causality. The effect on poverty reduction among all cultivators, including the small and marginal farmers, was also positive and significant. This was the experience in Africa, where trading margins are much higher than in Asia, partly because of the thinness of individual surplus and partly because of lack of rural roads and transportation.

Many empirical studies have brought out the contribution of infrastructure to agricultural transformation and the consequent impact of new agricultural technology widely adopted during the 1960s and the 1970s on the growth of income, income distribution and poverty reduction in the green revolution regions in many Asian countries. One of the earliest studies was by Bell, Hazell and Slade on the experience of Malaysian development. The study brought out that infrastructural development had direct effect on increasing income and also led to large indirect benefits through the operation of multipliers. The multiplier effect, in the context of a Malaysian rural area, was equivalent to 75 cents out of a dollar's worth of incremental income that was the indirect effect of an original investment in infrastructure.

The impact of the green revolution in India has been intensively studied by various scholars. Once again, all of them have stressed the important role that irrigation and other rural infrastructure played in bringing about technological transformation in many areas in India. In their study, Bhalla et al. brought out that because of sectoral linkages associated with rapid agricultural growth, several sectors of the Punjab economy were generating high input, output, and consumption multipliers. For example, in the case of dairy products, the value of direct, indirect and induced income multipliers was as high as 16.5 and for textiles 14.2. The authors concluded: "Punjab was able to pioneer the green revolution and thereby transform its agriculture. Its rapid agricultural growth was due primarily to the state's large investments in irrigation, power, roads, communications, and other rural and urban infrastructure".

The positive correlation between the levels and growth of agricultural development and availability of irrigation has been extensively noted by scholars. Irrigation promotes growth first, through increasing intensity of cultivation, second, by leading to yield increases, and third, through its impact on cropping pattern. The elasticity of area increase with respect to irrigation was found to be as high as 0.5 by Dhawan for the country as a whole. But, most important, assured irrigation was considered a precondition for the adoption of high-yielding Borlaug seed-fertilizer technology.

In a detailed study of Indian agriculture, Kumar and Rosegrant first computed the growth of total factor productivity (TFP) and then decomposed the growth of TFP into several components like infrastructure, canal irrigation, balanced use of fertilizers, terms of trade and research and extension (through a regression analysis). Market infrastructure, research, canal irrigation and balanced use of fertilizers were found to be the most important sources of growth of TFP. The marginal returns to public investment in research on various crops like rice were found to be very high, particularly in the eastern and southern regions.

Barker and Hayami put forward a hypothesis that improvements in physical and institutional infrastructure were the best vehicle for achieving self-sufficiency in commodity production in the long run. Since they require large investments and long gestation periods, subsidies and price support may appear to be attractive alternatives. Important steps in the prescription of Barker and Hayami for improving physical and institutional infrastructure were technological improvements, easing credit constraints in the case of small holders and dissemination of scientific knowledge through research and extension. Some authors pointed out that since irrigation was essential for the adoption of new technology, it had to be developed through canals and tubewells. Tubewell irrigation was credited with being less capital intensive than canals, more flexible, and less wasteful of water. But, being costly, to begin with, only rich farmers could afford to dig tubewells.

Vaidyanathan found that because of extensive use of new technology under irrigated conditions, productivity was much higher in irrigated tracts as compared with unirrigated tracts. According to Rao, between 1970-71 to 1989-90, 43million tons of additional foodgrains output could be attributed to irrigation. The uneven spread of assured irrigation across regions was the main reason for large variations in their agricultural development. That irrigation leads to greater stability is also brought out by several scholars. Dhawan found that the coefficient of variation of yield declined during 1971-1984 for irrigated crops compared with the unirrigated crops. Rao also concluded that irrigation per se led to reduction in instability. It is also argued that by generating more biomass, irrigation contributed to ecological conservation and sustainability. On the negative side, excessive irrigation could lead to submergence of forests, waterlogging and salinity. On balance, with appropriate intervention, it was possible to reap the benefits of irrigation and bring about higher sustainability.

Some scholars have also argued that irrigation serves the interest of equity. For example, Rao feels that to the extent irrigation results in higher agricultural growth and more employment, it leads to reduction in poverty. Rao has also argued that irrigation from public sources like canals and state tubewells has been more equitable than irrigation through private tubewells which are biased towards the rich farmers.

Further, studies conducted in several Asian countries and areas like Taiwan Province of China, mainland China and India (Punjab) confirm that the best strategy for strengthening farm and non-farm linkages and development of rural non-farm activities is investment in rural infrastructure, in general, and in rural road networks, in particular.

Finally, rural infrastructural development leads to interaction with the outside world and movement of people which results in the gradual removal of many superstitions and taboos. This, in turn, tends to weaken many of the attitudinal barriers to growth and modernity.

Indicators of Benefits of Infrastructural Interventions

A rural infrastructure project generates several direct and indirect developmental impacts. For example, a rural road project when completed results in increased accessibility, development of secondary and tertiary activities, and a decline in the incidence of poverty. Again, the initiation of special programmes for marginal and small farmers in countries like India, Bangladesh, Nepal and the Philippines yields numerous direct and indirect benefits in the form of improved farming practices; better repayment performance; and increased income, employment, self-reliance and family welfare. Specific indicators have been suggested for measuring the degree of achievement in each of these areas.

The indicators of development or of poverty reduction could be direct or indirect. For example, increase in accessibility due to road construction could be measured by the reduction in cost of transportation. Economic development could be measured directly by increase in per capita income. The indirect indicators of development could be increase in life expectancy, increase in the level of living and self-reliance.

In many countries, the debate on poverty has generated a vast literature on the appropriate definition of poverty, development of measures of incidence of poverty and development of indicators capable of capturing the impact of any programme on poverty reduction. The direct indicators of the incidence of poverty are based on the minimum threshold level of living (known as the poverty line) defined in terms of the ability of a household to meet minimum per capita calorie requirement or the equivalent in terms of minimum per capita income or per capita expenditure per day. Among the direct indicators, "head count ratio", defined as the proportion of population below the poverty line is the most commonly employed indicator of poverty. The other direct indicators are the "Sen index", "poverty gap index", "squared poverty gap", and "per capita income or expenditure", which capture the depth and severity of poverty among the poor and their level of living. On the other hand, the indirect indicators of poverty reduction include increase in employment, improved production practices and increased self-reliance. The impact of rural infrastructure investment on poverty reduction can be traced through both direct and indirect indicators of poverty by comparing the changes therein before and after or with and without the project situations. The indicators of development or of poverty reduction could, therefore, provide extremely useful information for supplementing benefit-cost analysis.

Monitoring and Evaluation of Anti-poverty Programmes

In most developing countries large resources are being devoted to anti-poverty programmes, and there has emerged in some of these countries an elaborate system for evaluating many of these programmes. The two most important indicators frequently used are the extent of financial and physical achievement. Financial achievement is often measured by looking at the expenditure incurred as a percentage of total allocation made for the programme. The physical performance gives much better idea about the benefits flowing from infrastructural investment. For example, in an employment scheme, the total employment generated is an important indicator giving the extent of benefits from the scheme. Similarly, the additional employment generated and the number of employees belonging to economically and socially backward sections of the population (like Scheduled Castes and Scheduled Tribes (SC/ST) in India) and the number of women employees, are the other relevant indicators. The infrastructural services generated in physical terms, such as kWh of electricity generated, irrigation potential, number of rooms constructed in a school or beds in a hospital, also give a measure of the project's benefits.

Detailed evaluation procedures have been laid down for the two most important anti-poverty programmes, namely, the Integrated Rural Development Programme (IRDP) and the Jawahar Rozgar Yojana (JRY) operating in India. The IRDP is one of the oldest anti-poverty programmes initiated in 1980 with the objective of providing credit based productive assets like milch animals, irrigation equipment, carts, handloom, shops, etc. to the identified poor in rural areas in order to enable them to augment their income and, thereby, rise above the poverty line. In the case of IRDP, there could be several financial and physical targets. The more important among the latter are the number of beneficiaries crossing the poverty line through the incremental income generated, the recovery rate of the loans advanced by the banks, and the subsidy credit ratio which measures the extent to which these programmes are becoming dependent on credit rather than on subsidy. The negative benefits could be measured by the percentage of the defaults in debt repayment.

The second programme, namely, Jawahar Rozgar Yojana (JRY), is an employment-generating programme initiated in 1989 by combining several earlier such programmes. The main objective is to provide wage employment to the rural poor and unemployed for creation of community assets like roads, tanks, irrigation bunds and watershed development. Recently, the Million Wells Programme and the Indira Awaas Yojana (Housing Programme) have become the most important components of JRY. In the first round, the number of wells dug under the Million Wells Programme and the total houses built for the poorer sections under the Indira Awaas Yojana are useful indicators of direct benefits. In the case of infrastructural investments, indirect benefits should also be calculated from additional agricultural output obtained from digging out a well and the imputed value of rent generated as a consequence of building a house. Similarly, the benefits of minor irrigation works created through an employment programme like the Watershed Development Programme could also be measured by looking at increased agricultural output due to the availability of irrigation. Watershed development also has an impact on the improvement of the environment, prevention of soil degradation and afforestation. Suitable indicators for each of these outcomes would need to be devised for calculating the overall impact of a watershed development project.

The experience in many countries brings out the importance of a broader approach for monitoring infrastructure projects in rural areas. For example, in India, the Ministry of Rural Development has evolved a comprehensive system of monitoring and concurrent evaluation of major rural development programmes like the Integrated Rural Development Programme, Jawahar Rozgar Yojana, Employment Assurance Scheme, Land Reforms and Rural Drinking Water Supply Programme. Concurrent evaluation studies are contracted out to independent researchers to assess the impact of poverty alleviation programmes. The Ministry undertakes the following types of monitoring:

- *Progress reports*. These consist of monthly indicator sheets and six-monthly comprehensive progress reports.
- *Release procedure*. This consists of receipts of matching grants from the states, utilization reports and audit reports before release of the next instalment.
- *Intensive inspections*. These consist of inspections by senior level state and implementing agency officers.
- *Review and monitoring*. This is done by committees and groups of high level officers at the state and central levels.
- *Review meetings*. These take place at the headquarters.
- *Concurrent evaluation reports*.
- *Standing committees and consultative committees of the Parliament*.

Some of the procedures mentioned above are used extensively for evaluation and monitoring of project performance.

Impact Monitoring and Performance Indicators

Some scholars have developed impact monitoring and performance indicators for evaluating the impact of transport infrastructure which offers numerous benefits to the rural poor. These methods can also be used for measuring the benefits of other infrastructural investments for poverty reduction in rural areas. Two general approaches are the cost surrogate method, and the behavioural approach. The cost surrogate method is quite simple and is widely used. But to use it, one ought to know the income distribution among the affected persons before the project and also the level of use of road and infrastructure service by each group. The benefit desired by each income group is estimated by multiplying the average level of use by the particular income group and the unit cost of providing the service. This benefit is then compared with pre-project income level as an indicator of welfare improvement among the various income groups.

The behavioural approaches resulting from the project could be measured within a general equilibrium framework. However, for this, the data requirements are very demanding. This is particularly true in the case of transport which has very wide linkages in the flow of benefits to various classes, including the poor. Because of their huge data demands, both the impact monitoring and performance indicator methods are not very cost-effective.

An alternative suggestion is to use a small set of performance monitoring indicators which can give information at low cost. Three categories of indicators are suggested: (a) input indicators that measure the means by which the project is implemented; (b) process indicators that measure the extent to which the project is delivering what it is intended to deliver; and (c) impact indicators that measure the project's impact upon the living standards of the project beneficiaries. For most transport projects, the indicators that measure the poverty impact fall into the third category.

The selection of a set of indicators will differ from one project to the other depending on their objectives. In general, it is always better to have a few key indicators for evaluating the performance of a project. For a rural road transport project that aims to improve accessibility to basic social services, a key indicator would be the average travel time and cost of travel to facilities, such as markets, schools, health care facilities, and primary transport networks (rail station, long-distance bus station) for different trips by different modes. Another measure would be the reduction in the number of days per year when travel is not possible, say, due to floods or bad weather.

Independent Indicators Approach

An infrastructural investment in rural areas generally results in promoting growth through increasing factor productivity and in providing basic services like education and health to the rural population. Its impact on poverty reduction depends on the extent to which it is able to provide productive employment and higher income to poor households and raise their living standards. While investment in physical infrastructure like irrigation directly augments earnings of the poor farmers and landless labourers by increasing land productivity, investment in social infrastructure, like rural schooling, indirectly helps the poor in augmenting their earning capabilities and hence enabling them to rise above the poverty threshold in the long run. Therefore, the poverty ameliorating impact of rural infrastructure can be examined by measuring the changes brought about by it through various household specific socio-economic indicators particularly designed for the poor households.

Indirect Indicators

The direct measures of poverty discussed above have been criticized for introducing a mechanistic approach to poverty alleviation. It has also been argued that the income, consumption, and nutrition approach fails to capture the changes in the access of the poor to services like education, health, safe drinking water and sanitation or other qualitative changes, such as perceived well-being and self-reliance of the rural poor, introduced by the project investment. An alternative measure of poverty is the lack of ability to attain a minimum standard of living. This broader approach supplements income- or consumption-based poverty measures with other indirect indicators of well-being such as life expectancy, mortality rates (both infant and under 5) and other health related indicators, and school enrolment rates.

In a paper presented at an ESCAP Workshop, Islam presented a group of indicators that could be used to measure the benefits of the rural scheme, Small Farmers Development Agency (SFDA), in Bangladesh. These indicators related to income, employment, self-reliance, family welfare, people's participation, repayment performance, self improvement, improved production practices, command over fixed production assets, impact on other agencies and involvement of women.

The importance of the broader approach has been demonstrated by several studies. For example, a resurvey of two villages of the state of

Rajasthan in India brought out that even though real per capita income in the terminal year declined, there were significant improvements in other indicators of economic well-being, such as expanding economic opportunities, increased consumption of goods with high income elasticity, investment in lumpy consumer durables and reduced reliance on patrons.

The supplementary indirect indicators, other than those based on income or consumption, that can be included in the broader approach to evaluate the poverty reduction impact of project investment, are described below.

Employment

Direct employment benefits are (a) additional employment generated by the project; and (b) its positive effect (if any) on rural wage rates.

Direct employment benefit indicators are employed for concurrent evaluation of employment generation programmes (such as Jawahar Rozgar Yojana) for the rural poor in India (India 1994).

Indirect or secondary employment benefits of infrastructural investment that flow in the long run include (a) occupational diversification from primary towards secondary and tertiary sector jobs, (b) increase in the wages of rural workers due to labour migration to urban and sometimes prosperous rural areas, (c) increased female work participation, (d) decreased male-female wage differentials, etc.

These indirect benefits are specially relevant for infrastructural investment like rural transport, rural schools and training institutions.

Improvement in agricultural production practices

Indicators of improvement in agricultural production practices include (a) increased proportion of cultivated area under high-yielding seeds, (b) increased per hectare chemical fertilizers, pesticides, weedicides, etc., (c) increased area under irrigation, (d) increased use of machinery, (e) increased area under high value commercial crops, and (f) growth in total factor productivity.

Improvement in non-agricultural production practices

Increased use of machines and other elements of new technology by village artisans and rural industries.The indicators for agricultural and non-agricultural production practices are useful for evaluating project investment undertaken to improve the well-being of the rural producers, such as village artisans and small and marginal farmers who constitute a significant proportion of the rural poor in developing countries. For example, Small Farmers Development Agency (SFDA) and Marginal Farmers and Landless Labour Development Agency (MFALA), which were set up in India to improve conditions of these target groups, yielded positive results in improving the productivity of assets belonging to the rural poor.

Self-Reliance

The main indicators of self-reliance are (a) acquisition of fixed production assets like land, milch animals, poultry birds, agricultural machinery, and implements like tubewells, tractors and other implements by agricultural households and productive assets by village artisans, (b) release of mortgaged land or other assets, (c) increased proportion of household expenditure as also of productive investment met from own resources, (d) decrease in interlocking of factor and product markets, e.g. a decrease in the degree of bondedness of labour and advance sale of crops, (e) increased access to institutional credit, and (f) timely repayment performance of advances or loans. These indicators can be utilized to evaluate the benefits from infrastructural investment. In fact, self-reliance of the poor is a very robust indicator of the long-term poverty reduction impact of any infrastructure in general and of rural credit in particular.

Improved housing

Shelter being one of the three basic needs of humans (the other two being employment for food security and minimum clothing), improvement in housing conditions is a sure sign of the improved well-being of the poor. The main indicators of improved housing are (a) increased ownership of dwellings, (b) improvement in the structure of the dwelling house, e.g. from mud-walls to bricked or semi-bricked or wooden structures with proper ventilation and natural light arrangements, (c) use of electricity for lighting purposes, and (d) additional per capita covered area.

The improved housing conditions capture the benefits from almost all projects but assume added significance in housing related infrastructural investment. Indira Awaas Yojana (provision of housing to poor households belonging to the scheduled castes and scheduled tribes) is one of the important investments under the anti-poverty employment generation programme in India.

Drinking water and sanitation

The main indicators are (a) increased access of the poor to sources of safe drinking water, (b) improvement of rural sanitary conditions for the poor (measured through improved water drainage, sanitary latrines, etc.), and (c) increased availability of public curative measures such as anti-malaria drive and immunization.

Health and family planning

The main indicators that can be usefully employed to capture increased well-being of the poor in this regard are (a) increased accessibility to health and family welfare services (resulting in time saving and, hence, reduced delivery cost of the line agency services), (b) decline in both infant and under-five mortality rates, (c) decline in morbidity rate among the poor (measured as number of days saved due to reduced sickness as well as savings on account of lesser expenditure on curative medical treatment), (d) increased longevity (or life expectancy), and (e) decline in birth rates due to adoption of family planning practices by the fertile age group couples. These indicators are specially relevant for infrastructural investment in public health and family planning projects. However, some of these indicators like reduction in morbidity and mortality rates are also related to increased availability of safe drinking water and improvement in sanitary conditions.

Nutrition

Apart from the direct indicators of overall nutrition deficiency (proportion of population below minimum level of nutritional requirements), the indirect indicators of nutritional deficiency, specially among the children and pregnant mothers, are also closely related with the prevalence of poverty. Some of these indicators are (a) decline in the proportion of underweight children (measured alternatively as weight-for-height, weight-for-age), (b) decline in the proportion of population suffering from anaemia (specially pregnant mothers), and (c) decline in the proportion of low weight by birth babies (an indicator of maternal malnutrition). These poverty related indicators of malnutrition are specially relevant for evaluating the projects aimed at improving the nutrition level of the poor, in general, and of the children and pregnant mothers, in particular.

Human capital indicators

The main human capital indicators related to increased well-being of the poor are (a) increased net enrolment rates among the primary and the secondary school age group children of poor households, (b) decline in the school drop-out rates, (c) increase in the literacy rate specially of the secondary and above level of education, and (d) increase in the proportion of technically trained personnel.

The above indicators are specially important for evaluating project investment in education and training infrastructure. It may, however, be noted that besides investment in education, etc, these indicators also reflect the secondary impact of almost all income augmenting infrastructural investments like irrigation, rural credit, and rural transport. In fact, the human capital index is one of the three indicators used to calculate the composite index of well-being, like the "human development index" and "public quality of life index".

People's participation or empowerment

(a) Increased representation and participation of the poor (especially women) in the decision-making process in rural democratic institutions, (b) increased rights of accessibility to the poor (especially women) to village common property resources like collection of firewood, grasses for the cattle and cattle grazing rights on common grazing lands, (c) increased involvement of the poor in project planning, implementation and management, in general, and in poverty eradication projects, in particular. These indicators are specially relevant for evaluating the poverty reduction impact of projects related to the development of common property resources like integrated watershed development projects in India.

Environment

(a) Increased area under forest and other common lands, and (b) declined degradation of soil, forests, water and biological resources. This is not an exhaustive list of indicators that try to capture the poverty ameliorating impact of project investment. The list is amenable to modification with the addition of some area-specific or project-specific indicators. Similarly, all these indicators may not be relevant for all the rural infrastructural projects. The choice of indicators for evaluating the poverty reduction impact depends on the availability of data and their relevance in a particular situation.

Combining Indicators

The individual indicators such as an increase in per capita income and employment provide a useful measure of impact of project investment for reducing poverty from different angles. However, to provide an overall index of poverty reduction, these are required to be combined into a simple composite index capturing the overall effectiveness of project investment on numerous variables. But formulation of such a composite index is not so easy. Combining of various independent indicators involves two problems. The first problem is related to the scale of measurement as different indicators are measured in different units/scales. The second problem is related to the assigning of weights to different indicators in formulating a composite index. The problem of scale effect can be removed by conversion of the chosen variable to a discrete scale or by standardization or by converting it to normal scale with zero mean and unit variance or normalizing it with respect to mean. Once the bias in measurement is removed, the crucial problem is of assigning weights to each indicator in the composition to reflect its relative importance. One simple solution to the weightage problem is to assign equal weights to all indicators as has been done in computing the Human Development Index and Public Quality Life Index.

However, an equal weightage scheme could lead to misleading conclusions and ambiguous policy decisions. For example, giving equal weights to primary education, reduction in child mortality and provision of safe drinking water involves strong value judgement which may be difficult to defend in a given socio-economic context. It is more appropriate to derive weights on the basis of degree of association (correlation) of indicators with the phenomenon under consideration. The "principal component analysis" is one of the approaches that can be usefully applied in determining the weights. This method enables an analyst to determine a vector (known as the first principal component) that is linearly dependent on constituent variables and has maximum squared correlation with variables. It can be shown that this vector explains the maximum possible variance among the constituent indicators. The composite index can, therefore, be obtained by linearly combining the standardized (free from scale bias) variable values with weights given by the eigen vector associated with the largest eigen value of the correlation matrix.

The main advantage of a composite index is that it provides an easy decision rule for the policy makers. However, being aggregated, it fails to give information on its various components which may be quite revealing and important.

References

Ahluwalia, M. S., (1978). "Rural Poverty and Agricultural Performance in India"; *Journal of Development Studies,* vol. 14 (2).

Bhagwati, Jagdish, (1998). "Poverty and Public Policy", *World Development*, vol.16, No.5.

Dasgupta Partha, (1998). *The Economics of Poverty in Poor Countries*, DERP No. 9, London: London School of Economics and Political Science.

Evenson, R. E., (1986). "Infrastructure, Output Supply and Input Demand in Philippine Agriculture: Provisional Estimates", *Journal of Philippine Development,* vol. 13(23), pp. 62-76.

Owen, Wilfred, (1987). *Transportation and World Development,* Baltimore: Johns Hopkins University Press.

World Bank, (1976). *The Economic Analysis of Rural Road Projects,* World Bank Staff Working Paper No. 241, Washington, D.C.: World Bank.

5

Strategic Planning for Rural Communities

Healthy communities require constant attention and nurturing. Communities become what they are based on choices people make over a long period of time. They are shaped by the decisions we make or fail to make. Some are made with knowledge about their impacts, but others are not. Some lead to unanticipated outcomes. But, the lack of a decision also has consequences. The strategic plan is a useful tool for any community that wishes to change and grow. A plan will help you see where you want to go and help you make decisions on how to get there.

The community development process consists of three phases:

1. strategic planning,
2. implementation, and
3. evaluation

Strategic planning looks at the big picture and helps you decide what is important. During implementation, you do the things which will get you where you want to be.

Strategic Planning

There are many ways to develop a strategic plan. These six steps will guide those who are not familiar with the process.

1. Develop a Vision Statement

Start thinking about your vision by creating a list of shared values in the community. Ask yourselves, "What is important to our community? What values will guide our activities?" For example: "We value creativity and innovative ideas," "We value self- sufficiency and helping ourselves," and "We value everyone's opinions and contributions."

Begin crafting a vision statement. Describe how you want your community to be in the future. Use a 10- to 50-year timeframe. Think about how your economy, environment and people will interact. What will be different from today? Describe the end result you want. At this point, you do not have to describe how you will get there. That will be decided later.

Involve as many people as possible in this process. You may choose to have a larger group brainstorm about ideas and then ask a few people to try to combine those ideas into a short and clear vision statement.

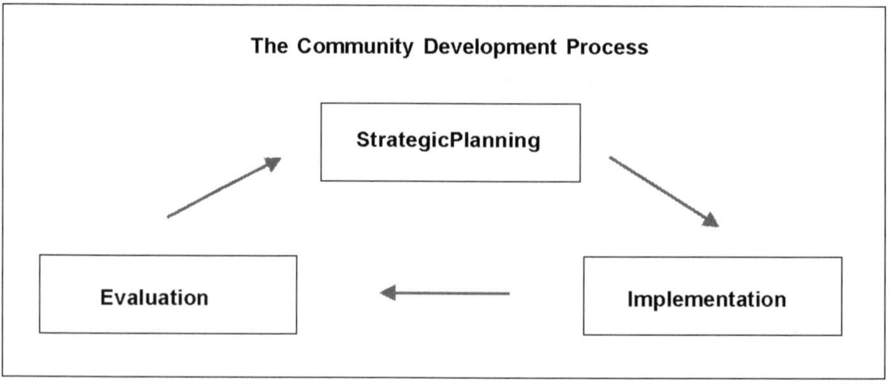

2. Assess the Community

Once you have agreed on a common vision of the future, look at what you currently have. Prepare a profile of your community that describes its economy, environment and people. Some of this information may already be available from government agencies, colleges and universities, planning departments, utilities or local businesses.

Describe trends affecting your community, the problems it faces, and the opportunities ahead. What are the barriers to change and the assets you can rely on? Has there been a lot of growth? Are a lot of people leaving the community? What businesses are doing well and what businesses are doing poorly? Look at the resources in your community. What kind of businesses are there? What do they sell? To whom do they sell? Where do people and local businesses buy the things they need? What churches, health centers, schools, parks and other public facilities serve yourcommunity? What are community landmarks or attractions? What are the things your community is most proud of?

This community profile will help you see where needs are not being met and identify people and resources needed to carry out your plan. The chart given bleow includes some major areas in which to identify your community's strengths, weaknesses, opportunities and problems.

Issue Category	***Examples***
Arts/Recreation/Culture	Facilities, programs, after-school activities, festivals
Basic Needs	Food, housing, clothing, household goods, equal opportunity.
Business Opportunities	Large and small businesses, self-employment, and second jobs.
Education	Preschool, primary, secondary, trade schools, colleges
Environmental Quality	Quality of air, water, land. Noises, odors, pollution.
Health	Physical, mental, dental, emergency care, drug abuse.
Housing	Affordable, safe, with basic services
Jobs	Unemployment, wage levels, training and job placement
Family and Youth	Parenting and communication skills, abuse or violence.
Physical Assets	Natural environment, parks, land use, roads, airports, water and sewer, telecommunications
Safety/Security	At home, school, work, in the community.

After preparing the community profile, examine the root causes of problems you identified. Ask why this problem exists and continue asking until you find the root cause. Imagine you are the manager of a store and have a problem with an employee.

Why is there a problem?	The employee shows up late to work every day.
Why is the employee late?	She takes her child to the day care across town.
Why does she take her child there?	There is no day care close to work.
Why can't she find any?	There is the only one facility in the community.

By asking "why?" several times, you will realize that the root cause of the problem is not that you have a lazy employee, but that there are not enough child care services in the community. Asking why can save you a lot of time and money in getting at the real cause of problems.

3. Analyze Resources

After completing the community assessment, look at available or needed resources such as people, organizations, money, facilities, equipment, and other things that can be used to carry out your plan. What Federal, State, local, foundation and private resources could you apply for? Can a religious group raise some of the needed money through a yard sale? Will a large employer match any funds you can raise? Think about creative ways to find additional resources, especially those that do not involve money. Can local or regional businesses donate excess equipment? Committed and motivated people are just as important as money.

4. Rank Problems and Opportunities

During the community assessment, you identified opportunities and problems and their root causes. Now rank the issues in order of importance. Rate each problem on one or two factors: the *severity* (seriousness of the problem) and *magnitude* (number of people affected). Assign a value to each problem, ranging from 1 (low) to 5 (high). Multiply the severity number by the magnitude number to get a score for each problem. Opportunities can be ranked be the likelihood of success, how much benefit you will get or other factors. Limit the amount of time for discussing each problem in public meetings to focus on the most important concerns. Differences of opinion and lack of resources may mean some highly ranked problems or opportunities are left out of the strategic plan in the short run. But these issues can be included in later updates of the plan.

5. Determine Long-term Goals

What does the community want to change or achieve in the next 10 years? A strategic plan should include goals for each highly-ranked problems and opportunities. It is not necessary to begin working on every goal in the first year. In some cases, more information may be needed about a problem before you can begin to solve it. When you develop goals, you are setting the direction for your community. Any specific action you take later should relate directly to one of your goals. Describe your goal in enough detail so that everyone will know when you get there. For example: By the year 2010, the high school graduation rate in the community will be 80 percent. In this step, you do not need to say how you will achieve the goal.

6. Select Strategies

Next, decide the best way to achieve your goals. You should brainstorm as a community about different strategies to achieve your goals. You will be more likely to identify creative strategies when a diverse group of individuals are involved in the process. This will help you identify and avoid any negative or unintended consequences. For example, to reduce unemployment, you could use any or all of these strategies: increase the amount of loans available to existing businesses; set up a job training program; recruit new businesses into the community; start a small business center; or come up with another creative idea.

After you have developed a list of strategies, evaluate them to decide which ones will be most effective. Here are some questions to help you think about the impacts that a strategy could have. If negative impacts are identified in any of these areas, you can brainstorm about ways to minimize or avoid them.

- Does the strategy attack the root causes of a problem?
- Is it a powerful method for change?
- Does it involve partnerships among all sectors?
- Will the strategy promote community empowerment in decisionmaking?
- Will the strategy distribute benefits widely in the community (Consider age, gender, race, income and disability)?
- How will the strategy affect the community's economic diversity and vitality?
- How will the strategy affect the community's self-reliance and vulnerability to outside influences (e.g., global trade, severe weather, economic downturns)?
- How will the strategy affect the community's resilience or ability to adapt to changing circumstances?
- How will the strategy impact existing public services, such as schools, police, roads, water, and sewer?
- What is the net impact on community finances (revenues vs. long-term costs)?
- How will the strategy affect the community's natural resources (air, water, energy, and land)?
- Will the strategy enhance the more efficient use of community resources (financial, man- made, natural)?
- How much waste or pollution will the strategy create?

- What will be the cumulative effect of this and other related actions (i.e. approving a subdivision may contribute to a gradual loss of farmland.)?
- How will this action further the community's long-term vision and goals?
- What impact will this action have off-site (neighboring communities or the larger region)?
- How much risk does this action involve? Consider whether it puts all of the community's eggs in one basket or if some aspects of the action could succeed while others do not.

Implementing the Plan

No strategic plan is complete just because it gets written. The hard work of implementation comes next. Everything cannot be done at once, so a strategic plan should be divided into several programs of work. Divide a 10-year plan into five 2-year work programs. Each two-year work program describes who will do things, to or with whom, what will be done, at what cost, and how success will be measured.

Select goals and strategies from the strategic plan that you will begin during the first 2-year period. The work program must contain realistic estimates of expenses and income, describe tasks that need to be done, identify who will do the tasks, and set a timeframe for completion. Although this information may change under unexpected circumstances, your work program should be as detailed and realistic as possible. Next, decide how to measure your progress and select "benchmark targets" for the first 2 years. These targets help evaluate your progress and report on outputs.

Implementation may be the most difficult but most important phase in the community development process. It is in this phase that the planned-for resources can be lost, partnerships become either close or distant, projects are started and then managed, and results become visible. Experience shows that successful communities usually do these things:

- Start with a smaller project that has a high chance of success,
- Manage their resources wisely and get the most value for every dollar,
- Act responsibly so their supporters have confidence in the community's ability to deliver the promised results,
- Keep citizens informed and constantly involved,

- Set benchmarks to measure how well they are doing,
- Evaluate progress regularly and publicly,
- Change their plans when conditions change or new opportunities arise, always keeping in sight the long-term vision,
- Use every opportunity to learn from experience, and
- Celebrate successes publicly.

Evaluation

A strategic plan is never really finished. It will change as your community's needs, resources and priorities change. Your first version will change over time as you learn from your experiences and improve it. Think of your plan as being in a looseleaf notebook, not as a hardcover book which never changes. Constant evaluation will help you see how well the community is doing, understand the benefits and impacts of certain activities, and make decisions based on better information.

1. Continuing Public Involvement

After the initial enthusiasm of developing a community vision and strategic plan, many communities find it difficult to maintain public interest and involvement. This dropoff is normal, but over the long term, a strategic plan cannot succeed if it relies on only a few people to implement it. The plan should describe how the community will involve the public. The community always needs a large pool of motivated people. For example, some communities establish working committees or hold regular town hall meetings. It is especially important to reach out to those segments of the community that have not been very active in past community functions.

2. Progress Reports

How will successes be publicized? As the strategic plan is being implemented, it is important to have constant communication with the public and agencies that have provided resources to the community. It is easy to forget to tell everyone what you are doing when you are so busy doing the work. However, the individuals and agencies that support the community need to know that their time and money are well spent. The strategic plan should describe how and when you will provide progress reports to the public and other partners. This will help maintain good partnerships and ensure continued support from inside and outside the community.

3. Strategic Plan Review and Amendment

How and when will the community review its strategic plan? This review can look at both "How is the community doing?" and "How well are the plan's goals being carried out?" It can consider unexpected circumstances and scan the environment for new problems or opportunities. The review team could include some of the people that developed the strategic plan as well as members of the public. The review may identify things that need to be changed in the strategicplan. Perhaps you thought you could build a new airport, but you later learned that your proposed site was a toxic waste area. As your situation changes, so will your plan.

However, you should not immediately revise your strategic plan every time you identify something that needs to be changed. Planning experience has shown that an annual review cycle works well and no more than two per year should be allowed. Constant changes can weaken the plan and lead community members to lose interest in the process. The strategic plan should describe an official, public process to change the plan. This will allow those who helped develop the plan to learn about the proposed changes and participate in refining and approving them. Just as the whole community participated to create the plan, they should also help improve it.

4. Continuing Evaluation

Every once in a while, you should stop and look at what went right or wrong, learn why it happened and try to prevent similar problems in the future. The strategic plan should describe how and when the community will evaluate the process, outputs and outcomes of the strategic plan. If you already know who will do your evaluations, include them in the planning process. They can tell you what kind of data is needed to do a good evaluation.

Process

Did people complete their tasks on time and within budget? A process evaluation helps answer questions such as "What changes are needed in how we are carrying out our plan?" and "How can we do it better?" It may be possible to do a process evaluation at the end of the first year or it may be more effective to do it during the strategic plan's annual review and update.

Outputs

An output evaluation asks, "How much of what we planned to do did we actually accomplish?" Outputs are usually things that can be counted and that you can see completed in a short timeframe. They result from activities in the strategic plan and work programs. (e.g., jobs created, houses built, programs started).

Outcomes

In evaluating the end results of implementing a strategic plan, ask "How successful were we in tackling the long-term problems in our community?" or "How successful were we in achieving our long-term goals?" Outcomes are usually long term (e.g., fewer people living in poverty) and linked to problems and goals. They are hard to evaluate because many factors that influence a community's well-being are out of its control (e.g., weather, the world trade).

Strategic Plan Elements

What is the product of the strategic planning process? Unless required by a specific program, the plan does not have to follow any specific format. Here are all the major elements of a strategic plan:

1. Vision Statement

- What values will guide our activity?
- What kind of community do we want to become?

2. Community Assessment

- Trends/conditions (economic, social, etc.)
- Problems and barriers, their root causes and their magnitude/severity
- Community strengths and opportunities
- Ranking or prioritizing of problems and opportunities
- Existing resources, assets, capabilities and new resources needed

3. Goals

Group goals under key issues, such as housing, transportation, employment, and environment and under each major heading, describe:

- What are out long-term goals?
- What is our desired condition?
- What do we want to change (condition, problem, barrier, opportunity)?

4. Strategies

- How can we best achieve each goal?
- How will partnerships help us achieve our goal?

5. Evaluation Process

- How and when will the strategic plan be reviewed and updated?
- How will the community report on progress every year?
- How will the community evaluate its process, outputs and outcomes?
- How will members of the community be kept involved and informed?

References

Flora Jan, *et al.*, (April 1991). *From the Grassroots: Profiles of 103 Rural Self-Development Projects*. USDA/ERS Staff Report 9123. Washington: U.S. Department of Agriculture, Economic Research Service.

Hornbeck, J.F. (October 12, 1993). *Empowerment Zones: Can A Federal Policy Affect Local Economic Development.* Economics Division of the Congressional Research Service.

Kretzmann, John P., and John L. McKnight. (1993). *Building Communities from the Inside Out: A Path Toward Finding and Mobilizing a Community's Assets.* Evanston, Illinois: The Asset-Based Community Development Institute, Northwestern University.

Reeder, Richard J. (November 1990). *Targeting Aid to Distressed Rural Areas: Indicators of Fiscal and Community Well Being.* USDA/ERS Staff Report AGES 9067. Washington: U.S. Department of Agriculture, Economic Research Service.

U.S. Department of Agriculture, (September 25, 1996). *Rural Empowerment Zones and Enterprise Communities: A Status Report.* Washington: U.S. Department of Agriculture, Rural Development, Office of Community Development.

6

Rural Energy and Development

Generally, there is a high degree of correlation between energy use, economic growth, and level of development. In the context of rural development, the traditional view of the productive use of energy is that it is associated primarily with the provision of motive power for agricultural and industrial or commercial uses. For example, motors are used to grind grain, operate power tools, irrigate farmland, and facilitate many commercial activities. It was believed that the motive power made possible by electricity would result in tremendous productivity gains and economic growth, thus transforming the underdeveloped rural landscape. In other words, the emphasis has been on the direct income-generating uses of energy.

The traditional conceptofproductive usesofenergy for rural development needs to be revised for primarily two reasons. First, there is a growing realization that although energy is a necessary condition for rural development, it is insufficient by itselftobring about the desired socioeconomic impact. Second, thereisasignificant shift in the understanding of what is meant by rural development, especially in the context of the Millennium Development Goals (MDGs) used by the major donors and international development agencies.

The MDGs emphasize not just poverty reduction in terms of income, but they also highlight the importance of improved health, universal primary education, women's empowerment, and gender equality. The very goals of development are to raise incomes of the poor and also to ensure that they are educated and healthy, and treated equally. Thus, an enhanced understanding of what is a productive use of energy must take into account not only the direct impact of energy on raising incomes, but also the indirect impacts that energy can have on education, health, and gender issues.

Productive Uses of Energy in Rural Areas

For rural development, energy was, and in some cases still is, looked at as having two distinct uses: residential and productive. Residential uses of energy are expected to positively impact the rural quality of life or improve rural living standards. The productive use of energy in rural areas is expected to result in increased rural productivity, greater economic growth, and a rise in rural employment, which would not only raise incomes but also reduce the migration of the rural poor to urban areas.

With respect to agricultural production, electricity would be used principally to provide motive power for agriculture-based industries and would power farm machinery, such as water pumps, fodder choppers, threshers, grinders, and dryers. This would resultinthe modernization of agricultural production. Electricity would bring an increase in irrigation, which in turn would result in an increase in the amount of required labor. The generous output of these modernized farms would provide inputs to large commercial enterprises such as rural cooperative sugar factories.

Another example includes the use of electricity as a source of driveshaft power and lighting, which is suitable for rural industries, for example, machine shops. In the past, a common belief was that once a rural region was provided with electrical service and access to modern energy, rural industries would expand and the quality of rural products would improve. Over the long run, the availability of modern energy services would provide significant indirect social benefits such as greater equity and improved quality of life. In short, if energy was used for productive applications, itwould transform an underdeveloped agrarian economy. Not surprisingly, the process has proved to be more complicated. One example of this is India.

India has a long history of supporting rural electrification for productive uses, in recognition of the potential benefits for the country in terms of poverty alleviation and food self-sufficiency. A major component of India's rural electrification program since the late 1960s has been to promote electricity for irrigation pumping by heavily subsidizing agricultural electricity rates. Since then, 13 million pump sets have been put in use for irrigation by Indian farmers. Partly owing to the high prices of other pumping alternatives such as diesel, and partly owing to the constrained capacity of the State Electricity Boards, today there are substantial waiting lists for irrigation pump-set connections in most Indian states.

Thus, this program in India has been relatively successful in promoting productive uses—particularly in the form of irrigation. However, electricity use by households has not kept pace with its use for irrigation pumping, and it is estimated that only about 44% of rural households actually have electricity in their homes. Bangladesh, by contrast, has witnessed a more balanced approach toward rural electrification. The rural electrification program in Bangladesh stressed both residential as well as productive uses of energy and has met with reasonable success.

Lack of adequate electricity for households has important gender implications as well. Because agriculture and cultivation are usually male domains (with homes being female domains), the traditional definition of productive use of energy has an inherent gender bias. This bias is evident in the rural marketplace as well. Even in rural areas where households have access to electricity, markets stock leisure items such as televisions and radios but not labor-reducing modern cooking appliances for women. Because men serve as the decision makers in households, the market tends to cater to their needs over women's.

In Indonesia, a survey of a relatively wealthy rice-growing region found that the rate of growth of pump sets was low and that most irrigation continues to be successfully accomplished through traditional, gravity-fed methods. Furthermore, the price of kerosene and diesel in Indonesia was heavily subsidized, making it less attractive for those farmers who used diesel pumps to switch to electricity. Thus, experience suggests that there are many different ways to promote productive uses of energy. This has important consequences not only in shaping the program but also in producing the types of benefits needed for rural areas.

Emerging View of Productive Uses of Energy

The view that the productive use of energy for rural development is primarily one of motive power is now changing. There are several reasons for this change. First, some recent studies have documented that lighting for rural nonfarm businesses actually improves productivity and provides additional income for rural people. Secondly, there is growing evidence that electricity use in rural homes is related to an improvement in education levels. And, because there is a well-documented relationship between lifetime earnings and education, a use of energy that positively impacts education can be considered productive. For instance, one study that stresses the value of human capital in development states, "The main engine of growth is the accumulation of human capital—or knowledge—and the main source of differences in living standards among nations is a difference in human capital. Physical capital plays an essential but decidedly subsidiary role".

Finally, access to modern energy services can lead to improvements in health. Although there are very few studies examining the relationship between electricity and health, there is a growing body of literature on indoor air pollution and its impact on both morbidity and mortality. And because people who are unhealthy cannot work as much as people who are healthy, surely improved health will lead to higher incomes. Thus, the uses of energy in homes or businesses, which can have a positive impact on social development in many contexts, are also productive.

In June 2002, the Global Environment Facility (GEF) and the Food and Agricultural Organization (FAO) held an expert workshop on the productive uses of renewable energy. The fact that the traditional concept of productive uses as motive power for farms is under scrutiny was revealed as the assembled international experts grappled with developing a working definition of productive uses. In the end they settledonthe following definition: "In the contextofproviding modern energy services in rural areas, a productive use of energy is one that involves the ap-plicationofenergy derived mainly from renewable resourcestocreate goods and/or services either directly or indirectly for the production of income or value".

It should be noted that the above definition is specifically for renewable energy; however, it can apply to energy derived from all sources. The workshop participants admitted that the meaning of productive uses of energy in the context of human development is difficult to establish. They felt that a use of energy that is instrumental in bringing about an increase in income is clearly a productive use. They also felt that the use of energy for increasing education and/or life expectancy is also a productive use; however, the impact that energy can have on these two is an indirect one. They argued that educated and healthy people will possess greater potential for income generation than a comparatively unhealthy and uneducated people. Thus, uses of energy to enhance education and life expectancy should be considered productive uses.

However, some argue that applications of energy for home lighting and entertainment cannot be considered as productive applications, because even though they improve the quality of life, their linkages to the Human Development Index are less obvious and almost impossible to quantify. In a review of renewable energy markets Martinot et al. use a definition similar to the one developed by the GEF/FAO workshop. Both not only include the uses of energy that have a positive impact on income generation, but also include the uses of energy for indirect social benefits such as education and health. Finally,K.Kapadia, in an unpublished World Bank paper , cites three primary reasons for the emphasis on productive uses of energy: maximization of the economic and social benefits, catalyzed by access to energy; facilitation of the Millennium Development Goals; and improving the economic sustainability of rural electrification projects and renewable energy markets.

Although all of the above-mentioned reasons for choosing the definition of productive uses are extremely pertinent, they preclude a broader understanding of what is meant by development. Amartya Sen stresses the importance of thinking of development as the process of expanding the real freedoms that people enjoy. Specifically, he notes that the growth of individual incomes is important "as *means* to expanding the freedoms enjoyed by the members of the society." In addition, he provides a wide list of freedoms, e.g., political freedom, opportunities to receive basic education, opportunities to receive health care, and freedom to participate inthe labor market.Itisoften asked,hesays, whether these freedoms are indeed conducive to development. This question, however, unfortunately misses the point that these very freedoms represent what development aims to achieve.

In the context of energy, many of the uses of energy that are seen as consumptive (e.g., home lighting or television) in fact may be uses that help achieve the goal of freedom allowed by development. For instance, television viewing is considered traditionally as a consumptive or unproductive use of electricity. However, a recent study in Bangladesh revealed that women in households with electricity were much more aware about gender equality issues than women in households without electricity. Furthermore, these women cited the television as their chief source of information for gender equality-related knowledge. In the discussion above on the definition of productive uses of energy, energy projects that have a positive impact on education and health are included because improved health and education increase people's incomes. A broader understanding of development would suggest that improved health and education are goals and ends in themselves.

This is not to suggest that an emphasis on income generation is misplaced. However, if the only productive uses of energy are those that facilitate income generation, then any use of energy which does not must therefore be an unproductive use. Although energy professionals and specialists may understand that "productive uses of energy" is mere substitute nomenclature for "income-generating uses of energy" and does not in any way pass a value judgment on the "unproductive uses of energy," some may mistakenly believe that only energy projects that increase income are valuable. Thus, it may be worthwhile to consider revising the nomenclature for income-generating uses of energy from "productive uses of energy" to what they really are, namely, "income-generating uses of energy."

Quantifying the impact of energy services on human development is not easy. However, a lack of quantitative data does not suggest the absence of a relationship but rather the need for further analysis and research.

Linking of Energy with Development Goals

The energy sector has a significant and productive role to play in achieving the goals related to income and poverty, education, health, and gender issues. More than half of the world's population and more than 70% of the world's poor are found in rural areas. Energy access can have a substantial positive impact on rural growth and livelihoods. In terms of economic development, it provides the basis for improving productivity by facilitating income generating activities and improving the business climate. In terms of human development, the energy sector can assist in reducing child mortality, maternal mortality, and other diseases by facilitating better health services. It can also encourage the development of higher literacy rates, gender equality, and women's empowerment. It is not surprising that a number of statistics show a very strong association between increasing commercial energy consumption and human welfare.

The MDGs adopted by the UN member states commit the international community to human development and are key to sustaining social and economic progress in all countries. These goals are now almost universally accepted as a framework for measuring developmental progress. The MDGs seek to eradicate poverty and hunger; achieve universal primary education; promote gender equality; empower women; reduce childhood mortality;

improve maternal health; combat HIV/AIDS, malaria and other diseases; ensure environmental sustainabil-ity; and develop a global partnership for development. The UNMillennium Project, which offers a practical plan to achieve the MDGs, has also recognized the importance ofenergy services. Ithas mentioned the provision of electricity for all schools and hospitals as one of the quick-win interventions that can be implemented immediately and has the potential to bring vital gains in well-being to millions of people.

Energy and Poverty

Energy services can help reduce poverty and raise incomes in a variety of ways. The traditional thinking about the productive uses of energy considers only the impacts on farm incomes by substituting machines for animal and human labor. However, energy services impact incomes in other ways too, such as saving time and resources, indirect benefits due to lighting and communication, and numerous other positive impacts on the nonfarm business environment. An expanded definition of the productive uses of energy would provide a greater emphasis on these benefits of energy.

Electric-powered farm equipment has tremendous benefits for rural farm incomes. As discussed above, farm machinery, such as water pumps, fodder choppers, threshers, grinders, and dryers, increase average yields per acre, improve cropping intensities, are more dependable, increase cost efficiency and productivity, decrease labor time consumed, increase areas for cultivation, and result in higher crop growth. Several studies have documented these benefits.

Onesuch studyinIndia demonstratesthat the additionofanelectric pump to a typical farm without electricity can result in an approximate income gain of about 11 thousand rupees (Rs) annually. This compares quite favorably to the farmers' electricity expenses (excluding electric pump capital expenditures), which average between 2 and 3 thousand rupees per year. Given existing agricultural subsidies, an irrigation pump appears to be a good investment for most small, medium, and large farmers with available groundwater resources. Same may not be true for marginal farmers, who gain only about 5600 Rs, as this sum may not cover capital costs. Therefore, it is quite reasonable that most of the farmers in this group have not yet invested in irrigation.

Apart from raising farm incomes, modern energy services can improve the more informal aspects of rural incomes by reducing much of the necessary daily drudgery that pervades the lives of the rural poor. For example, the rural poor spend a considerable amount of time each day collecting fuelwood, dung, and water. Because biofuels are a poor source of energy (particularly for an activity such as cooking), they consequently have to be collected in large quantities. If the rural poor had access to improved stoves and modern cooking fuels, this time could be spent on income-generating, educational or other activities.

On the extreme end of the spectrum, studies in South Indian villages have revealed that families spend 2–6 hours each day collecting 10 kilograms of wood over distances of 4–8 kilometers. A survey in the Himalayas found that although the hilly areas of Nepal provided an abundant supply offuelwood, women still had to spend more than an hour each day collecting biomass. The survey also revealed that the amount of time they were able to spend on agricultural activities was reduced likewise (compared to other people who were not dependent on these fuels). Surveys in Africa have shown similar results. Some evidence from India suggests that even if households continue to cook using biomass fuels, lighting enables timesaving food preparation.

Time is not the only precious resource that is wasted by the rural poor owing to a lack of modern cooking fuels. Using dung and crop residues as a fuel reduces the amount available for use as a fertilizer for growing crops, thus reducing income from crops. The dung used as fuel in India would be worth US$800 million per year if it were used as fertilizer.

Also, the importance of lighting and the many benefits that it provides is oftentimes ignored. Without lighting, livelihood activities cannot be continued beyond daylight hours, thereby reducing the total number of productive hours available. If the rural poor had access to lighting, they could work in the evenings and nights. For example, some poor Indian households that operate small cottage industries increased their income by 10 Rs per day using light to extend their productive hours after nightfall. In Indonesia, solar home systems provided lighting, which not only had a direct impact on income-generating activities such as office and store hours but also on activities related to household chores.

Another often overlooked impact is the facilitation of information and communication technologies. Rural energy services allow farm and nonfarm sectors access to modern communication, enabling them to receive accurate and current market prices. Lack of adequate information hurts sound business decision making and lowers income. For example, telephones in rural Thailand have enabled farmers to check prices in Bangkok regularly, significantly increasing their profits. Also, in India, the "*e-choupal*" initiative has succeeded in providing farmers with accessto Internet-enabled computers, which helps them obtain current information on market prices and good farming practices and allows them to order agricultural inputs. This initiative has resulted in improvements to the quality of their produce and also ensures that they receive better prices for their produce.

All of the above-mentioned benefits of improved energy services result in an improved business environment for small farm and nonfarm businesses. An example of the links between productivity and electricity is provided by a recent study in the Philippines, which found that small home businesses were more active in areas with electricity and made a greater contribution to family income than those in areas without electricity. Overall, 25% of households with electricity operated a home business, compared to about 15% of the households without electricity. The businesses with electricity, furthermore, were more productive than those without electricity. Most of these businesses were small general stores.

Bundling the delivery of electricity with other services or coordinating rural electrification with other development programs has been shown to magnify its effect on income. A household survey in India, for instance, revealed that while both education and electricity can result in higher nonfarm income, when the two services are delivered together the effect is amplified by as much as 2.3 times (or 25,000 Rs of annual household income). The traditional definition of productive uses of energy does not take into account these types of synergies.

Education

Modern energy services can have a positive impact on the time children spend at school and also improve the quality of the schools and the teaching. Electricity also provides lighting for rural homes, which increases the number of hours children have to study. In fact, children in rural areas are often unable to go to school because they must perform household chores and/or income-earning activities. For example, collecting cooking fuel can be an important component of a child's daily household chores; and if children are in school, they are unable to assist the household in this activity. Similarly, children may be involved in certain income-generating activities.

This income could be vital to the economics of the households, thus acting as a disincentive for the parents to send their children to school.

As discussed above, lack of access to modern cooking fuels in rural areas forces villagers, often girls, to spend considerable amounts of time collecting firewood. If there is access to modern cooking fuels or better stoves , then children need not spend hours every day collecting firewood and can take courses at school instead. In Morocco, road improvements made butane more affordable. This reduced the need for girls to collect firewood, giving them more free time and opening up new opportunities for education, work, and other activities.

A comprehensive survey in India was able to quantify the complex relationship between electricity and education. Although the positive influence of rural electrification on education is fairly well established, it was found that one of the main benefits of electricity is a very high amount of quality light compared to that provided by kerosene. This high quality light in the evening creates an atmosphere in which reading is possible for adults and children, who can more easily pursue their studies.

Furthermore, the likelihood of having electricity is directly related to the level of education and the level of income. Households in the rural energy sample with low levels of income earn about 13 thousand rupees per year and only 30% of them have electricity. This contrasts with close to 30 thousand rupees annually for the more than 80% of households that have electricity and have an adult with a high school education.

Particularly interesting was the finding that with every year of education, electricity seems to have a greater impact on income compared to those households without electricity. In other words, the combination of electricity and education has a greater effect on income than each variable taken separately. This finding has potentially important policy implications because it implies that education and electricity are mutually supporting programs.

Providing education without electricity is not going to have as much impact as providing education with electricity. Similarly, providing electricity by itself without schools or other educational facilities will not have as much impact as having both of them present in a community. This is supported by a study in Peru that found the bundling, or joint provision, of services was very important in creating positive impacts and increasing returns. To illustrate, the study found, in an analysis of identical households, that those households with access to basic services such as electricity and water "had a significantly higher growth rate of per capita consumption than households that did not have such access".

Rural schools throughout the developing world typically lack electricity and clean fuels. Many development assistance programs will paytobuild school houses and provide books, teaching materials, and basic furniture, but electricity is rarely part of the package. With modern energy, these schools can much better serve the needs of students and their families by providing space heating, clean water, good meals, and educational facilities that include decent lighting, audio/visual equipment, computers, and information and communication facilities. The use of electricity, modern fuels, and thermal energy services for schools is described in a detailed manual from the National Renewable Energy Laboratory.

Electricity and clean water are also essential services if schools are to offer decent living and working conditions for teachers. Retaining qualified teachers in remote rural areas is a challenge. For example, there is an ongoing crisis in teacher retention faced by the Papua New Guinea Department of Education and the various Provincial Divisions of Education. At present, there are approximately 36,000 primary, elementary, and secondary school teachers posted throughout the country. Over 90% of the teachers are in rural locations and serve the predominantly rural population. Most primary and elementary school teachers have little or no provision for power supply. Primary schools in particular typically do not have electricity or communications, and teachers posted to these schools and their families suffer from a lack of basic amenities. Not surprisingly, poor teacher retention directly contributes to low levels of access to education and poor educational outcomes.

An example of how this problem is being addressed is the proposed World Bank and GEF-assisted Teacher's Solar Lighting Project in Papua New Guinea that will provide a modest financing package, making the purchase of solar lighting kits affordable for teachers and eventually for health workers and the general public. It is intended to improve delivery of education in rural Papua New Guinea through longer retention of teachers posted to remote areas. The project will provide the financial remediation necessary for the PNG Teachers Savings and Loan Society to offer long-term (five-year) fixed-rate loans that make purchase of a Solar House Lighting kit by school teachers possible.

Electric lights in schools and homes permit evening study and classes. These greatly encourage adult education because adults are busy during the day. Educated adults, especially women, ensure educated children. Lighting also allows for a reduction in household accidents such as paraffin poisoning and burns associated with other commonly used fuels such as kerosene. According to some estimates, in Sri Lanka, one person dies every two days as the result of burn injuries associated with unsafe bottle lamps.

A study in the Philippines examined the social and economic impact of rural electrification. The most important finding was the clear link between electricity and education. Rural households perceived electricity to be important for children's education because it improved study conditions during the evening. This was borne out by the increased number of hours spent by both children and adults reading in rural homes, where electricity was available. Children from electrified households gained about two years in educational achievement over children from nonelectrified households. A household survey in Vietnam produced similar results.

Distance education is widely used in secondary schools (grades 7–9) throughout Mexico. The *Telesecundaria* program provides education to children who live in rural and indigenous communities where access to modern education services is limited. The educational program uses 16-minute televised lessons transmitted from Mexico City via the EDUSAT satellite. Rural teachers use the broadcast in combination with related texts and other teaching materials for a total educational segment of 48 minutes. The television sets are used for about 2 hours during each school day. Both grid electricity and photovoltaic (PV) power systems are used to ensure reception by all communities.

The Mexican program is not just about energy; it is a comprehensive distance education program developed over more than three decades, and it is a major initiativeinbringing thepossibilityofuniversal primary and secondary education to Mexico. Other developing countries are using various energy-enabled methods for distance information and education, including both low-cost radio (e.g., Mali) and television. The integration of modern energy with schools and effective curricula is emerging as an essential approach to achieving improved education in rural areas of developing countries.

The evidence of correlation between electricity and education is strong, but we must caution that the difficult issue of causality has not been fully resolved. There is fairly strong evidence that electricity is related to improvement in school attendance, literacy, and level of education, but this could be caused by the decision of educated households to adopt electricity as well. These are issues that require further investigation and may be assisted by the inclusion of energy questions in national multisector surveys, a topic addressed below.

Health

Rural social and economic development depends significantlyon the state of health of the population. For rural people to be productive farmers, fishermen, and workers, they must be healthy and well nourished. As mentioned previously, it can also be argued that better health has an intrinsic value and, irrespective of its impact on income generation, is a desirable goal. Indeed, energy has a significant role in improving public health in rural areas. Modern energy services improve health service delivery, increase access to safe drinking water, provide clean fuels that reduce indoor pollution, and can make available various communication tools (e.g., radio, television, and the Internet), which can be utilized effectively against AIDS and other diseases.

Rural health clinics are the front line against disease and in the promotion of health in rural communities. Yet few rural health clinics in the developing world have access to electricity, modern fuels, clean water, or telecommunications. Provision of electricity, heat, and kerosene or liquefied petroleum gas (LPG) to rural health clinics allows cleaner and safer environments, power for operating lights, water pumping and heating, sanitation, sterilization of medical equipment, medical refrigerators, other laboratory equipment, and telecommunications equipment. Handbooks are available that provide detailed information on the electrical and thermal (e.g., clean fuel) requirements of rural health posts, together with information on alternative means for providing the required energy services.

Without electricity for lighting, it is difficult to present health and medical information to local families and communities at night (when the men are back from the fields); yet providing such information and education is central in the war against the triple pandemic of HIV/AIDS, malaria, and tuberculosis. Deaths at birth can be reduced with improved delivery conditions, such as proper lighting. In the absence of a good lighting source, doctors are unable to perform operations at night or even examine patients. In health clinics, energy makes it possible to refrigerate vaccines (e.g., measles and tetanus toxoid vaccine) and operate medical equipment. Telecommunications equipment is essential in contacting physicians and in locating and obtaining emergency sources of medicines (e.g., antisnakebite serums).

Without electricity and fuels, such as kerosene or LPG, for rural health clinics and the residences of nurses and doctors, it is extremely difficult to attract, much less hold, trained health workers in rural areas. In Ghana, a primitive rural primary health care facility in the community of Binde evolved into a district hospital with the introduction and expansion of electricity (primarily from PV systems) and useofLPG for heat and sterilization.AsofMay 1998, 170 rural clinicsinthe remote mountain regions of Cuba were electrified with PV systems. These systems have reportedly increased the quality of life and decreased the infant mortality rate in those areas. All the systems include lights, a vaccine refrigerator, and other medical equipment, such as electrocardiographs and x-ray machines. Because each clinic has a live-in doctor, the systems include a television and radio.

It is for some of these reasons that maternal mortality rates tend to be lower in urban areas than in rural areas in most parts of the world because urban residents have easier access to appropriate medical services. One study illustrates the beneficial effects that electricity can have on an area's infant mortality rate. The infant mortality rate in electrified Bangladesh households was 4.27%, whereas nonelectrified households in electrified villages and nonelectrified villages experienced rates of 5.38% and 5.78%, respectively. For further perspective, the infant mortality rate in households with electricity is 25% less than the national average (5.7%) and 35% less than the national rural average (6.6%). The study's estimates show that if access to electricity is expanded to 100% of rural households, the annual number of infant deaths that could be avoided would number roughly 36,818, i.e., a savings of 101 infant deaths everyday.

Access to modern energy services also can improve access to clean water, and this, in turn, can make a significant difference in the fight against all kinds of diseases. Energy allows the use of mechanized pumps to tap water from deep wells, and energy can be used to boil or filter available water resources to make it safe for drinking. Energy for pumping and treating raw water provides numerous health benefits for communities as well. And, by reducing the cost of boiling water, access to modern cooking fuels not only improves hygiene but also reduces deaths from diseases such as diarrhea.

Exposure to biomass smoke is a significant cause of health problems, such as acute respiratory infections, chronic obstructive lung diseases, lung cancer, and pregnancy-related outcomes. Indoor air pollution affects children and women the most. In fact, indoor air pollution is estimated to kill 2 million women and children every year: There are about 500,000 deathsinIndia, roughly the sameinChina, with the other million inother developing countries. It is also estimated that indoor air pollution causes 500 million incidences of illness each year among women and children in India alone. In Nepal and India, studies of women exposed to biomass smoke—but who did not smoke themselves—found that their death rate from chronic respiratory disease was similar to that of heavy smoking males.

The exposure to smoke is quite high in households that cook with biomass fuels in traditional stoves. For instance, a study in the Guatemala highlands indicates that households using open fires for cooking have average particulate exposure levels of over 700 micrograms per cubic meter of air over a period of 24 hours. For households with an improved stove (*plancha*) or those that use LPG, the exposure levels are 100 to 200 micrograms per cubic meter. As a reference, this level can be compared to the United States Environmental Protection Agency's recommended maximum exposure level of 50 micrograms. Therefore, developing country households that used open fires or three stone stoves have very high levels of exposure to particulates.

There is strong evidence of causal linkage between biomass combustion emissions and acute respiratory infections in children. Children are particularly vulnerable because they spend a lot of time indoors close to the women who are doing the cooking. A study in the Gambia, for example, examined the health of 500 children under five years old. It found that girls, who were carried on their mother's backs as they cooked in smoky huts, were six times more likely to develop acute respiratory illness than other children. World Health Organization figures indicate that 20% of the 10.9 million deaths of children under five years old in 1999 were due to acute respiratory infections. In Bangladesh, a study found that a child's exposure to indoor pollution could be halved simply by increasing their time spent outdoors from 3 to 6 hours per day and by concentrating this outdoor time during peak cooking periods.

Information and communication facilities also play a crucial role in improving health. Rural health clinics benefit from radio-telephone communications capabilities, including single-side-band radios, two-way radios, cellular phones, and satellite phones. In Cuba, clinic electrification resulted in significant health improvements in local communities. However, owing to the remoteness of clinics, doctors had no way to communicate with ambulances or hospitals. Radio communications were added to each clinic. Of the 170 clinics, 130 have radiotelephones, allowing them to communicate with hospitals in the larger towns. The radiotelephones have already saved numerous lives and have been used for many purposes, including during hurricanes and floods to request ambulance or helicopter assistance; to inform relatives of the condition of a patient in a hospital; to inform hospitals about the status of vaccination campaigns; to ask for specific medicines needed by the clinic; and to solicit help from medical specialists. Importantly, the communications equipment adds only slightly to the cost of the total PV system.

Apart from having direct impacts on health (as described by the examples above), energy services also provide indirect impacts on improving health by increasing literacy, reducing malnutrition, and promoting women's empowerment. For instance, a rise in women's literacy and education has a strong impact on reducing child mortality, maternal mortality, and HIV/AIDS. Educated women take better care of children and increase a child's chances of surviving. Grant in "The State of the World's Children" has shown the relationship between female literacy rate, contraceptive prevalence, the crude birth rate, and the maternal mortality rate. The higher the female literacy rate, the lower is the maternal mortality rate. The education of young people merits the highest priority in a world afflicted by HIV/AIDS because education is the most effective—and the most cost-effective—means of prevention.

Increased energy access can have an indirect impact on reducing malnutrition. About 95% of staple foods need cooking before they can be eaten. Thus, lack of access to energy may render some, otherwise edible, products inedible and increase hunger. Malnutrition plays a role in more than half of all child deaths. Experts agree that malnutrition leaves many women unable to meet the physical demands of pregnancy.

Gender Equality and Women's Empowerment

Lack of women's empowerment has a direct impact on women's health issues. It is not an exaggeration to say that a maternal death is the outcome of a chain of events and disadvantages throughout a woman's life. A UNICEF publication titled *The Lesser Child* highlights the disadvantages of being born a female. For example, girls are likely to be breast fed less often and for a shorter period of time than boys, resulting in malnourishment from the beginning of their lives. They also are subjected to heavy work both within and outside the house at an early age and, when ill, are less likely to receive medical help. Energy services in rural areas can have a significant impact on women's empowerment (one of the MDGs), thus indirectly impacting women's health issues too.

Energy projects are often seen as having no impact on gender equality , however, as it is assumed that energy services impact men and women in similar ways. This assumption does not reflect reality in most developing countries. Consequently, several energy projects have not been as successful as they should have been because they failed to recognize the differences in energy usage patterns between men and women.

As a matter of fact, rural markets in developing countries often do not provide appliances that cater to women's needs. Although these markets stock leisure items such as televisions as well as video and audio players, they do not provide labor-saving cooking devices for women, e.g., mixers, grinders, and cookers. One of the reasons this occurs is that men are the decision makers; hence, markets are biased toward goods that serve their interests. Women benefit from televisions and radios too, but many of the labor-saving devices that are of greater benefit for women are not considered a priority.

Many of the benefits that stem from modern energy services disproportionately benefit women more than they benefit men. This is largely true because it is women and girls who spend the most amount of time and effort cooking, collecting water, and collecting fuelwood and other biomass resources. Thus, any improvement in energy access will disproportionately benefit them. By reducing the time women must spend cooking and collecting water, electricity allows women and children to spend more time on educational, social, and income-generating activities. This additional time can have a dramatic effect on a woman's level of education, health, economic opportunities, and involvement in community activities.

Limited access to modern energy remains an issue of gender equity in much of the rural developing world because 70% of all poor are women. A study of the impact of electricity on rural women in India showed that women from households with electricity had more time for leisure activities than women from households without access to electricity. There also is evidence that suggests the probability that a woman will read is very strongly related to the presence, or absence, of electricity in the home. In fact, regardless of income level, virtually no reading takes place in households without electricity.

The Indian experience was mirroredin Mali, where modern energy services derived from a multifunctional platform project showed that after the implementation of the project women were spending less time milling cereals and dehusking rice. They also were generating greater revenue from the sale of agricultural goods and foodstuffs and were producing and consuming greater amountsofrice. Perhaps most relevant to the subject of women's empowerment is that the total proportion of girls completing primary school increased as did the girl-to-boy ratio in primary schools. Additionally, from a health perspective, the number of prenatal visits that women made to health clinics also increased.

The successful integration of renewable energy with economically productive uses in the rural Philippines is providing income to many women at a small coconut development cooperative. This enterprise employs 200 families; 90% of the employees are women. Not only have employees doubled their household incomes, but previously unemployed rural women are now earning a regular income and, in many cases, have become the principal wage earners. Rural women have been empowered by becoming bona fide (with voting privileges) members of the local coconut cooperative. The Philippine Government and others are supporting replication of this activity in other coconut growing areas of the Philippines.

In Bangladesh, a study revealed that women in households with access to electricity were much more aware of gender equality issues than women in houses without access to electricity. Barkat's case study of Bangladesh provides a "women's knowledge score of gender equality issues" for electrified and non-electrified households in electrified villages and nonelectrified houses in villages without electricity. The effect of electricity on women's empowerment through a combined knowledge score based on three indicators: (*a*) women's freedom in mobility, (*b*) participation in the family decision-making process, and (*c*) knowledge about gender equality issues. Women in households with electricity had a higher empowerment score (0.662) than women in nonelec-trified households in both electrified and nonelectrified villages (0.533 and 0.499, respectively).

The same study also found that poor women in electrified households were more knowledgeable (79%) about gender equality issues than even the rich in the nonelectrified villages (64%). This indicates that household access to electricity can greatly improve a poor woman's knowledge of gender issues.

Women in electrified households, compared to those without, are more aware and knowledgeable about the selected gender equality issues and that electricity (via television) can play an important role as a primary source of this knowledge. This has important implications for the definition of productive uses of energy. In the traditional thinking about productive uses of energy, use of energy for television is considered a leisure or nonproductive use. However, if watching television encourages gender equality and gender equality is one of the goals of development, then energy used for television is energy used productively.

Public lighting improves women's safety and encourages evening community and commercial activities. Clean cooking fuels minimize indoor air pollution and the associated morbidity and mortality of women. Women are at greatest risk from indoor air pollution because of their gender roles, household responsibilities, and behavior. Modern energy services can increase agricultural productivity and women's incomes. Electricity and fuels for lighting, refrigeration, entertainment, and a host of other purposes permit women to develop small enterprises and increase their income and social power.

In conclusion, an updated approach to the productive uses of energy would emphasize that energy services should be part of a suite or package of rural infrastructure services that together can provide a base for substantial economic and social development. For instance, it was found in Peru that when the infrastructure includes electricity, water, and other development programs the various parts actually work together rather than separately to promote economic growth. The result is that the causal effects of electricity and other energy services are sometimes hard to disentangle from other causes. However, this is really an empirical issue for further research rather than an argument against the relationship between energy and rural productivity.

Effect on Public Policy

The most obvious impact of considering all the productive uses of energy is to realize that even though the MDGs do not explicitly mention energy, without the provision of energy services, the MDGs cannot be achieved. This has strong implications for public policy. Development strategies, whether formulated by the developing countries themselves or by international development institutions, must include a greater role for rural energy. In the past, energy was either assignedamarginal roleornot mentioned at all in important strategy documents. Such an approach will only serve to repeat the mistakes of the past. Energy services also cannot be thought of in isolation. Changes in the understanding of the productive uses of energy for rural development have meant that public policy also must consider the following: An emphasis on simply providing electricity coverageinrural areas without adequate forethoughttoopportunities for business development and poverty reduction is not only undesirable, but in the long run is unsustainable as valuable resources will be wasted. Moreover, promotion of productive uses, in addition to its poverty reduction impacts, can also improve the efficient utilization of energy infrastructure. For example, a rural electrification project in Indonesia included a component to promote rural business services by targeted marketing interventions and price incentives and also addressed information constraints and business needs of small enterprises in rural areas. The rural business service program demonstrated that these promotional efforts led to better daytime utilization of utility electricity generation and distribution assets. In fact, the program supported 66,000 rural enterprises and led to an increase in employment of 22,000, as well as an increase in electricity consumption by these enterprises of 180 GWh/year.

Energy services, to be most effective, have to be applied in a way that they improve the delivery of services from various other sectors such as health, education, information, and communication. This in turn has several implications. To a certain extent, the work on productive uses of energy has overconcentrated on the role of electricity. This is not to diminish the importance of electricity, but to improve maternal health, for example, improved cook stoves and modern cooking fuels are needed to reduce indoor air pollution. Also, it is important that public policy recognizes the interdependence of the various sectors by employing a mul-tisectoral approach. For example, in the case of India, this suggests that the rural electrification program should have a broader focus—one that seeks to improve not only the supply and quality of electricity to households, businesses, and farms, but also to improve access to services. This broader focus implies that within the developing countries, as well as in the international development institutions, development professionals need to have greater cross-sectoral interaction and competence. Energy professionals need to provide greater outreach by engaging planners and implementers within other sectors. By doing so, this will help ensure that an understanding of the important role of energy in delivering services ranging from healthto education to communication is held among all professionals across all sectors.

Although energy professionals often maintain that their colleagues from the health and education sectors, for example, do not grasp the importance of energy services, more often than not they themselves are guilty of not having made an attempt to understand the education and health sectors. To be sure, it is of critical importance that a better understanding of the linkages between energy and other sectors be found. In spite of anecdotal evidence, there is a lack of sufficient quantitative data on this aspect. However, it is important to emphasize that the lack of quantitative data does not indicate the absence of linkages but rather only indicates the need to study these linkages further.Thus, it is important to improve and systematize the collection of information on uses of energy and its impact on income generation, health, and education.

REFERENCES

Barkat A. (2003). *Rural electrification and poverty reduction: case of Bangladesh.* Presented at NRECA Int. Conf., Sustain. Rural Electrif. Dev. Ctries.: Is it Possible, Arlington, VA

Barnes D, Sen M. (2004). The impact of electrification on women's lives in rural India. *Energia News* 7(1):13–14.

Energy Sector Manag. Assist. Program. (2002). Rural electrification and development in the Phillipines: measuring the social and economic benefits. *ESMAP Rep. 255/02*, World Bank, Washington, DC.

Siddhi P. (2000). *Making solar affordable to the poor*. Presented at Village Power 2000, World Bank, Washington, DC.

World Bank, South Asia Energy, Infrastruct. Unit. (2004). *Access to Electricity: Strategy Options for India*, pp. 1–56.Washington, DC: World Bank.

7

Sustainable Rural Development Policy in Europe

Rural development has been an increasing focus of European policy over the past decade. It was initially pursued through the Structural Funds and related Community Initiatives as one aspect of regional development. The EU has now given it new prominence in its Agenda 2000 reform of the Common Agricultural Policy (CAP), with the birth of the Rural Development Regulation 1257/1999, and the SAPARD programme for accession states in central and eastern Europe. For the most part, the Member States and accession countries have responded positively to these developments. However, among the nations in Europe the policy goals of rural development are understood in different ways, and a variety of approaches has been pursued. Terms like 'integrated rural development' have a range of possible interpretations at national and local levels, and the motivation for different actors and stakeholders becoming involved in these initiatives can be equally diverse. The question therefore arises as to how such variety is likely to influence the development of these policies at national and European levels.

WWF and the Land Use Policy Group of the GB countryside agencies are working to identify and promote a new model of rural development for Europe that is more sustainable in environmental, social and economic terms. An important part of this will be to achieve a European policy framework that will enable and foster the evolution of such a model. In undertaking the study, the research team has been guided by a concept of sustainable rural development which involves the protection and enhancement of environmental capital; the fostering of viable rural economies; and the strengthening of rural communities and the cultural values that they possess. In this, there is also a concern to ensure stakeholder participation in development policies and processes. This concept is drawn from the broad principles embodied in key international agreements and statements, notably the Rio agenda.

This chapter aims to give readers an understanding of this variety of approaches and experiences of rural development. It also provides a comparison of a range of European countries including EU Member States and accession countries and also Switzerland in order to provide the perspective of a non-EU country with its own distinctive approach.

Driving Forces Behind Rural Change

Europe's rural areas have been experiencing significant socio-economic and environmental changes over recent decades. In this section, we briefly outline the main driving forces behind change in rural Europe. Together they provide the context, or starting point, for efforts to progress sustainable rural development.

Social and Economic Changes

Population

Low population density is one characteristic common to Europe's rural areas, but what counts as 'low' differs markedly from region to region. Densities of more than 100 people per km can be found in rural parts of southern Germany while in the most northern counties of Sweden there are less than 4 people per km. Similarly, the proportions of national populations that live in rural areas differ greatly: from under 10% in the UK, 25% in France and Spain, to over 30% in Austria.

Until the 1970s, the dominant population trend across Europe was urbanisation – the concentration of populations in larger urban centres, driven by the concentration of employment there. The rural concomitant of this trend was rural depopulation, and particularly the loss of younger and more economically active people. This was partly a result of the 'pull' of growing urban economies, but also as technological changes allowed agriculture to shed labour. Since the 1970s, the overall pattern has become more complex. Depopulation is the dominant trend in many parts of rural Europe, particularly in more geographically peripheral areas and in part of the

CEECs. Because it tends to be younger people that move away, problems of an ageing and less economically active population are heightened. In contrast, other rural areas are experiencing population growth, largely through urban out-migration. This sometimes leads to considerable pressure on open countryside. In Germany, strong interregional migration links these two processes: while West Germany's population grew by 4.8 million between 1980 and 1997, that of the Eastern Länder fell by 1.1 million. At least two forms of counterurbanisation can be distinguished. The movement of predominantly middle class families to accessible rural areas that occurs in many prosperous regions of Western Europe contrasts with the departure of often unemployed workers from some of the industrial cities of the CEECs who are attracted by the possibilities of a subsistence income and cheaper housing.

Some more accessible parts of rural Europe, particularly those closer to larger urban centres, have experienced counterurbanization as more affluent people choose to move from towns and cities into rural areas, either to commute to work, to retire, or to work in new or growing business sectors in the countryside. Migration patterns can be complex, with causes of migration being either economic in origin, or to do with changes in lifestyles and social aspirations. Rapid political and economic changes such as those experienced in many CEECs in the 1990s can also have dramatic consequences in terms of population distribution. While depopulation continues, particularly in more remote rural areas, it is no longer a universal rural phenomenon in Europe. However, for many parts of southern Europe and the remoter mountainous regions of central and northern Europe, one of the key challenges for sustainable rural development is likely to continue to be population decline.

Social Factors

In some parts of southern Europe, the transition from peasant forms of social organisation is still a significant process. In many countries, changing gender relations are altering the nature of, and aspirations around, local rural development strategies. For example, in Sweden, a country with a strong welfare-state tradition and women's movement, women dominate the public sector, which is a major employer in rural areas. Women are also very prominent in rural development organisations and gender equality is a major feature of development programmes. In some countries, particularly among the CEECs, national and cultural identities are gaining new prominence.

Common among many rural areas are the long term challenges posed by an ageing population, as well as the opportunities enjoyed by populations that benefit from continually rising living standards. Similarly, we might identify a general trend towards a greater emphasis on amenity and quality of life concerns, such as a new environmental ethic, as living standards rise. However, quality of life expectations can also favour further outmi-gration, especially of skilled people, where rural services, transport links, education and health are not of the same standard as in urbanised areas. Such trends can be observed especially in the least populated areas of economically weaker regions, in southern Europe in particular. All these trends shape the context for rural development in the different regions of Europe.

Economies

All rural areas of Europe begin from distinctly different starting points in terms of their development. There are substantial regional differences in rural GDP and a sharp divide between the western countries and the CEECs. The urban/rural divide is much sharper in the CEECs, which have seen the collapse of much of the formal economy in rural areas; industrial output per head in the rural areas of Latvia is a quarter of that in the urban areas. In contrast, it is possible to find some rural regions in every EU Member State that figure among the most economically dynamic in their country. Unemployment in many of the more developed EU Member States (such as Germany, France and the UK) is lower in rural than in urban areas, although this is not the case in the mountainous areas of Austria or the forested counties of Sweden. In other Member States, unemployment in rural areas tends to be either similar to or somewhat higher than in urban areas. Unemployment rates are also significantly higher in the CEECs, particularly in rural areas. Official unemployment is 27% in the Latgale districts of Latvia, for example, while the actual level is considerably higher.

There are major variations in the economic importance of rural areas. In some countries the agri-food sector accounts for more than 20% of exports (eg Hungary), in others for less than 5 per cent. Agricultural employment ranges from under 2% of the national workforce in the UK to more than 10% in Greece, Ireland and Portugal. In some CEECs, there has been a dramatic decline in the numbers employed in agriculture in the last decade – dropping from 17.5 to 7.9% in Hungary since 1990.

The economic functions of rural areas have changed considerably in recent decades. There has been an inexorable decline in primary sector employment and traditional rural industries have been squeezed. However, new industrial and service activities have emerged, although not necessarily in those regions suffering the most from rural decline.

All the EU countries have suffered losses of primary sector employment over several decades. There are now few regions in the EU where agriculture contributes more than 10% of the regional value added and these are concentrated in Greece, Portugal and Ireland. Agriculture now accounts for only 5% of employment in the EU (Eurostat, 1998). Forces of mechanisation have widely affected not only agriculture, but forestry, fishing and mining too; and expansion of production has encountered problems of over-exploitation and over-supply. At the same time, processing and manufacturing activities once closely linked to the primary sector (such as farm machinery manufacture, food processing, the leather industry, timber processing, etc.) have undergone significant economic and geographical concentration and face growing competition from outside the EU. Many service activities traditionally found in rural centres have also experienced intensified competition from urban centres. The consequence of all these developments has been the loss of much localised employment from rural areas and regions.

Agriculture and Forestry

Agriculture and forestry are by far the most important land uses in European rural areas. Agriculture accounts for over 40% of the EU's total land area, although the proportion in Member States varies from less than 10% of national territory in Sweden and Finland to over 70% in the UK and Ireland. Likewise, while about 36% of EU land is forested, this varies from under 8% in the UK to 60% in the Scandinavian countries. In Central and Eastern Europe the pattern is similar, with agriculture dominant in southern and central countries and forestry among the Baltic states.

The dominant trends in agriculture over the past half-century have been the intensification and specialisation of agricultural production, encouraged by technological developments and subsidised commodity prices. Within the Common Market for agricultural products there has also been a concentration of production in favoured and central regions and a marginalisation of production in less favoured and peripheral regions. Thus some 80% of the EU's intensive agricultural production occurs in coastal zones of the North Sea and the English Channel, in a corridor stretching from Brest to

Copenhagen and around Rouen and Rotterdam. On the other hand, Less Favoured Areas (LFAs) cover more than half the total farmed area in the EU.

In the CEECs, agricultural systems have experienced dramatic changes since the late 1980s. The dismantling of state structures of management and control, the privatisation and restitution of landownership and the sweeping market reforms of the early 1990s massively disrupted agricultural production in the short term and have greatly diminished the intensity of production in the medium term. The decline in output was most pronounced in livestock production as consumers switched to cheaper staple products and export markets were lost. In most countries, cattle and sheep numbers fell to about half their former level and there was a decline of 30–35% in pig and poultry populations.

Crop production fell by up to a third compared to 1989 but there has been an increase in average yields and production in most countries recently. Overall, a great deal of capital and labour have been withdrawn from the agricultural sector. Without support for marginal areas or farmers, processes of marginalisation are leading to extensive land abandonment, particularly in regions where growing conditions are poor and which are peripheral. These developments have been exacerbated in some cases by the way the privatisation of land has been handled. Privatisation of the state owned and collective farms generally has resulted in a dual farm structure. Often there is a large number of small semi-subsistent family farms, subject to rapid amalgamation in some areas, which exist alongside a group of larger units comprising co-operatives, limited companies and state farms.

To some extent, the pattern of change in European forestry in recent decades has mirrored that in agriculture, with a general trend towards intensification of forest management and increasing specialisation in forest outputs. Also, this has in turn engendered a critical appraisal of the impacts of the sector upon the environment and a move in recent years to redress the balance by seeking more multipurpose forestry which delivers environmental and social benefits, including initiatives to add value to forest products and conserve local distinctiveness and biodiversity. In the accession countries, a degree of privatisation of former state forest has occurred, which has led to some of the same stagnation in management activities as has affected agriculture. It is probably fair to say that in many respects, the changes in forestry and woodland management have been less swift and potentially less damaging than in farming because of the longer product cycles involved. They have also been tempered by the continuing significance of state ownership and management in this sector, in both EU and accession countries. One external factor which has had a particular influence on the state of forests in Europe has been air pollution from urban and industrial sources, which continues to be a concern in many countries.

Other Sectors

New economic functions have emerged for rural areas. Indeed, new firm formation rates and employment growth have tended to be higher in small towns and rural areas than in large urban centres. There has been a net increase in employment in all non-metropolitan regions of the EU with the exception of Greece and Finland (OECD 1996). In some cases growth is due to the decentralisation of productive activities, but very often it is due to indigenous industrialisation. Furthermore, in more accessible rural regions, certain service activities have also relocated to rural areas, thereby accentuating an employment pattern already heavily weighted towards the service sector.

Tourism has become a major growth sector for many rural regions. In some regions it has come to play a key role in maintaining rural livelihoods and landscapes. Austria is a prime example, with 15% of its GNP from tourism. The Austrian Alps have a highly developed tourism economy which is strongly related to the agricultural sector and helps to support a complex system of small-scale pluri-active farmers providing accommodation, tourism enterprises, handicrafts, etc. In other parts of Europe, the development particularly of mass tourism has seen a radical transformation of local economies, landscapes and settlements, as has been the case in what, in the 1950s, was the small Spanish fishing village of

Benidorm. There is no doubting, however, that leisure and tourism are still widely regarded as a significant development option for rural economies in much of Europe, particularly as active holidays (skiing, hiking, cycling, climbing, etc) gain in popularity. For example, some 69% of project proposals under the LEADER I programme in Spain were tourism-related.

Since the opening up of the CEECs to Western visitors, tourism has developed quickly there too. The number of international arrivals showed a sharp increase of 180% in the period 1985 to 1996 (compared with 60% for Europe as a whole). The outlook shows a continuous growth of tourism of about 60% between 1996 and 2010 which is also stronger than the predicted growth of about 50% for Europe as a whole. For example, over twenty million tourists visit Hungary each year, which makes it the eighth most visited country in the world (ahead of countries like Austria and Switzerland). However, although the cultural and natural qualities of rural Hungary offer considerable tourist potential, rural areas have largely not yet benefited because of the lack of infrastructure.

Technological Change

As in the past century, technological change will continue to be an important motor of change in Europe's rural areas in the coming years. Recent years have seen increasing interest in the possible implications of new Information and Communication Technologies (ICTs) and new biotechnology such as new crop varieties, leading recently to the planting of genetically modified crops albeit on a small scale at present. ICTs have the potential to alter the geographies of both work and trading. Some have interpreted this as the potential 'death of distance' with the implication that rural areas will be able to compete more effectively in the 'new economy' associated with ICTs. However, it is just as plausible for the ICT revolution to reinforce the competitive advantages of some larger urban centres to the detriment of peripheral rural areas. New biotechnology and developments in agriculture also have the potential to alter the geography of agricultural land uses in Europe, as well as the nature of agricultural input use. Many have postulated a further polarisation in Europe between areas of intensive, increasingly specialised production with more widespread adoption of 'integrated farming', and more marginal, extensive agriculture. In parallel, the effects of climate change and of measures to reduce greenhouse gas emissions may create both new constraints, and also new opportunities, for agricultural land uses.

Political Factors

Probably the most important motor of change in the rural areas of Central and Eastern Europe has been the process of social and economic restructuring, prompted by the political reforms of the last decade. The transition from centrally planned economies, and the preparations for accession to the EU, are key drivers shaping rural transformation. Important among these changes are the reform of local government structures and legal reforms concerning land ownership and the process of privatisation. These are profoundly altering the structure of local and regional economies as well as prompting significant movements of population.

In Western Europe too, the evolution of the policies and institutions of the EU are an important influence upon the socio-economic conditions of many rural areas. Over the past decade or so, the growth of the EU's cohesion policy has meant, for example, the targeting of considerable public funds for rural development and structural adjustment in rural regions covered by Objective 1 in countries such as Ireland, Spain and Portugal. The importance of EU co-funding for structural policies has led to a considerable influence of EU programme objectives on national policy making for rural areas, in particular with regard to important infrastructure investments. EU Structural Funds programming procedures have introduced a certain rigour with regard to the integration of environmental considerations into programme planning but also bind considerable administrative resources and can limit flexibility.

Environmental Changes

Different patterns of land use will shape development paths. In general, across Europe, natural habitats are now rare and frequently under pressure. Wildlife depends heavily on semi-natural habitats in every country and the management of farmland and commercial forests is a critical determinant of the status of a large range of habitats and the species that they support.

Environmental issues can create both constraining factors that inhibit rural development, and positive opportunities to be exploited. Often, specific problems such as pesticide contamination of drinking water have come to public and political attention as a result of the EU's establishment of pan-European systems of environmental monitoring and regulation.

The ten national studies reveal a familiar catalogue of environmental pressures on the countryside, with many threats now diffuse and cumulative, as opposed to large development proposals, which are less prominent today. Most countries share certain concerns, as follows.

- There has been a progressive degradation in semi natural and farmed habitats, driven by a combination of intensification and abandonment.
- In central Europe abandonment has taken place on a large scale; in Hungary one million hectares of farmland is expected to be affected.

- In the EU intensification is generally perceived to be a greater problem, with exceptions such as remoter parts of Spain, northern Sweden, patches in France, Germany and elsewhere.
- Degradation of soils and water quality continue to be associated with intensive farming and there are a number of distinct regional issues, such as excessive water abstraction and pollution associated with irrigation in southern Europe.
- Continued urbanisation, and the progressive fracturing of rural landscapes and disruption of habitats and rural tranquillity by infrastructure projects are reported in most countries, especially in the developed zones of north west Europe. A few countries, such as Germany, pay particular attention to the impact of development on soils and water supplies.
- Forest management is a concern in many countries although the issues vary considerably. They include inappropriate afforestation in Spain, insensitive commercial management in Sweden and excessive felling on private land in Latvia.

In areas of more intensive agricultural practices, the risk over the longer term is that environmental degradation progressively undermines farming's underlying productive resources, for example by water pollution or soil erosion. Similarly, land that is developed for housing or large infrastructure projects is unlikely to be restored for other uses. Thus environmental change can constrain future development strategies in some places and limit their scope. Constraints may also arise in the future as a result of the impacts of climate change on European land uses and transport patterns, or the requirement that rural land makes a contribution to addressing greenhouse gas emissions through exploiting carbon sink functions, or growing new and renewable energy crops.

Extensive farming systems on often marginal farmland contribute most to agricultural biodiversity, the so-called 'High Nature Value' farming. However, such systems remain under strong economic pressure and continue to suffer intensification, simplification or outright abandonment.

At the same time, there is evidence of environmental progress. Throughout the EU there has been a large increase in the area of land under agri-environment schemes. In Austria nearly 80% of farmland now benefits from this measure and even in the UK, at the lower end of the spectrum, the area of land enrolled increased fifteen fold between 1987 and 1998. Organic farming has enjoyed a boom in many countries in recent years, partly driven by new markets and partly by support from CAP and national measures. In Austria about 20,000 farms, nearly 10% of the agricultural area, are now organic, although growth has levelled off in recent years.

High Nature Value farmed habitats are increasingly coming under systems of special protection and management, which may create a basis for new local economic development strategies. In many countries rural development initiatives attempt to capture higher added value for High Nature Value Farming products by marketing their special quality and healthy image.

The relatively rapid growth in EU policy measures to protect and enhance the rural environment will continue to influence the trajectory of rural development in future. Already, the Birds and Habitats Directives have become an important influence upon EU funding for rural development, and other environmental regulations are increasingly being linked to agricultural support policies in general. The implementation of the Water Framework Directive is likely to strengthen these influences in future.

Approaches to Rural Development in Europe

General Concepts

Rural areas are characterised by generally low population densities and by relatively extensive land uses such as agriculture and forestry. Yet beyond these simple characteristics, Europe's rural areas are extremely diverse in their socio-economic conditions and their physical geography and, therefore, in the nature of their development prospects and problems. Because of this diversity, there is no single, over-arching 'rural problem' for rural development policy to address. In the past, the broad parameters of what constituted 'rural development' were easier to agree and tended to be defined in terms of 'modernising' agriculture and rural services in order to catch up with the standards of urban areas. Nevertheless, in recent years it is increasingly agreed that the development of rural areas should *build upon and conserve their intrinsic qualities and assets.* So what may be required in one rural locality may differ sharply from prevailing needs and opportunities in another.

Post-war Approaches

In broad terms, two contrasting models of rural development have characterised European rural development. The classical formulation of rural development, dominant in post-war Europe, was an *exogenous* model ('driven from outside'). The function of rural areas was primarily to provide food for the expanding cities, and the development problems of rural areas were diagnosed as those of marginality. Rural areas were distant technically, economically and culturally from the main (urban) centres of activity. In all of these respects they were 'backward'. From this perspective, the basic policy response was a combination of subsidising the improvement of agricultural production, and the encouragement of labour and capital mobility.

However, these measures helped create new social and economic problems, not least the depopulation of peripheral areas. The 'balanced development' of national territory thus became a preoccupation of policy in countries such as France, Sweden, Austria and Switzerland. A second phase of exogenous policy, typically focussed on peripheral regions, sought to address this issue through attracting new types of employment into rural areas. Processing facilities were established and manufacturing firms were encouraged to relocate from urban areas or to set up branch plants. As well as financial and fiscal inducements, development agencies concentrated on providing infrastructure, including improvements in transport and communications, power supplies and the provision of serviced factory sites. Most European countries adopted this approach, but it was particularly strongly pursued in France, Ireland, Italy, the UK and across Scandinavia. In some regions (eg the Mediterranean) the emphasis was on the development of tourism.

By the late 1970s the exogenous model was falling into disrepute. The continued intensification and industrialisation of agriculture came up against the saturation of domestic markets and environmental limits. The recession of the early 1980s also resulted in the closure of many branch plants. Areas that had experienced rapid expansion of tourism also came to realise its seasonal and cyclical fluctuations as well as the destructive impact on local cultures and environments of mass tourism. These difficulties encouraged the exploration in the 1980s of so-called *endogenous* approaches to rural development ('driven from within') based on the assumption that the specific resources of an area – natural, human and cultural – hold the key to its sustainable development.

Endogenous Rural Development

Endogenous development ideas drew on four sources. *First* was the recognition that during the 1970s and 1980s certain rural regions, with previously unrecognised internal dynamism, had achieved remarkable progress – the 'Third Italy' was the most celebrated example. The question arose of what was the key to success for these regions and whether it could be replicated elsewhere.

A *second* source was regionalist movements and agencies seeking to overcome previous policy failures by promoting forms of local development less dependent on external capital, including rural diversification, support for indigenous businesses, and the encouragement of local initiative and enterprise. Prominent examples of this kind of approach can be found in the work of development agencies in Ireland, France, the Scottish Highlands and Islands and in rural Wales (UK), in mountain community projects in Italy and Austria, and in village development groups in Northern Sweden.

The *third* source was the debate about rural sustainability. The sustainability concept seeks to bridge not only the conventional divide between economic development and environmental protection but also embraces the viability of localities and communities on which the maintenance of both the environment and economic activity ultimately depends. Thus, there has been a growing awareness that a conserved countryside must be socially viable and is therefore dependent on the vitality of rural communities.

The *fourth* source of ideas came from notions of self-reliance promoted by two groups -radical greens and development activists working with particularly marginalised groups. The former elaborated the 'small is beautiful' thinking of Schumacher into the field of community economics, seeking to reassert local control over economic activities to protect local communities from the forces of globalisation. Where possible, they have argued, local production should seek to supply local needs, and strategies should be pursued for retaining value added from the use of local resources within the area. Development activists working with marginalised groups have also promoted notions of self-reliance. Thus a feature of community development in peripheral regions, such as Southern Spain and Northern

Sweden, has been the promotion of community enterprises and community ownership and management of natural resources.

Integrated Rural Development (IRD) is a term that has been increasingly used to describe the modern perception of the endogenous model, emphasising a perceived need at the local level to break down barriers between sectoral policy making in the fields of economy, society and environment. In the UK, the Countryside Agency defines IRD as 'a way of working that seeks to deliver sustainable development in rural areas by benefiting social, economic and environmental objectives, bringing equal benefits for all three wherever possible, whilst seeking to avoid damage to any one of them.' IRD embodies principles of:

- *integration* (where packages of policies are designed both to harmonise different interests and to achieve economic, social and environmental objectives);
- *individuality* (where locally distinctive characteristics and priorities are suitably acknowledged); and
- *involvement* (where local communities are actively included, and the emphasis is upon self-help rather than reliance on external action).

Policy Development at EU Level

The evolution of European Community policy has followed, incorporated and influenced these changing conceptions of rural development. In the 1960s and 1970s the dominant preoccupation was with agricultural modernisation. Since the 1960s, the CAP has included an agricultural structures component to assist the workings of the common market through a process of agricultural modernisation. This agricultural structures policy was funded through the Guidance Section of the EAGGF - the European Agricultural Guidance and Guarantee Fund. It was used primarily to assist rationalisation in agriculture and in the processing and marketing of agricultural products. In the 1970s, it took on more of a social dimension, with measures added to support early retirement and young farmer schemes, and to provide compensation for farming in Less Favoured Areas (LFAs). The accession of Spain, Portugal and Greece to the European Community prompted a more fundamental rethink of the relationship between agricultural and rural development. Each of these countries had a large farming population and a clear need for investment in its rural areas.

Agricultural structures policy began to be shifted away from enhancing productivity to improvements in the quality of, and establishing new markets for, agricultural products. At the same time it was apparent that the modernisation of agriculture in Southern Europe would need to be accompanied by large-scale investment in infrastructure, services, and non-agricultural sources of rural employment. This view informed the major reforms to the Structural Funds in 1989 and 1993. The new Objective 1 designation was intended to channel European funding into the regional development of the so-called cohesion countries - Spain, Portugal, Greece and Ireland. It was also recognised that certain agriculturally dependent regions within the rest of the Community would need assistance to begin to diversify their economic base away from uncompetitive farming - the intention of the new Objective 5b designation. The reforms of the Structural Funds sought to combine the different funds (the EAGGF, the European Social Fund and the European Regional Development Fund) in regionally targeted and coordinated programmes. As part of this process there was a major expansion of the Guidance section of EAGGF, most of which became part of a broader territorial approach to integrated development, with new partnership and decision-making arrangements for programme management put in place between the European Commission, Member States, and sub-national actors.

Alongside the main Structural Fund programmes, the community also established a large number of much smaller 'Initiatives' for particular purposes. Of these, the LEADER Initiative was set up to promote 'bottom up', integrated and innovative approaches to rural development at local community level.

In 1988 the European Commission set out a strategic re-think of its rural policy entitled *The Future of Rural Society* which stressed the need for an approach that stimulates development *from within.* The Commission explained that rural development policy 'must... be geared to local requirements and initiatives, particularly at the level of small and medium-sized enter-prises, and must place particular emphasis on making the most of local potential'. This does not, the Commission argued, mean 'merely working along existing lines. It means making the most of all the advantages that the particular rural area has: space and landscape beauty, high-quality agricultural and forestry products specific to that area, gastronomic specialities, cultural and craft traditions, architectural and artistic heritage, innovatory ideas, availability of labour, industries and services already existing, all to be exploited with regional capital and human resources, with what is lacking in the way of capital and co-ordination, consultancy and planning services brought in from outside'. This thinking informed Objective 5b but more particularly LEADER, with its emphasis on innovation, community mobilisation and partnership building and direct funding of local actors.

The Cork Declaration and Agenda 2000

The mid-1990s saw increasing interest in combining the agricultural structures measures of the CAP with the partnership approaches to rural development employed in the Structural Funds. In 1996, Commissioner Fischler convened a conference on rural development at Cork in Ireland to try to widen popular support for his ideas on the building of an 'integrated rural policy'. Central to the Cork agenda was the notion that some element of the resources saved from future reductions in agricultural commodity support should be recycled within rural areas through agri-environment, agricultural structures and rural development spending. The 'Cork Declaration' pointed towards an expanded rural development programme with an emphasis on including the whole, farmed countryside.

The Commission's *Agenda 2000* proposals of July 1997 included such a programme in the form of the new Rural Development Regulation (RDR), hailed as the CAP's new 'second pillar'. Through this measure, rural development has been swept into the vanguard of European policy, as part of a policy model to be accepted in central and eastern Europe too. Four main sets of concerns inform this process:

- *first* is a desire to equip economic sectors and individual firms with the capacity to adapt to the market conditions of an increasingly liberalised system of world trade;
- *second* is a view that economic development should be sustainable, especially in environmental terms;
- *third* is the need to switch the weight of agriculture policy from commodity support to alternatives more acceptable within the World Trade Organisation talks;
- *fourth* is the view that development policies should be flexible and more locally tailored to meet the diverse needs and conditions in rural areas.

The *Agenda 2000* reforms were agreed in March 1999. Although the resources available for the RDR were widely regarded as disappointing, the arrangements for programming and implementing the policy represent a new model imported from the operation of Structural Fund programmes. Each Member State is required to draw up seven year rural development plans 'at the most appropriate geographical level' for the period 2000-2006. All rural development, forestry and agri-environment measures are to be integrated within a single plan. Although the former measures are optional, and a very broad-based menu of measures is allowable, the latter are compulsory with the result that each region has to have an agri-environment programme in accordance with its specific needs. The Structural Funds continue to be complemented by a Community Initiative on rural development, with LEADER+ developing the approach of past LEADER (I and II) programmes.

In effect, a fragmented set of EU farm structures, forestry and regional adjustment policies has been welded together, broadened in scope and elevated to a new strategic status. A wide range of institutions in the ten countries is influenced by this European mantle, while they retain their own perspectives. They can draw on a succession of European and more local models of rural development, creating a rich variety of conceptual and operational preferences.

EU Rural Development Today

In the EU, what constitutes 'rural development' has come to be understood as those activities eligible for support under the CAP's new Rural Development Plans and LEADER across the whole countryside, and the new Structural Fund programmes largely in designated rural areas. A parallel process is underway in the CEECs through the SAPARD programmes. This is, of course, a highly particularised version of 'rural development' which reflects the current prevailing concerns of those responsible for EU agricultural, regional, cohesion and accession policy. It differs from other notions of rural development, which have either characterised past EU policies, or which continue to characterise national or local understandings of rural development in different parts of Europe.

Under the Rural Development Regulation, what now constitutes the 'European model' of rural development has widened significantly to embrace the agri-environmental measures introduced in 1992. Prior to Agenda 2000, agri-environment policy and rural development policy were far less integrated. Now these two policy areas have come together under the Rural Development Plans. On the one hand this process could be interpreted as a broadening of the scope and the Europeanisation of the scale of rural development policy. However, on the other hand, the fact that Member States are able to draw up their own programmes from a menu of measures means that what constitutes rural development still has the scope to vary, within this framework, from place to place.

Different Perspectives at National Level

An Agrarian Versus Rural Perspective

From our national reports, it is clear that one very important axis for interpreting different approaches to rural development is an agrarian versus rural perspective. Some policy makers and stakeholders would not recognise the distinction, but others would see it as fundamental. Some see rural development as an adjunct to agricultural policy; others see agricultural development as just one component of rural policy. Beyond simply confusion over terms, at the core of these disagreements is a debate about the continuing centrality of farming, socially, culturally and environmentally, to the future of rural areas.

In all the countries under study, agriculture represents a diminishing proportion of GDP and employment. In most countries, though, it is still the major land use shaping the national territory and regional geography, forming the rural environment and acting as a reservoir of cultural values. Agricultural policy was clearly once seen as a means to support rural areas. Conversely some now promote rural policy as a means to support agriculture and farming communities, while others see rural policy as a means to help rural areas overcome their dependence on a sector in decline. Relating to these alternative viewpoints are questions of:

- the legitimacy of public funding for farmers as environmental managers;
- the significance accorded to other economic and political actors in rural development;
- the relative importance given to farming and non-farming activities;
- attitudes towards farm structural change; and
- views about desirable alternative activities for rural areas.

There are different perspectives on these issues even within countries, but broad national differences are also apparent. Farming lobbies and agrarian ideologies are more powerful in certain countries than in others. For example, the central preoccupation of French rural policy has always been the outlook for agriculture and its changing role in rural areas. Likewise Austrian rural policy is built on 'the supposition that agriculture and rural areas determine each other' and there is an increasing homogenisa-tion of agrarian and local development perspectives on rural policy.

In contrast, the UK report refers to the 'historical separation' of a rural development policy, preoccupied with rural industries and village services, and a sectoral agricultural policy. Likewise, the Swedish report points out that agriculture 'constitutes only a minor part of rural development in Sweden': at least as important are 'forestry, fishery, reindeer husbandry, mining, hydropower and small enterprises of various kinds'. In addition, other major policies in Sweden are recognised as critically important for rural development, such as employment policies and social services. Even among the farming sector, the Swedish Federation of Farmers is described as an interest group which embraces a much broader rural constituency than its name would imply. Finally, the Hungarian report points out 'Hungary has a large rural population, but not everyone living in rural areas is a peasant or farmer. In fact, most of them have qualifications and are, or used to be, working in industry'.

Traditional Economic Development Versus Consumption/Recreation

Traditionally rural areas have been seen as areas of production and places of work. Increasingly, though, they have come to be appreciated as places to live in and as sites for leisure. This transition depends upon levels of affluence and the spread of post-materialist values in society. As people move beyond concerns with material security and embrace quality of life issues they place increasing value on the opportunities rural areas provide for living space, recreation, the enjoyment of amenity and wildlife, and a wholesome and pleasant environment. These tendencies are most marked in the most advanced economic regions of the EU which have large, middle-class commuter belts, but also in attractive peripheral areas which have developed functions for tourism, second homes, retirement and nature protection. In addition, there are different cultural norms operating – such as the appreciation of landscape and importance of recreational access, both of which are prominent in the 'consumption countryside'; for instance in Spain gastronomy and wine play a central role.

The Austrian report refers to 'a new concept of modernity in the rural world ... an innovative understanding of rural culture and lifestyles'. On the other hand, across much of rural Europe the preoccupation remains that of traditional economic development, and this clearly is the priority of the CEECs. The Latvian and Polish reports describe the impoverishment of rural society, lacking in basic services and infrastructure.

Policy Innovators/Adapters

Countries divide between those with a strong national agenda and institutional pattern, as opposed to countries more influenced by the driving force of EU policy. Some have long traditions of their own in rural development policy (eg Austria, the UK and Sweden). Others (eg Spain) have acquired a rural development role much more recently, generally in direct response to EU measures.

The Europeanisation of rural policy may pose difficulties for countries with established policy traditions of their own. The UK report refers to 'a risk that traditional rural development interests will become more marginalised'. The Austrian report criticises the restrictive interpretation of Article 33 of the RDR by EC officials as being too narrow for the Austrian approach to area-based, trans-sectoral development (linking, say, farm diversification, tourism promotion and craft enterprises). France and Germany are in a somewhat different position. They have been central architects of the CAP, and they have developed their own domestic agricultural and rural policies in tandem with the development of EU policies. For these two countries there is a much greater sense of accord between national and European policies and programmes. In the CEECs, in contrast, EU models and procedures are greatly shaping the policies and the institutional structures for rural development. Indeed, there is contention over the extent to which this properly recognises their real needs and priorities.

Bottom-up or Top-down

There are examples of both the top-down and bottom-up approaches amongst the ten countries although all now have some level of public participation and decentralised control of rural development. In France, despite the recent political impetus towards decentralisation, the central government plays a determining role in the majority of policy measures, sometimes with the assistance of a range of other stakeholders in a formal national forum. Sweden, by contrast, has an exceptionally dense set of local rural networks, with strong representation across the whole country. These are organised so as to provide a forum for community activity and participation at the level of individual villages and small communities. At the same time they are organised into national federations which can participate as appropriate in national level debates. Bottom-up participation is meaningful because there are effective channels between central government and individual localities. This is an attractive model, although it relies on an exceptional level of community organisation.

More typical is a pattern of partial regionalisation in which levels of real local participation vary. In some countries this may be partly because of the relative weakness of key local stakeholder groups – for example in Poland, where environmental NGOs are not very active in rural areas – but in many cases there is also an inference that the public administration has not been ready to work in a more devolved way. The central authorities themselves highlight the difficulty of developing participative local structures for policies when they are often under pressure to deliver concrete outcomes within a few years. In Spain, 'the already prevailing attitude of conservatism and subordination to public authority and initiative', compounded by high levels of public subsidy to rural areas in recent years, has led to 'a general belief that it is the State or other levels of government which should sort out rural problems and ensure a secure future, rather than the rural population itself'. This tendency has also been hinted at in some other countries, particularly in relation to more marginal areas.

Instruments for Delivering Rural Development

There are, naturally, very significant differences in the institutional structures in place in the ten countries and in the attitudes held by the main actors. Some of the most important divisions are between:

- Federal states and those with a more unitary structure;
- EU and Central European states;
- those where environmental authorities and perspectives have established a significant role in the rural policy community and those where the environment remains more marginal.

Nevertheless, the main instruments for delivering rural development policy in all countries studied here, with the obvious exception of Switzerland, are those derived directly from EU level policies and funding. This section therefore briefly discusses these European instruments before looking more closely at the structures and institutions that different countries have used to develop and deploy them.

The European Rural Development Framework

The EU Rural Development Regulation

The RDR is undoubtedly the most important instrument in EU rural development policy as it demands comprehensive rural development programming from all Member States, and has the largest overall budget and geographical coverage of all rural development measures. It aims to bring together different measures within an integrated planning framework. The RDR combines revenue orientated funding with capital investment

support. The former includes LFA payments, agri-environment measures, aid for young farmers, farmland afforestation and early retirement for farmers while the latter targets other forestry measures, training, marketing and processing, investment on agricultural holdings, and rural diversification under Article 33.

The Rural Development Regulation has proved a complex policy instrument for policy makers in Brussels and the Member States alike. During the planning phase it offered a nearly overwhelming range of measures, with little time for officials and stakeholders to deal with them properly. However, the Regulation potentially offers new opportunities for rural development over the next seven years. Whether plans are national or regional, most plans incorporate a significant degree of regional or sub-regional flexibility so that measures can be tailored to local needs and opportunities.

In spite of its shortcomings there is emerging agreement on common overarching principles and a growing recognition of the potential value of the Rural Development Regulation in the broader context of Europe's agricultural and rural policy. If it succeeds, the Regulation could play a key role in re-orientating the justification for support for the managers of rural land, strengthening the relationship between urban and rural members of society

The EU Structural Funds

The Structural Funds for economic and social development will continue to have an important, although reduced, influence upon rural development in Europe, through their deployment in rural areas which qualify for Objective 1 or 2 status under the new Agenda 2000 Regulations. Their influence during the past decade or so has clearly been significant in many Member States, both in shaping the institutional framework for rural development within a broader 'regional development' approach, and in stimulating change on the ground. While some countries (eg Spain) report that the Funds were overly concentrated upon public sector projects and large scale capital infrastructure, others have apparently deployed them for a much broader rural development agenda which has included community actions and support for SMEs (eg UK). In future, the European Commission hopes there should be increased emphasis upon using the funds in environmentally sensitive ways; however it is not clear whether this perspective is shared by the Member States to the same degree.

In 1999, the WWF European Policy Office (EPO) undertook a brief ex-ante environmental evaluation of the Objective 1 Regional Development Plans submitted by five EU Member States for the period 2000-2006: Germany, Greece, Spain, Italy and Ireland. Although in some Member States, the evaluation revealed signs of increased integration of environmental concerns compared with the previous funding period (1994-1999), the proposed Plans were found in general to fall far short of a sustainable approach to regional development. Some general conclusions were as follows (these do not all apply to every plan evaluated).

- The environmental focus is on the correction of specific types of environmental damage already done and on the limitation of damage through mechanisms such as EIA; there is very little emphasis in the plans on promoting sustainable systems of resource use or on the conservation of biodiversity.

  The descriptions and assessments of the environmental situation in the plans (an essential basis for the development of appropriate measures for sustainable development) are very varied, and in some cases extremely weak, leading to inconsistent objectives and measures.

  The environmental targets and objectives are not quantified and no clear criteria are proposed for measuring whether they are achieved.

> Transparency and public participation in the programming process has been highly variable. Apart from Germany, independent environmental organisations were excluded from the process.

Objective 1 and 2 designation give a regional focus to the European Rural Development Fund, the European Agricultural Guidance Fund and the European Social Fund. An additional structural fund is the Financial Instrument for Fisheries Guidance (FIFG), which supports structural change in the fishing industry and which is not targeted solely through these regional designations. In the past, FIFG expenditure has largely been concentrated on fleet modernisation and vessel decommissioning but since Agenda 2000 there is new potential for the fund to support positive rural development in coastal areas traditionally dependent on fishing. It remains to be seen whether FIFG will therefore assume more prominence in rural development, in future.

LEADER

The LEADER Community Initiative supports innovative rural development projects in relatively small, distinct rural areas across the EU. The project objectives and implementation are largely developed and managed by local action groups formed from representatives of the affected communities. LEADER thus represents a bottom-up, cross-sectoral approach. One strength of the LEADER programme is its emphasis on knowledge transfer and the exchange of experiences between different LEADER groups. This aspect is managed by the LEADER European Observatory in Brussels. Due to its innovative nature and emphasis on the sharing of experience the LEADER programme has had a significant impact on EU rural development policy as a whole, as seen for example in the Cork Declaration.

All national reports indicate favourable experiences with the LEADER II programme. The attractiveness of the LEADER approach is underlined by the fact that the Spanish government has introduced a similar programme, called PRODER, to make this locally focused, bottom-up model more widely available across its rural areas. This programme is planned to continue slightly modified during the 2000–2006 programming period.

In several countries, however, the current process was described as rather dominated by local government representatives and municipalities rather than involving local stakeholders directly. This is expected to improve under the new 'LEADER+' successor to LEADER II which requires representation by social and economic partners, i.e. the private or voluntary sector, of at least 50 per cent in future local action groups. Another aspect of LEADER II that was criticised by Spanish and French stakeholders was the fact that it was confined to the most marginal rural areas, often in Objective 1 regions. This situation is again expected to change under LEADER+ which extends the potential coverage of the programme to all rural areas in the EU, although limited funding will still mean that it cannot be made available everywhere.

EU Rural Development Measures in the Applicant Countries

SAPARD (Special Action for Pre-Accession Measures for Agriculture and Rural Development) is the EU pre-accession fund that supports rural development measures in central and eastern Europe. It is similar to the RDR in terms of measures and implementation, but also has another important objective – that of preparing the candidate countries for the implementation of EU agriculture and rural development policies after EU accession. Thus, the candidate countries also have to present national rural development plans under SAPARD, complete with prior environmental appraisal and public consultation. To disburse money for measures financed under SAPARD they also have to establish national paying agencies that operate in accordance with the EAGGF Guarantee procedures, the same fund that finances RDR measures in EU Member States (outside Objective 1).

SAPARD can fund a total of 15 different measures that range from re-structuring and modernisation of the agri-food industry, land consolidation, investments in agricultural holdings to diversification of economic activities, protecting the environment and cultural heritage, training and technical assistance. Five of these measures have been chosen by all three countries investigated in this study – investments in agricultural holdings, improvement of processing and marketing, development and diversification of economic activities, environmentally friendly agricultural methods and technical assistance. Although SAPARD is an important measure its total budget is small compared to the needs of the countries and it is also criticised in some countries for focussing too much on the adaptation of administrative and rural structures to the EU framework instead of addressing the particular rural development needs of the accession countries.

PHARE (Poland and Hungary Assistance for Economics Restructuring Programme), the oldest and largest pre-accession fund, also provides support for agriculture and rural development programmes. These projects focussed on direct assistance to rural areas during the early 1990s, eg agricultural restructuring or infrastructure measures, but most current measures also support preparation for EU accession in the form of institutional capacity building and training. However, critics of PHARE believe that it has not adequately addressed the broader social side of rural development, being too focussed upon providing money for plant, infrastructure and, more recently, capacity-building within government administrations. Insufficient scope has been available under the measure for activities which could build confidence among local populations.

Policies in Switzerland

Swiss rural development policy is an integral part of a strong regional policy, which dates back to the 1930s when the first focused measures were introduced to deal with the particular problems of mountain areas. However, since then a range of instruments has been built up which has similarities with the kinds of policy promoted within the EU. Some notable differences of particular interest to this study include:

- the use of investment loans and loan guarantees, rather than just grant aid, for many areas of rural development activity;
- a fully decoupled agricultural policy where all direct payments to farmers are linked with a clear environmental commitment which goes beyond the observance of environmental regulations;
- a suite of laws and institutions designed to ensure co-ordination between authorities in the area of regional policy and, increasingly, to promote sustainability;
- 30 years of regional development planning and programming in response to 'global' allocations from the federal level, in the mountain regions.

Institutions Responsible for Rural Development

In every country, the institutional map for rural development involves a hierarchy from the central government ministries down to the local or regional authorities. In the federal countries the regions/Länder/autonomous communities play a prominent part in the cascade of responsibility, and may be involved in devising as well as implementing policy. The role of local authorities, particularly municipalities and their Mayors, is variable. In the majority of countries they have recently become more active in the implementation of rural development measures, especially where LEADER II has been funded on a significant scale.

A second axis runs from the core group of critical actors, generally led by central government ministries, to a succession of more marginal stakeholders, like the skins of an onion. Agricultural interests, particularly farm unions, are a major force in most countries. A combination of private sector interests, environmental NGOs, forestry institutions, education and training bodies and others typically make up the outer layers.

In Central Europe the dominant actors are nearly all governmental and the custom of consultation with other organisations is not very developed. The critical influence of political parties and individual political leaders in shaping the direction of policy in countries that are still in transition is very apparent. This contrasts strongly with the EU where the role of political parties is rarely mentioned in national reports. In Poland, for example, where the government is largely unconstrained by the CAP, there has been a succession of major changes in agricultural policy during the 1990s with continuous debate about the merits of government support for farming and agrarian society more widely.

In Hungary and Latvia land privatisation has been a central concern, also subject to changing political influence. In Hungary, regional and environmental institutions and groups such as the Hungarian Rural Parliament appear to have established more influence than the other two accession countries.

Within central government, the agriculture ministry or its equivalent is usually the key actor in developing and delivering rural development policy. A few ministries are consciously broadening their remit with new names, eg the Hungarian Ministry for Agriculture *and Rural Development,* or new mission statements as exemplified by MAFF in the UK. Agriculture ministries almost invariably control the expenditure on EU RDR measures, a role which flows naturally from their past involvement in agricultural structures policies. Not all are comfortable with this new role. MAPA, the Spanish ministry, is amongst those that favour a stronger focus on agriculture and production support within the CAP and less emphasis on rural development measures.

In Sweden, however, where just 9 per cent of the land area is in agriculture, but 60 per cent is in forestry, the leading Ministry regarding rural development is not the Ministry of Agriculture, Food and Fisheries but the Ministry of Industry, Employment and Communications which is responsible for regional development policy and the Structural Funds and which oversees, inter alia, the National Rural Development Agency and the National Board of Forestry.

Agriculture ministries are not free actors within central government. Not infrequently there is another ministry responsible for the overall coordination of the funds as is illustrated by the deployment of the Structural Funds, such as the Ministry of Economy in Spain. In Latvia, the Ministry of Environmental Protection and Regional Development coordinates work on the national Rural Development Programme, although the Ministry of Agriculture is responsible for the national rural development plan under SAPARD. Such ministries may have a strategic role in the distribution of funding and others may intervene at a high level. In Austria, over the last 20 years the Chancellery has played an important role in testing the Austrian concept of 'Endogenous Regional Development'. It created a national programme with a fund to support innovative projects in rural areas and bring together the local actors and funding institutions. This was replaced in the 1980s by similar structures operated at regional level. In France and the UK, where modulation has been adopted as an option, the involvement of the Prime Minister was unavoidable. In most instances finance ministries also play a critical role.

Few countries report that the ministry of the environment has been a key actor in driving rural development policy. In several cases they have been scarcely consulted in the process of drawing up rural development plans and other key documents. In this sense, integration has made alarmingly little progress. There are exceptions. In the UK, the environment ministry and countryside agencies were extensively consulted on certain aspects of the RDP and appear to have influenced some decisions, including the critical choice of modulation. For many years the agencies have been key players in the development of national rural policy. In Spain, the environment ministry has acquired funding for a number of relatively modest programmes with a strong environmental or biodiversity emphasis.

At a local level, the new agenda has stirred the ambitions of some existing actors, including the mayors of smaller towns and, where programmes such as LEADER have been in place, provided resources for substantive initiatives. The rural development debate has quickened at a time when many communities have become ready to assert a stronger view and seek fresh fields of engagement. In France, there has been a political movement to promote intercommunal groupings to strengthen grassroots rural development initiatives. In Spain, local action groups established under both LEADER and the major national programme PRODER have been the trigger for two new networks of local rural development groups, although often dominated by governmental bodies. In Hungary, voluntary associations of villages with their own local development agencies have been a significant factor in starting to strengthen grassroots participation in rural development projects and policy development. In Germany, new local coalitions between traditional rural interests such as farmers, local government and environmental groups are emerging to promote sustainable rural development. In Austria, the establishment of 25 local development management agencies to facilitate project development under the Structural Funds is seen as a valuable innovation at this level.

These relationships are not easy to capture in an institutional map. Most national reports include an institutional diagram of some kind, typically showing the distinctions between the central government, regional and local levels.

The Federal Countries

In the context of this report Austria, Germany, Spain, Switzerland and the UK can be classified as federal countries. Each has its own constitutional arrangements and the role of the regional authorities (including the Länder and the constituent countries in the UK) varies considerably. At the same time, there are important similarities, not least a strong debate about the respective role of the central and regional authorities in determining rural development policy as well as delivering it on the ground.

In each case the dialogue on rural development takes place alongside a wider debate on the role of the regions and the dynamics of regional policy. It is not always clear where regional policy ends and rural development policy begins. In several cases, including Austria, Spain and the UK the central government retains control over the direction of rural development policy and limits the resources and scope for independent initiatives available to the regional authorities. This is a dynamic and contested arena. The autonomous communities in Spain appear to have won a larger role implementing the RDR than its predecessors. Although presented with a national framework by MAPA for developing programmes they have often deviated and pursued to their own preferences. Some regions (eg Galicia, Andalusia) are developing their own independent strategies for rural development. In the UK devolution has given new autonomy to the Scottish parliament and Welsh assembly to determine their own programmes under the RDP and they have chosen a different pattern to that adopted in England, although the limits of their autonomy have yet to be really tested.

In Austria and Germany there are well established institutions for co-ordinating the work of central government and Länder authorities. In Austria the ÖROK (the Austrian spatial co-ordination conference), which involves social partners as well as the two layers of government, acts as a secretariat for the monitoring committees of several structural fund programmes as well as co-ordinating spatial planning activities. The German system, however, represents the most delicate balance between national and regional authorities, underpinned by Article 91a of the constitution. The federal government and the Länder

share certain 'Common Tasks', including the improvement of agricultural structures and some other regional economic structures. The former, the GAK (Gemeinschaftsaufgabe Agrarstruktur und Küstenschutz – common task for agricultural structures and coastal protection), has a central role in determining national rural policy which is then implemented by both the Länder and government agencies in their own spheres. The GAK procedure applies to the RDR, with funding for individual measures divided between the Länder and agriculture ministry. Länder have the freedom to develop their own programmes within the national framework and the more affluent Länder have the option of developing their own programmes without money from the central government.

The Unitary States

Devolution of power from the centre is also a theme in countries with a unitary structure. France is an outstanding example of a country in the process of, often cautiously, transferring powers from Paris to the regions, particularly in the details of rural development initiatives, while retaining central control over the main lines of policy.

The question of devolution of rural development policy formulation and implementation to regional and local institutions is crucial in the context of adapting RD programmes and measures to local needs and ensuring the necessary involvement of local populations in the development of their own territory. Due to strong community traditions, an open approach to government and support at various levels successful local participation appears to be a key feature in the development of rural regions in Sweden. In contrast, attempts at encouraging a bottom-up process in France, in the form of the contrats territo-riaux d'explotation (CTEs), have shown difficulties in engaging the farming population. These problems could be due to the history of top-down planning in France which leads to a lack of experience with bottom-up participation.

In the accession countries, all three investigated in this study are establishing regional government structures as part of overall democratic reform. However, institutions at both national and regional levels will need time, training and resources before they can assume a full role in the formulation and delivery of rural development policies. In Poland, some regional administrations have a single department for agriculture and the environment, which should enhance sustainable development. In Latvia, emerging Regional Development Agencies should assume a stronger role in rural development policies of the future.

Issues in Rural Development

There is continued diversity of institutional definitions of 'rural', and of 'rural development' across Europe. Policies have been driven by quite different concerns and developed in quite different institutional contexts.

The preoccupations of different institutions range from the traditional, such as the need to increase employment, promote agricultural modernisation, maintain rural populations, reduce rural poverty and improve infrastructure to a newer agenda which includes building social capital, tackling gender imbalance, seeding local enterprise, supporting organic agriculture and improving monitoring and evaluation. In the more affluent northern countries, such as Austria, Germany and the UK the second set of concerns has gained more ground.

However, elements of this debate are already present in central Europe alongside the more immediate concerns of large-scale unemployment, land abandonment and under-investment in infrastructure. Education and training are leading concerns for many central European institutions; perhaps surprisingly they are accorded less priority in the EU. In Austria and, to a lesser degree, Germany there is a preference for improving regional economic links and food sourcing, with support for greater regional self-reliance in some cases. In the UK, by contrast, the regional element in policy making and the sense of regional identity is markedly less developed, but is an emergent feature.

Sustainable rural development is a concept enjoying increasing support from environmental organisations in most European countries but there has been more limited progress in implanting it into governmental institutions responsible for rural development. The majority of these retain a more agrocentric view of rural development and some have clear reservations about the new European framework embodied in the RDR and SAPARD. However, this framework and other political changes at national as well as the EU level in recent years have spawned a new set of institutional relationships and a sense of change in the rural agenda.

Table 1. Dominant Concerns Emerging from National Rural Development Policies

France	– maintaining the multifunctional role of agriculture
	– improving the sustainability of rural communities
England	– reducing environmental pressures on the countryside
	– promoting economic restructing and the agricultural sector
	– improving rural services
Spain	– promoting the sustainable development of farming
	– addressing environmental degradation
Austria	– the ecological modernisation of agriculture
	– diversifying the rural economy

Role of the Environment in Rural Development

In principle it is widely accepted that good management of the environment is a critical element of sustainable rural development. In practice, however, many of the institutional actors responsible for developing and implementing rural policy have yet to internalise the environment very deeply in their own priorities. Environmental sustainability implies a set of challenges, many of which have yet to be fully articulated and addressed.

A clear sense emerges from the national reports that the rural environment is not a high priority on national agendas, particularly compared with other issues such as the distribution of EU and state aids, the maintenance of farm populations and income or revitalising marginal economies. There are exceptions, such as Sweden, where the environment seems to have become more deeply woven into the fabric of rural development. In the UK, the maintenance of rural landscapes and habitats remains a high profile issue, supported by a powerful phalanx of NGOs and substantial government agencies which have few counterparts in other countries. This was a factor in securing the government's recent agreement to modulation, thereby increasing the flow of funding into agri-environment schemes.

Nearly all countries in central and eastern Europe also pay considerable attention to maintaining their rural environment and heritage which has been neglected in the past. For example, in Hungary there is a tripartite 'National Environmental Council' (NEC) with representatives from industry, environmental NGOs and academia, which has the right of preliminary assessment of any new law. The annual congress of environmental NGOs selects 7 representatives to be members of the NEC.

Generally, one can detect a certain pattern of richer north-western European countries giving greater attention to environmental priorities than Spain or other southern European Member States. In Austria, the national report states that it 'has become unthinkable' to have agriculture without a strong environmental accountability, whereas in Spain, the government's approach to environmental integration and sustainability is 'considered minimalist' by stakeholders. However, one specific environmental issue has made an impression on a number of institutions, which is the need to implement the EU Natura 2000 network, particularly by designating candidate Sites of Community Interest. The European Commission has been forceful in insisting on the presentation of such lists before it will approve Objective 1 programmes and is also requiring assurances in relation to Rural Development Plans. This form of cross compliance appears to have focused attention in a way that the exhortations of NGOs have not necessarily been able to do.

The rhetoric of rural development policy has for some time had a strong focus on environmental sustainability, and individual measures within and outside rural development programmes have furthered that goal in practically all countries investigated. Measures that can be mentioned in this regard include agri-environment schemes, the promotion of organic farming and 'local product cycles' (production, distribution and consumption in a single locality), environmental training and demonstration projects. All these measures have a positive impact. For example, in Poland the 'coalition for development of ecological agriculture' was developed in 1998 and involves 21 institutions supporting organic farming in a variety of ways. One of the coalition's successes has been the launch of government support for organic farming and the drafting of a new law on ecological agriculture.

The Swiss report has made an interesting analysis of areas of rural environmental concern where there is consensus or difference among the different stakeholders, which indicates a relatively high degree of environmental awareness. This concludes that:

> Surprisingly, widespread consensus exists in some major areas of influence.....(this analysis) enables us to identify the areas with positive ecological effects (eg direct marketing and environment-friendly, sustainable tourism) in which it would be possible to achieve a political consensus. Moreover, it should be possible to prevent or influence those developments about which consensus exists with respect to negative ecological consequences, for example competition in tourism. Similar consensus-generating actor constellations were behind the development of today's agricultural policy, the new water philosophy (whereby flowing water bodies are given more space rather than being encroached upon), the new Alpine rail system (NEAT)....and ecological tax reform.

Overall, however, the national reports do not suggest that the institutions surveyed have all grappled with the long term limitation imposed by the environment or with some of the trade-offs inherent in a sustainable development approach. For example, the challenge of maintaining and enhancing biodiversity in the face of adverse trends fuelled by changing agricultural practice is not a high policy priority. There is a general hope that more organic farming and greater investment in agri-environment schemes may relieve some environmental pressures but little concrete analysis to support this. Similarly, the

problems of traffic congestion, unsustainable transport patterns, poor forest management, excessive water abstraction and development/tourism pressures in some coastal regions are not receiving the attention that they merit.

The Austrian report states that:

> Massive farm decline can be observed especially in peripheral areas. No one knows where and how it will end. Many interview partners in Austria think that product revenues alone will not suffice for sustaining farms through

> the next generation. One possibility lies in the de-coupling of farm support from production and the payment of compensation for providing services for society as a whole (environmental and social/infrastructure). On the other hand, survival based on transfer payments alone does not meet farmers' traditional perception of their role in society, so this approach may not halt the decline of farming.

This comment is made despite the fact that Austria provides notable evidence of environmental integration in practice through its use of the Rural Development Regulation, namely:

- from 2002 onwards it will use Article 16 to make payments to farmers in areas with environmental restrictions due to Community environmental protection rules, such as the habitats Directive;
- more than 90 per cent of farmland in Austria is covered by agri-environment agreements under the RDR;
- specific environmental objectives have been developed for training measures under Article 9 of the RDR, including raising awareness of environmental and nature conservation goals in rural areas, promoting environmentally friendly farming methods, and professional qualifications in nature conservation and landscape management;
- measures under Article 33 of the Regulation include aid for clearing scrub from overgrown meadows and (re-)building traditional landscape elements such as stonewalls or terraces.

Social Values in Rural Development

The prevailing ethos in the rural development debate is that partnership between official agencies and between them and a wider range of social actors should be one of the foundations for all policy. This has been reinforced by the RDR and the EU Structural Fund Regulations and the popularity of LEADER. This ethos seems to have won widespread acceptance amongst government bodies in most of the countries which have been studied. However, there are variations in the way in which it is interpreted and efforts to implement it in practice have been subject to several different limitations, including the great pressure on Member States to complete and subsequently amend rural development plans within very tight timetables laid down by the Commission. There is also a growing sense that it is necessary to involve local people more directly in policy formation, without much sense of how this can be done in practice other than by replicating the LEADER approach which empowers local groups to develop their own initiatives and devolves financial autonomy to a relatively local level. In a few countries, though, there is a long tradition of local participation in the formulation and implementation of rural development programmes, for example Sweden.

The question of engaging regional, and particularly local, actors in rural development policy formulation and implementation remains a key issue to be tackled in the further evolution of European rural development policy, both in unitary and federal countries. The author of the French report points to a conflict at the heart of the current debate. This is 'between a tradition of central state-managed normative and procedurally dominated universalist public policy and the growing need for a more differential, locally generated, project-oriented and partnership based rural development policy that takes this diversity into account and builds upon it.' While the order is changing, new partners are still not fully accepted either in France or most other countries.

Several reports indicate that the concept of widespread consultation in advance of agreeing new policies is quite new for many agriculture and economic ministries. The record in consulting stakeholders other than the farming community appears to be patchy. In the UK there is a stronger tradition of consulting outside organisations in rural policy questions and several consultation documents have been issued relating to the RDP, modulation and individual policies, such as Less Favoured Area (LFA) aid. Nonetheless, many stakeholders felt that they should have had more opportunity to comment on the overall balance and direction of the RDP and some were pleading for greater advance notice to enable them to respond more fully. In Spain, some negotiations between the Ministry of the Environment, farmers organisations and environmental NGOs about new programmes focussed on Natura 2000 sites were suspended due to strong disagreements between the participants.

In Central and Eastern Europe limits on public participation are also evident. Several stakeholders in Poland felt it was difficult to participate in vital policy developments arising from enlargement, including SAPARD. On the other hand NGOs and independent experts have clearly played an important part in developing and supporting agri-environment initiatives in several countries, including Hungary and Latvia.

A lack of transparency in developing recent rural policy initiatives was a failing noted by many stakeholders outside the government network, not least in Germany where procedures are particularly complex. This is a serious concern for many environmental NGOs with limited resources. Where should they best place their limited capacity to influence new policies, such as the RDPs?

Another common thread in the national reports is the interplay of different sectoral interests within rural development policy. Farming organisations are concerned to retain the maximum level of rural funding within their own community whereas other interests, such as local authorities and environmental organisations support greater expansion of measures benefiting a wider range of actors. Environmental NGOs support the new culture of partnership, participation, monitoring and evaluation. They also argue for environmental safeguards, including a set of basic environmental standards for farming in many countries. It is less clear whether NGOs have an important influence on policy design. In Germany they have been influential in the acceptance of compensatory payments on habitat Directive sites – the new Article 16 in the RDR. Environmental lobbying for a new, more environmentally sensitive approach based on area payments rather than headage payments for LFA support took place in the UK before the Agenda 2000 package had been agreed. However, much of the debate stimulated by national ministries has been conducted with farming rather than environmental partners.

Overall, the relationships between institutions appear more fluid than in the past. The community of actors is growing and now embraces environmental and wildlife concerns, still weakly in some countries. However, partnership is seen as a challenge often putting stress on bureaucratic systems used to more autocratic procedures. There is a widespread sense that a new agenda and change in style requires more institutional adaptation than has yet taken place. Institutional reengineering is seen as critical by many of the actors most committed to a more integrated and sustainable rural policy.

Rural-urban Interface

In several of the national reports, it has been stated that rural development policy cannot be sustainable on its own as rural areas are strongly interlinked with urban regions in economic, social and environmental terms. This relationship needs to be understood and recognised when designing more holistic RD policies, but this has apparently not been the case in many areas. Understanding the many and various interconnections and interdepen-dencies between rural and urban areas, whether neighbouring or spaced apart is one of the keys for interpreting sustainability in a coherent and holistic way. Furthermore, a range of non-rural policy sectors, such as transport, energy and spatial planning, need to be sustainable for sustainable rural development to be feasible. This issue has begun to be recognised and incorporated in some of the countries in this study – eg Switzerland and Sweden – but many countries still lack sufficient trans-sectoral policy making structures or traditions to enable this to occur. The Swiss report describes some of the related tensions of this situation:

> … agricultural policy remains an influential actor which, however, is also being joined by players from other policy areas. Overall, the number of actors in rural areas is increasing and this has something to do with the wave of privatisation in the area of basic infrastructure (regional transport, post office, telecommunications, electricity). These new actors, who are assuming state tasks, are at least as motivated by the interests of profitability and shareholders as they are by the general economic interests of providing comprehensive basic services… and this is reflected in the quality … of the development concepts and planning, which are sometimes a more accurate reflection of economic desires than an integrated perspective.

Austria is another country where there is growing awareness that current programmes and policies are not furthering interlinkages between rural and urban areas as much as they could. There can also be problems with the language traditionally used to describe rural areas and values:

> According to some interviewees slogans like *'the preservation of rural cultural heritage'* or *'tradition and folklore'* do not have enough attraction to motivate young people towards a creative and future-oriented interpretation of rural life. An innovative understanding of rural culture and lifestyles has to link up to existing values but carry with it a modern self-awareness and be attractive to farming as well as non-farming communities. It should emphasise local characteristics and conceptualise itself as being complementary, and not contradictory, to urban lifestyles.

Policy Delivery, Resources and Administration

In spite of the goal of the Agenda 2000 reform to achieve administrative simplification of rural development measures all national reports show that the EU rural development framework remains very complex. Arrangements such as different funding sources for the same rural development measures between Objective 1 and non-Objective 1 areas or the differential treatment of the accompanying measures as part of rural development programmes in most areas but as separate inside Objective 1 areas are not easy to understand. If one adds to this the necessary co-ordination with LEADER+, other Structural Fund and national measures the overall complexity of rural development support in the EU becomes apparent.

Austria and France may be most advanced in integrating and thus reducing this complexity at local level due to the existence of co-ordinating institutions at higher level (Federal Chancellery in Vienna) or new policy instruments (Loi d'Orientation Agricole in France) that aim to integrate environmental, agricultural and economic objectives. However, all reports from EU countries point out the considerable administrative resources required for understanding and following the new programming procedures. In some cases this can impact on the capacity for working on the best design of rural development measures. Similar issues with the EU planning process were also apparent in the reports from the applicant countries. Further attention needs to be given to this issue in the future.

It is clear that the Member States have approached the planning and implementation of the Rural Development Regulation (RDR) in a wide variety of ways, using existing and new ways of funding and administration. However, there are common issues emerging which relate to the administration and delivery of the new plans. A few are discussed below.

- There is a common concern about the shift of funding for these kinds of measure from the Agricultural Guidance to the Guarantee budget, which has created some tension between a desire to devolve implementation and allow flexibility at local level, and the need to reassure the Commission and national auditors about how money is being spent. EAGGF Guarantee budgets have traditionally been subject to a much more restrictive set of accounting and administrative procedures than has been applied to the Structural Funds, which has meant that certain delivery options under former rural development programmes (eg Objective 5b) are apparently no longer available under the RDR. For example, whereas 5b projects could be led at local level by public authorities and could involve delegated payment of EU funds to farmers via these authorities, the same arrangements seem now to be unacceptable. Also, guarantee section budgets must be spent annually, whereas structural funds could be allocated over a period of several years. These difficulties from a rural development perspective have led to some stakeholders in Member States (eg Austria, Spain, UK) commenting that the RDR could prove to be a backward step in policy terms.

- Decisions about whether to programme separately in Objective 1 and 2 regions and how to co-ordinate RDP funds with Structural Funds have been difficult, and there are some concerns about the complexity of arrangements that seem to be emerging in this area. France has had particular difficulties in agreeing its proposed Objective 2 rural development delivery procedures with Commission Officials.
- The complexity of RDR programming procedures has proven a big burden on regional authorities in southern Member States in particular, to the degree that the wide range of options under the Regulation could not be explored completely, that possibilities for policy integration have not been exploited to the full and that the adaptation of programmes to local needs has proven difficult.

One consistent thread in the reports is the traditional set of conflicts between the different layers of administration. Most government agencies acknowledge the influence of the EU and the shift in direction signalled by the RDR on their own policies, although some agriculture ministries are uncomfortable with an enlarged rural development role. Central European governments, such as Latvia, are critical of a lack of clarity in SAPARD and the way in which it has been presented and explained to them. They would prefer a model which was more flexible, easier to adapt to their own priorities. There is a sense of an EU model, supporting EU interests, distorting the direction of rural policy in all three CEECs.

A lack of sufficiently strong regional and local structures of government may also become an important factor in the development and implementation of RD policies in the applicant countries. Local democratic structures were not a feature of the previous political system in which state co-operatives and collectives conducted many of the service functions of local government. As a result of the breakdown of collective farm structures after the introduction of market reforms new local institutions had to be developed that could assume the role of local service provider and interest representative.

Predictably, there are tensions between national, regional and local authorities in all the countries studied. These include frustration by regional bodies at the extent of policy control from the centre and rising expectations at a local level which may be hard to satisfy in the current structure. The Spanish agriculture ministry is not alone in worrying about the conformity of regional authorities with a national framework and about the administrative efficiency of delivery systems. Local and regional authorities often point to long delays in the clearance of their schemes and bottlenecks in the payment of funds.

Table 2. Distribution of the French Rural Development Plan Budget by Measure, 2000–2006

MEASURE	*M EURO*	*% of Total*
Investment in agricultural holdings CTE	1496,29	10,2
Installing young farmers	2053,73	14,00
Training	116,78	0,8
Early retirement CTE	380,23	2,7
Less Favoured Areas	2839,13	19,3
Agri-environmental measures CTE	4207,17	28,5
Improving processing and marketing of agricultural products	2490,00	17,0
Afforestation of agricultural land	120,41	0,8
Other forestry measures	525,17	3,6
Farm-land improvement	16,17	0,1
Land parcel reorganisation	106,71	0,7
On-farm replacement services	0	0
Commercialisation of quality agricultural products CTE	55.83	0,3
Services for the rural economy and population	0	0
Renovation&development of villages and heritage protection CTE	33,50	0,2
Farm diversification CTE	55,83	0.3
Protection of water resources used in farming CTE	33,50	0,2
Development and improvement of agricultural infrastructure	0	0
Encouraging tourism	0	0
Environmental protection CTE	180,04	1,3
Reconstituting agricultural potential following natural disasters	0	0
TOTAL	*14 710,50*	*100*

Whilst integration is widely seen as desirable, few agencies are anxious to cede any autonomy to other actors. Forestry policy institutions for example are often semi-detached from those concerned with other land uses and policy is not always coordinated with other measures.

All the Member States investigated have developed individual mechanisms and instruments for the implementation of EU rural development programmes. These national administrative frameworks and policy traditions are having to respond to, and in turn are shaping, the implementation of EU rural development measures to a considerable degree.

Most rural development measures in the EU still show signs of the quite rigid CAP policy framework within which they have evolved. This is also reflected in the fact that a large part of spending under the RDR still does not finance rural development as such (i.e. investment to open up new income opportunities and aid the economic diversification of rural areas). Instead a large part is revenue spending that supports the agricultural community and/or the preservation of public goods, generally the rural environment (via agri-environment schemes, LFA measures, early retirement), although there are interesting contrasts between countries in the balance between these measures. Ultimately, both revenue and investment funding are probably necessary, because a number of societal goals cannot be achieved by market-led investment alone. The right balance and design of public spending is the issue here.

In taking forward the findings from this scoping study, any further work should bear in mind the following points.

- New models for sustainable rural development will need to be sufficiently robust to take account of the different institutions and perspectives that will shape policies and outcomes in each country, at both national and more local levels. They need to address some of the key concerns that have been clarified through this initial study, in relation to goals, environmental and social concerns, and policy delivery, as well as vital resourcing issues.
- In preparing the national reports for this study, the team has identified a number of factors hindering sustainable rural development which are worthy of further investigation and analysis. At the same time, many positive examples have emerged which together may provide practical solutions and point to new directions for sustainability. A more detailed appraisal of a range of these examples would therefore seem to be a valuable next step.

References

Barke, M. and Newton, M. (1994) A new rural development initiative in Spain: the European Community's LEADER plan, *Geography 79*, 366–71.

Commission of the European Communities (1988) *The Future of Rural Society*, Commission Communication 29 July 1988 [COM(88) 371 final], Brussels: Commission of the European Communities.

European Environment Agency 1998. *Europe's Environment: The Second Assessment.* EEA. Copenhagen.

Eurostat (1998) *Agriculture: Statistical Yearbook.* Eurostat, Luxembourg.

Organisation for Economic Cooperation and Development (OECD) (1996) Rural Employment: 'Territorial Indicators of Employment: focusing on Rural Development'. OECD, Paris.

8

One Village One Product Movement

The 'One Village One Product' (OVOP) movement was initiated in Oita Prefecture, Japan, in the late 1970s, and aimed to vitalise the prefecture's rural economy. The original concept of OVOP was to encourage villages in Oita each to select a product distinctive to the region and to develop it up to a nationally and globally accepted standard. In recent years, this concept has been transferred into neighbouring Asian countries and to other developing areas, including Africa and Latin America. In the course of these transfers, it has evolved more into a direct state-involved policy for poverty alleviation, differing somewhat from the movement of Oita, which was to prevent rural depopulation. OVOP development is seen as a way of enhancing local communities' entrepreneurial skills by utilising local resources and knowledge; creating value adding activities through branding of local products; and building human resources in the local economy. In particular, the use of local resources and knowledge is a critical element of OVOP development, which also can be associated with endogenous development theory.

This chapter describes how the OVOP movement has developed in Thailand and asks what have been its effects. In Thailand, local government administrative structures can be divided into four levels: 76 provinces, 876 districts, 7,255 sub-district (called '*tambon*' in Thai) and 79,830 villages. In 2001, the Thai government introduced the scheme at the sub-district level, the so-called 'One *Tambon* One Product' (OTOP), in order to stimulate the rural economy of the country. We rely mainly on a wide range of secondary and survey resources, including the Japanese literature, and our understanding of OTOP generated by a programme of qualitative interviews of producers in 2011. We supplement these by a small and preliminary sample survey of firms in Chiang Mai province in Thailand, and by a case study of an OTOP enterprise.

Theoretical Framework

The One Village One Product (OVOP) movement aims to encourage rural development through community-oriented activities by employing local resources and knowledge. Thus, this development could be viewed as having 'endogenous', rather than 'exogenous' elements as its key features. The original concept of an endogenous model of development appeared in the late 1970s, advocated by Friedman and Weaver and Stohr and Taylor in association with those who researched the 'Third Italy', the area centred on Bologna and famous for its industrial clusters of small and medium enterprises, in particular in traditional sectors such as shoes and leather products in the 1970s.

In this context, researchers paid special attention to the geographical proximity of firms, the specialisation of small industries, close inter-firm relationships, their socio-cultural identities, and socio-institutional system which facilitated trust, active self-help organisations, and the supportive role played by the regional government. Endogenous development theorists take the view that local economic development can be determined not by the capacity of the region to attract foreign firms, but the capacity of the region to generate the conditions of transformation of its own productive structure.

Most recently, this concept of regional development has evolved further to include more societal, cultural, environmental, and human elements. For instance, Friedman identified seven elements of regional assets necessary for endogenous development: basic human needs, organised civil society, the heritage of an established environment and popular culture, intellectual and creative assets, regional resource endowment, the quality of its environment, and infrastructure. In addition, the endogenous development concept influences practical movements for local development by non-governmental organisations (NGOs).

Social Capital and Community-Based Enterprises

Social and small business entrepreneurs have been increasingly playing an important role in complementing government in the field of poverty alleviation as well as sustainability in local rural society in developing countries. Social entrepreneurship has emerged as a form of social development strategy for dealing with social needs. Community-based enterprises (CBEs) are formed as a result of a local community's entrepreneurial activities, by employing their social resources, structures and networks.

According to Peredo and Chrisman, CBEs are defined as a community acting corporately as both entrepreneur and enterprise in pursuit of the common good. In short, CBEs are collective business ventures that are created by local communities, and aim to contribute to both local economic and social development. Social capital is a community's major resource. One of the most significant sets of actors in OVOP in Thailand are community-based enterprises, although their existence pre-dates the introduction of OTOP. In Thailand, the over 7,000 tambon (sub-districts) organise their own CBEs, which employ approximately 1.5 million people in rural communities. In Thailand, approximately 68% of OVOP producers are CBEs and 34% of CBEs in the country are engaged in OVOP activities.

In relation to entrepreneurship and CBEs, there are many links with the concept of social capital. Whereas, human capital is an individually-related resource, social capital, in contrast, is based on the relations between individuals/actors. Coleman identified the difference between social capital and private resources, arguing that "as an attribute of the social structure in which a person is embedded, social capital is not the private property of any of the persons who benefit from it".

Putnam *et al.* further elaborated Coleman's approach, viewing 'social capital' as a feature of social organisation, such as networks, norms, and trust that facilitate coordination and cooperation for mutual benefits. Subsequently, the concept of 'social capital' has begun to be employed to explain community development, particularly in relation to local entrepreneurship.

In particular, a study conducted by Kilkenny *et al.* revealed that the interaction effect of an entrepreneur's service to the community, and reciprocated community support of a business, make a significantly positive contribution to a business's success in rural areas. They concluded that social capital, which can be measured by participation in the community, has a positive influence on economic performance at the micro level.

Oita's OVOP Experiences

The original OVOP movement was initiated in 1961 by a small mountain town, Oyama, in Oita prefecture in Japan. Harumi Yahata, the president of the Oyama agricultural cooperative, encouraged the diversification of the town's agricultural practices, and directed farmers from traditional rice production to plums and chestnuts, and later to high-grade mushrooms and herbs as well as a variety of processed agricultural products.

Due to Oyama's geographical disadvantage as a mountainous location, each farmer's rice field was very small, with consistently low incomes for the farmers at that time. In consequence, many young people had left the town to search for employment in the cities. The town was facing a serious population problem.

Plum and chestnut were generally viewed as the most appropriate commercial agricultural products due to the fact that they already grew wild around the town. The idea of a NPC (new plum and chestnut) movement came from the farmers' struggle to escape from poverty. The movement was mainly supported by young farmers, as opposed to elderly conservative farmers and the state's agricultural policy, which encouraged rice production. The NPC movement re-vitalised the town: its population, which had dropped from 7,000 to less than 4,000 before the movement, stabilised thereafter.

Importantly, the people of Oyama town believed that 'resources are limited, but wisdom is unlimited'. This encouraged the practice of using 'local wisdom' as a key to the successful development of higher value added activities – a critical element for success. Farmers realised that the distribution of profit from raw agricultural products was unbalanced: For instance, if the price of an agricultural product to the customer in 260 yen (retail price), an Oyama farmer typically would receive 100 yen. Therefore, farmers developed a variety of processed agricultural products, including plum wines and *umeboshi* (plum pickles), and later engaged in an organic restaurant business that used locally available resources. Consequently, Oyama's agricultural cooperative (with 848 household members) generated 5.49 billion yen of sales output in 2008, becoming one of the most successful rural enterprises in Japan.

Inspired by Oyama's success, the governor of Oita prefecture, Morihiko Hiramatsu, subsequently introduced the OVOP movement into the whole prefecture in 1979. The OVOP movement involved each village within the prefecture specialising on the production of one distinctive product. It aimed to develop products or services within a community by adding value to locally available resources, and also to enhance local community's capability and sustainability through engaging the activities by improving local leadership and human resources.

Hiramatsu advocated the importance of locally-led development rather than heavy dependence on the government. His ideal concept of the role of the local state in the OVOP movement was as a catalyst for local communities, rather than providing subsidies for poor farmers. He acted as a salesman for Oita products, organising Oita foods fairs, promoting particularly Oita's local *shochu* (spirits) in luxury restaurants in Tokyo, and once even taking Oita beef to the Tokyo meat market.

The OVOP movement targeted value creation and the establishment of brand names for local products. For instance, *kabosu* limes are not only distributed as a primary agricultural good, but also processed as juices, salad dressings and other value added products. Through the creation of their Oita brand, '*Seki Saba*' (mackerels caught in the Saganoseki area) are traded at almost three times the price of mackerels caught in the ocean of the adjacent prefecture, located just 30 km away from Saganoseki. In addition, the movement encouraged human resource development by establishing a number of training schools, designed for particular needs. These included an Agricultural Training School, a Commerce School, and a Tourism School to educate potential entrepreneurial leaders.

OTOP in Thailand

Thailand has employed policies to induce foreign direct investment inflows, stimulating industrialisation and export expansion though multinational corporations, and achieving a high rate of economic growth. These policies favoured rapid industrialisation and development in urban areas. Income inequalities and inequalities in wealth distribution between urban and rural areas emerged as a critical social problem in the country. In such an economic environment, the Thai government has promoted CBEs for an additional source of income for in rural and farm households since the 5th National Socio-economic Development Plan (1982–1986). Several government agencies had been involved in strengthening these rural economic units, including the Department of Agricultural Extension, the Department of Livestock, the Department of Industrial Promotion, and later the Department of Rural Development.

In 1997, the Asian Crisis affected rural poor farmers as well as the urban economy. As a result, the dichotomy between rich and poor became one of the most controversial issues in Thailand. In particular, social movements such as the Assembly of the Poor, comprised predominantly of small farmers, forced Thai policy makers to realise the importance of tackling poverty alleviation in rural areas. As a result, the government of former Prime Minister Thaksin Shinawaratra (2001-2006) issued a moratorium on farmer's debt payments for three years and loaned up to 1 million baht to every Thai village for development projects. At the same time, the government established a Village and Rural Revolving Fund, which now serves as a source of capital for the OTOP project. Furthermore, the 9th National Socio-economic Development Plan (2002–2006) was introduced using the Thai King's philosophy of 'Sufficiency Economy', stressing a more balanced, holistic and sustainable path of development, which could alleviate the economic and social impacts of the crisis.

The concept of 'Sufficiency Economy', the social movements of the Poor, and the existing CBEs paved the way for a new rural development strategy in Thailand. Oita's experience of OVOP influenced the Thaksin government to introduce a Thai version of 'One Village One Product', namely 'One *Tambon* One Product' for stimulating rural development in the country. CBEs became a foundation for the OTOP scheme in 2001 when the government then adapted the concept of OVOP to CBEs and later to include other small and medium enterprises (SMEs). In the implementation of the OTOP project, Prime Minister Thaksin led a mission to Oita in order to study Oita's experiences. Japanese national government organisations such as the Japan External Trade Organization (JETRO), the Japan Overseas Development Corporation (JODC) and the Japan International Cooperation Agency (JICA) also provided assistance, including the promotion of the scheme's products in the Japanese market and the dispatch of design experts.

Administration of OTOP

Compared to Oita, the Thai government plays a rather different role in the OVOP/OTOP movement. In Oita prefecture, local government has played a catalytic role; in Thailand it is the national government that has been playing a central role. In fact, as a strategy of the TRT party, OTOP was used as a policy which would enhance the influence of the central government *vis à vis* local governments. In principle, local governments were subordinated to the national government in the implementation of projects. The Thai government established a three-layer OTOP administrative structure, which is based on the national, provincial and district levels.

At the national level, the National OTOP Administrative Committee (NOAC) and the OTOP Office were established under the Prime Minister's Office in order to conduct the OTOP project. Also, both provincial and district levels of OTOP Administrative Committees, headed by the governor or district major, and their sub-committees were established in the local areas of the country.

At the provincial and district levels, local OTOP sub-committees play an important role in selecting outstanding products, and integrating the provincial plans and budget for the development and quality development of OTOP in their areas.

Overview of Thai OTOP Policy

The OTOP policy has been modified and refocused from time to time since its inception in 2001. In 2002, the policy was designed to identify OTOP products in parallel with various government-led marketing activities. Government programmes were mostly geared to post-production activities and OTOP exhibitions in various places in Bangkok. Furthermore, large numbers of events and fairs were set up in major provinces in all regions.

Table 1. OTOP Focus Activities from 2001 to 2010

Year	*Activities*
2001	Ministerial Integration
2002	Search for OTOP Products
2003	OTOP Product Champion (OPC)
2004	Standard Champion
2005	Marketing OTOP
2006	Search for Excellent OTOP and OTOP Village Champion (OPC)
2007	Knowledge-Based OTOP
2008	Entrepreneur Promotion
2009	OTOP Tourism Village
2010	Sustainability of OTOP

Since 2003, more concentration has been placed on export linkages under the Department of Export Promotion. During these years, a logo for OTOP products, E-commerce, and the OTOP Product Champion (OPC) scheme were introduced.

In OTOP, the Thai government created a brand marketing strategy, which led participants to manufacture more value added products, and eventually enhanced OTOP's export capacity. This strategy has been based on the provision of OTOP certificates through the OPC scheme since 2003. Individual entrepreneurs, CBEs or SMEs, who are registered as OTOP manufacturers, are entitled to participate in the OPC contest. In this contest, OTOP registered products are graded from 1-star (the lowest) to 5- star (the highest) certificated products by an independent committee. The assessment criteria emphasise:

i) export potential through strong brand capacity;

ii) stability and production sustainability and stability of quality;

iii) level of consumer satisfaction; and

iv) the background of the product, particularly the use of locally available resources, knowledge and culture.

OTOP products are classified into five types:

i) foods,

ii) beverages,

iii) textile products,

iv) decorative items, handicrafts and souvenirs and

v) herbal products.

In 2006, the largest group of products (or 33.4%) was ranked at the quality level of 3-star, while the second largest group (28.8%) was graded with 2-star quality level and the third largest group (26.5%) was classified into 4-star quality level. 5-star quality level accounted for only 5.7%.

The first important element of the OPC scheme is to facilitate OTOP branding by labelling with the OTOP logo, which enhances consumer consciousness and recognition of OTOP. The second element of the scheme is linked to financial and other benefits.

In general, higher stars producers tend to be able to access better financial support, bank loans, marketing supports, training, and provision of tools and machineries. For instance, the Small and Medium Enterprise Development Bank of Thailand (SME Bank) provides loans to a maximum period of five years to the OTOP producers. Under this scheme, 3-star producers can access a maximum amount of 500,000 baht. By the same token, 4-and 5-starts producers can obtain a maximum amount of 750,000 and 1,000,000 baht, respectively . Furthermore, above 3-star producers are eligible to participate in OTOP EXPO, the so-called 'OTOP City' for grants (free of charge). However, export promotion benefit is limited to 5-star producers.

In addition, the 'OTOP Village Champion' (OVC) scheme was also introduced in 2006 in order to promote the local tourism industry in Thai rural villages by integrating with various OTOP related elements including unique OTOP products, nature, agriculture, health, culture, and craftwork..

To move the OTOP scheme forward, marketing promotion related activities remained key. In 2007, the government set up a so-called 'matching buyers to OTOP producers' project. It was an integrated effort of the Ministry of Commerce, Ministry of Interior, Ministry of Industry and Ministry of Agriculture and Agriculture Cooperatives as well as the private sector (marketing companies and exporters). In the same year, OTOP producers were provided training in business management and entrepreneurship development. In addition, Knowledge-Based OTOP (KBO) was introduced in order to enhance idea, technical and scientific and managerial skills in OTOP activities.

OTOP implementation during the first five years received widespread criticism, however. The major shortcoming was the OTOP project's efforts in enhancing producers' capability in self-reliance and creativity. Subsequently, to reduce this weakness in human resource as well as organizational development, in 2007, the OTOP project has continued under a new policy entitled the 'Master Plan for Promotion of Community and Local Products (OTOP) B.E.2551-2555'.

The sustainability of CBEs and SMEs has become a major challenge within OTOP. The Thaksin government targeted the development of marketing strategies and provided a substantial finance to rural villagers; subsequently, some CBEs came to depend heavily on government support. As a result, OTOP policy needed to shift its focus from a marketing oriented policy to 'Sufficiency Economy' (using more locally available resources and knowledge) under the current Abhisit government in 2010. In addition, the 10th National Economic and Social Development Plan (2007-2011) also emphasises the importance of 'Sufficiency Economy' concept in parallel with facilitation of CBEs for social and economic security as well as promotion of new entrepreneurs.

The Bureau of Budget directly allocated an annual budget for OTOP to related agencies in 2001-2002. However, this financing system shifted to SMEs promotion funds in order to support OTOP projects in 2003. Both allocated budget and actually-used budget decreased rapidly after the peak of 2004. In 2008, the actually-used budget accounted for a mere 46.6 million baht, 3.6 % of 2004.

Overview of OTOP Activities and their Impacts

The OTOP project has been contributing to the rural economy in Thailand, particularly in terms of employment creation. Over 22,762 villages nationwide participated in the project with 37,840 OTOP producers and over 1.3 million members and employees, especially housewives and older people, who enjoyed increases in household earnings. The OTOP project also has provided opportunities for participation in community activities, which allowed villagers to work together, applying 'local wisdom' in their production, facilitating learning about other communities' products and skills too. By contributing to increasing villagers' income, fewer villagers were forced by economic circumstances to migrate to cities.

Type of OTOP Producers in 2010

A total of 33,228 producers were registered under OTOP in 2010, of which community-based enterprises (CBEs), single owner enterprises, and small and medium-sized enterprises (SMEs) accounted for 66.8%, 31.1%, and 2.2%, respectively. According to the Community Development Department, approximately 65,000 groups were registered as CBEs in Thailand. Thus, it is estimated that 34% of CBEs in the country are currently engaged in OTOP activities.

Types of OTOP Products

The total of 85,183 items were registered under OTOP products, of which decorative items, handicrafts and souvenirs accounted for 36.8%, textiles for 25.1%, foods for 23.9%, herbal products for 10.9% and beverages for 3.6%.

OTOP Sales Output

Sales output of OTOP products has increased considerably since 2001 – by over 4.6 times in the period of 2002-2008 in current price terms; or nearly 3.8 times in real terms. Domestic sales and exports accounted for 86% and 14%, respectively, in 2008.

Study of OTOP in Chiang Mai Province

Overview of Chiang Mai

Chiang Mai Province is located in the Northern region of Thailand, with a population of 1.7 million. The province produces a number of well-known horticultural products including some organic ones and some high quality rice and coffee. Chiang Mai province has been the tourist hub of the north and one of the country's most important tourist destinations, and tourism-related sectors such as hotels and handicrafts have developed rapidly.

OTOP Policy in Chiang Mai

Chiang Mai OTOP policy has set the following measures for OTOP development:

i) to improve the information system for strengthening trade and investment related to OTOP and SMEs;

ii) to enhance agro-related industry or value added products based on local industry, local identity, and local (Lanna) culture;

iii) to expand and support cottage-industry products as supplementary income sources or as a secondary occupation, and supporting product quality to meet standard acceptable in both domestic and overseas markets;

iv) to establish a central market as an assembling and distributing centre for OTOP products and farm produce for Chiang Mai, and hence, for promoting Chiang Mai to becomes the hub for the northern provincial cluster;

v) to enhance 'Village Fund' and 'Small, Medium and Large Village' (SML) programmes to their best performances, and networking OTOP with these programmes; and

vi) to support various professional groups toward sustainable development.

Local OTOP officers can access budget from three sources:

i) budget provided by the central office to be used for training in entrepreneurship (business planning);

ii) budget from the Chiang Mai provincial office available for activities related to the stated policies; and

iii) budget from the local administration (Or Bor Jor) available for Sunday OTOP Fairs and other activities.

One of the marketing strategies used in the OTOP project is to use the Star rating system for the OTOP Product Champion contest. In Chiang Mai, among 990 OTOP groups, 490 obtained above 3-star status. As in other provinces, Chiang Mai, the Community Development Department (CDD) provincial office set up a screening committee (including local personal from government, university and private sectors) to select products and recommend the list of 3-star, 4-star and 5-star product to regional and then nation level – committees for official certification. The Chiang Mai CDD office has put up a production development plan for those (490) groups. The plan aims at improving product design and business and marketing management, in conformance with central government policy.

Preliminary Survey of OTOP Producers in Chiang Mai Province

The aim of this survey was to overview the activities of OTOP producers, including business types, business conditions, start-up patterns and problems encountered. The survey was conducted in December 2009 – January 2010 with interviews with 32 enterprises in Chiang Mai. The 32 enterprises comprised two types: self-owned enterprises and Community Based Enterprises (including housewives' groups and farmers' groups), which accounted for 15 cases and 17 cases, respectively. The survey was random. The share of CBEs in the sample (53%) was somewhat lower than the national average (67%), but near to the average for Chiangmai (48%), Products of the sampled businesses covered a wide range but the largest category was textiles (25%, the same as the national OVOP), and handicrafts and wood products accounts (20%, compared to 35% for handicrafts nationally)

1) Background of Entrepreneurs

Of the respondent entrepreneurs, 20 (62.5%) were female and 12 (37.5%) male. 47% of the respondents were 30-50 years old and 53% were over 50.

However, at the age at business start-up, respondents were rather young, i.e. 65.6% set up business when they were between 18 and 41 years and 35.5% were younger than 34 years.

OTOP participants in our survey showed large differences in educational attainment. While 37% were university graduates, 34% had only completed primary school. Between these extremes, 15% of respondents completed secondary school and 12% had diplomas from vocational education. The survey interviews indicate that self-owned entrepreneurs have relatively high education compared to group entrepreneurs.

With regards to time commitment to business, 72% of OTOP survey participants worked full time.

2) Motivation for Starting-up Business

The motivation to start-up a business among the self-owned differed somewhat from that of the group entrepreneurs. For the self-owned, the important motives (in order of significance) were:

i) to have a free hand in work,

ii) to use their knowledge and expertise,

iii) to put ideas into practice and

iv) to have time with family.

By contrast, the motivation driving groups to run business was more related to public concerns. Their most important reason appears to be:

i) to enhance income of other in society and

ii) contribution of the group's activities to society, although presumably referring to people in their own group or community.

Although it is commonly believed that most groups are formed mainly to capture access to government support, this turned out to be less important than the above mentioned reasons.

3) Difficulties and Business Prospects

At the establishment stage, the entrepreneurs found two dominant difficulties. The top of the list was 'development of sale outlets'. Obtaining expert advice at the beginning of business was also problematic and ranked second. Others of importance were 'financial/capital shortage', 'marketing research', and 'acquisition of business know-how'.

With regards to how entrepreneurs obtained funding to start their business, own capital was the dominant source of start-up funds. Loans from the local government lending programme played only a moderate role for these sampled respondents.

Since business skill appears to be an important issue for business startups, acquiring advice and training support receives considerable attention from both government and promotion programme organisers. However, the survey indicates that entrepreneurs mainly depended on their own experience and self-learning. Customers' feedback ranked second as a source of learning experience followed by suppliers' feedbacks. Trainings and guidance given by supporting programmes ranked at the bottom of the list implying either there was no real need for training or that the provision of training was irrelevant or trivial.

4) Respondents' Assessment of the OTOP Project

One goal of this preliminary survey was to identify OTOP participants' knowledge of OTOP project and their attitudes toward this policy. Data from the questionnaire survey provide general evaluations of OTOP and participants' needs for future assistance. The highest proportion (53%) of respondents had a moderate knowledge of the OTOP scheme, while 22% and 12% reported they had good and very good knowledge, respectively. Only 3% of OTOP participant admitted to having no knowledge of OTOP.

Data from the survey reveal various types of support and level of involvement. A high proportion of participants (40%) did not receive 'technical matter' support, and 34% did not receive 'business procedural support'. Training in 'book-keeping' and 'packaging' are important elements for business success, but 31% of OTOP participants did not attend training in these areas. For those who received 'book-keeping' training, 31% were 'least involved' and only 12% and 3% attained the 'high' and 'highest' involvement.

The highest involvement in OTOP activities appears to be marketing-related: that is, product exhibition and marketing support. Apparently, OTOP participants value marketing related support the most. As a consequence, the 'OTOP City' exhibition in Bangkok has become the annual event and 'a must' that any government is obliged to organise.

Beside the OTOP scheme, OTOP participants can have access to other sources for financial and other supports. The *Tambon* Administration provides local budget to support group producers (but not individuals). In addition, the 'village fund' programme, launched at the same time as OTOP, allows a village's committee to consider loans for villagers' investment.

Furthermore, the SME Promotion Institute (SMEI) provides loans as well as technical and management know-how for self-owned enterprises. However, 75% of the respondents did not seek support from SME Promotion Institute (obviously only half of respondents are not eligible). One of common reasons for not obtaining SMEI support is its complicated application procedure, which requires substantial documentation.

The respondent were asked to identity their expectation from and appreciation in assistance provided by OTOP support. The top importance is placed on product exhibitions followed by marketing support and financial support. However, levels of expectation appeared to be much higher than levels of appreciation for all support programmes.

Enterprise Case Study: A Farm Women's Group

This is a case study of an OTOP enterprise, set up in an agricultural area in Chiang Mai province in order to process into potato chips locally grown potatos that have been rejected for direct sale. Originally established as a community based enterprise (CBE) in 1997, before the introduction of OTOP, it became an OTOP enterprise after OTOP's introduction in 2001. The project is shown to have provided employment to older workers, mostly women, who could not easily have secured other paid jobs in the area. OTOP is shown to have provided various means of support to strengthen this project, particularly on the marketing side. This account is based on two interviews, conducted in September 2010 and February 2011, respectively.

The Farm Women's Group (FWG) was established by 31 group members (29 women and 2 men) in a district of Chiang Mai province. FWG was awarded an OTOP 3-star in the OTOP Product Champion scheme, producing 2,000 bags of potato chips a week and accounting for an approximately 1.8 million baht sales output in 2010. The chairman of this CBE is a 63 years old woman with a primary school educational background, and was the wife of a potato farmer. FWG was formed when she was 50 years old.

Farmers in the immediate area began growing potatoes under an initiative started by the Thai king in 1986. Six months from the commencement of the potato-growing project, 'Lay' brand, one of the world's leading potato chip producers, and part of PEPSICO International, approached the *tambon.* As a result, all farmers in the area became contract farmers for PEPSICO International. Throughout the 1980s and 1990s,

PEPSICO International, as well as a local university in Chiang Mai, Maejo University, supported the improvement of potato quality for potato chip production, by importing seeds from the Netherlands.

One of the major issues in this *tambon* was the high proportion of rejected potatoes, and as a result, farmers could not sell large quantities of potatoes to PEPSICO International. The primary aim of the establishment of a CBE was to help the potato farmers. In 1997, the Ministry of Agriculture came to the *tambon* and to discuss this problem, encouraging farmers to start potato chip production with the provision of free leasing of machinery (valued at 100, 000 baht).

As a result, the wives of the farmers in this area created the initial capital of 300,000 baht by collecting 100 baht per share within group members and non-member villagers, and established a community-based enterprise, FWG in 1997. FWG members were allowed to individually purchase a maximum of 10 shares, while non-group members were only allowed to purchase a maximum of 50 shares through a savings group (non-member's investment group). Profits in CBEs are distributed to the shareholders at the end of year. FWG activities generated profits of 20 baht per share in 2010.

When they started potato chip production, there were a number of problems, such as the quality of products and management skills. The provincial government, provided support via the public health department and agricultural development office, particularly in regards to tasting and quality control. Also, Chiang Mai University and the local government assisted the CBE with the development of machinery and of accounting, respectively. As a result, FWG developed their own brand potato chips.

The OTOP project provided various business opportunities and assistance for this CBE. When the CBE participated in the OTOP Product Champions programme, and in OTOP City, with their own-brand potato chips, several Bangkok-based potato chips producers showed interest. Consequently, FWG became a supplier for two well-known Thai brands of potato chips. In addition, they gained access to additional free leasing of machinery as well as technical assistance and grants for packaging from the local and national governments.

Currently, farmers in the *tambon* sell raw potatoes for 11 baht per kg to PEPSICO International at arm's length prices. Rejected potatoes, which are assumed to have the value of 2-4 baht per kg, are passed on to FWG. FWG uses those reject potatoes in the first processing stage of washing and slicing by automatic machinery, followed by frying with palm oil manually, and flavouring (only for normal potato chips, not *Kanya* chips), and finally packing. FWG has two large potato chips buyers, which account for approximately 80% and 20% of their business, respectively. The profitability of their own brand is higher than the products subcontracted to the two national Thai brands. However, FWG prefers subcontracting, because most of theworkers are unfamiliar with the requirement of developing a brand to a higher level of business.

Of the total of 31 members of the CBE, 15 people are engaged in the production of potato chips; the remaining 16 members can be considered only as investors in FWG rather than workers. The wage level of workers, which is determined by the chairman of FWG in consultation with the workers, accounts for approximately 150-180 baht a day. The wage level is set in relation to that of local factories, to avoid its being inundated with job applications.

The FWG provides opportunities for older workers in the community (who in this case are mostly housewives, since the men are directly engaged in farming). It is a common practice for factories in the area to cap the working age at 40, leaving few such other few working opportunities, and the CBE fills this gap. Although it does not owe its existence to OTOP, OTOP facilities have strengthened it both on the marketing and the production side.

This chapter has surveyed the development of the OTOP (one *tambon*, one product) programme in Thailand, based on the earlier experience of OVOP (one village, one product) in Oita prefecture in Japan. OTOP has operated as a rural development strategy in the context of widespread rural poverty, whereas OVOP was conceived as a strategy to prevent rural depopulation in the context of a rapidly growing industrial economy. Nevertheless, the OTOP experiment has been a way of increasing the help to existing enterprises, including community based ones, as well as of helping new enterprises to establish. Employment for people, such as older women, who might not easily find jobs otherwise, have been a benefit of the OTOP scheme, and help with marketing has been a particularly important kind of support.

REFERENCES

Curry, Robert L, Jr and Sura, Kanchana (2007) "Human Resource Development (HRD) Theory and Thailand's Sufficiency Economy Concept and Its OTOP Program", *Journal of Third World Studies*, vol.24, no.2, pp.85-94.

JICA (2003) *The Study of Monitoring and Evaluation Model on the One Tambon One Product Development Policy*, Tokyo, JICA International Cooperation Agency (JICA).

Igusa, Kunio (2008) "The Problem of the Regional Revitalization in Asia and One Village One Product: Adaptability of Oita Model to Asian Countries", *Journal of OVOP Policy vol.1*, October.

Kaewmanotham, Malee (2008) "Thai ni Okeru OTOP Project to Jizoku Kanou na Hatten (OTOP Project and Sustainable Development in Thailand)", *Journal of the Faculty of International Studies*, Utsunomiya University, vol.26, pp.63-71.

Routray, Jayant (2007) *One Village One Product: Strategy for Sustainable Rural Development in Thailand*, CAB Calling, January-March, pp.30-34.

Bibliography

Ahluwalia, M. S., (1978). "Rural Poverty and Agricultural Performance in India"; *Journal of Development Studies,* vol. 14 (2).

Andre Beteille, (1999). "Empowerment" in *Economic and Political Weekly*, Perspectives, 6-12 March and 13-19 March.

Barkat A. (2003). *Rural electrification and poverty reduction: case of Bangladesh.* Presented at NRECA Int. Conf., Sustain. Rural Electrif. Dev. Ctries.: Is it Possible, Arlington, VA

Barke, M. and Newton, M. (1994) A new rural development initiative in Spain: the European Community's LEADER plan, *Geography 79*, 366–71.

Barnes D, Sen M. (2004). The impact of electrification on women's lives in rural India. *Energia News* 7(1):13–14.

Berry, R. A. and W. R. Cline, (1979). *Agrarian Structure and Productivity in Developing Countries*, Baltimore : Johns Hopkins University Press.

Bhagwati, Jagdish, (1998). "Poverty and Public Policy", *World Development*, vol.16, No.5.

Chambers, R. (1997). *Whose Reality Counts?* Intermediate Technology Publications, London.

Commission of the European Communities (1988) *The Future of Rural Society*, Commission Communication 29 July 1988 [COM(88) 371 final], Brussels: Commission of the European Communities.

Curry, Robert L, Jr and Sura, Kanchana (2007) "Human Resource Development (HRD) Theory and Thailand's Sufficiency Economy Concept and Its OTOP Program", *Journal of Third World Studies*, vol.24, no.2, pp.85-94.

Dasgupta Partha, (1998). *The Economics of Poverty in Poor Countries*, DERP No. 9, London: London School of Economics and Political Science.

Energy Sector Manag. Assist. Program. (2002). Rural electrification and development in the Phillipines: measuring the social and economic benefits. *ESMAP Rep. 255/02*, World Bank, Washington, DC.

ESCAP, (2005), *Energy services for sustainable development in rural areas in Asia and the Pacific: Policy and Practice,* ESCAP.

European Environment Agency 1998. *Europe's Environment: The Second Assessment.* EEA. Copenhagen.

Eurostat (1998) *Agriculture: Statistical Yearbook.* Eurostat, Luxembourg.

Evenson, R. E., (1986). "Infrastructure, Output Supply and Input Demand in Philippine Agriculture: Provisional Estimates", *Journal of Philippine Development,* vol. 13(23), pp. 62-76.

FAO Regional Office for Asia and the Pacific, (2003), *A handbook for trainers on participatory local development.*

FAO, (2007), *Role of agricultural cooperatives in biofuel development at community-level for rural food and livelihood security, regional workshop*, FAO and Network for Development of Agricultural Cooperatives in Asia and the Pacific (NEDAC), 2007

Flora Jan, *et al.*, (April 1991). *From the Grassroots: Profiles of 103 Rural Self-Development Projects*. USDA/ERS Staff Report 9123. Washington: U.S. Department of Agriculture, Economic Research Service.

Harris, R. W.(2005). *Building telecentre services.* APEC Telecentre Training Camp. (January 24-29, Taipei, Taiwan).

Hornbeck, J.F. (October 12, 1993). *Empowerment Zones: Can A Federal Policy Affect Local Economic Development.* Economics Division of the Congressional Research Service.

Igusa, Kunio (2008) "The Problem of the Regional Revitalization in Asia and One Village One Product: Adaptability of Oita Model to Asian Countries", *Journal of OVOP Policy vol.1*, October.

Jensen, M. & Esterhuysen, A. (2001). *The community telecentre cookbook for Africa – recipes for self-sustainability – How to establish a multi-purpose community telecentre in Africa.* United Nations Educational, Scientific and Cultural Organization, Paris.

JICA (2003) *The Study of Monitoring and Evaluation Model on the One Tambon One Product Development Policy*, Tokyo, JICA International Cooperation Agency (JICA).

Kaewmanotham, Malee (2008) "Thai ni Okeru OTOP Project to Jizoku Kanou na Hatten (OTOP Project and Sustainable Development in Thailand)", *Journal of the Faculty of International Studies*, Utsunomiya University, vol.26, pp.63-71.

Kretzmann, John P., and John L. McKnight. (1993). *Building Communities from the Inside Out: A Path Toward Finding and Mobilizing a Community's Assets.* Evanston, Illinois: The Asset-Based Community Development Institute, Northwestern University.

Organisation for Economic Cooperation and Development (OECD) (1996) Rural Employment: 'Territorial Indicators of Employment: focusing on Rural Development'. OECD, Paris.

Owen, Wilfred, (1987). *Transportation and World Development,* Baltimore: Johns Hopkins University Press.

Parkinson, S. (2005). Telecentres, access and development; experience and lessons from Uganda and South Africa. IDRC. Retrieved from Web: http://www.idrc.ca/en/ev-87255-201-1-DO_TOPIC.html

Reeder, Richard J. (November 1990). *Targeting Aid to Distressed Rural Areas: Indicators of Fiscal and Community Well Being.* USDA/ERS Staff Report AGES 9067. Washington: U.S. Department of Agriculture, Economic Research Service.

Roman, R. & Colle, R. D. (2002). Themes and issues in telecenter sustainability. In *Development Informatics,* Working Paper Series no. 10. Institute for Development Policy and Management, Manchester.

Rosenzweig, M. R. and H. P. Binswanger (1993), "Wealth, weather risk and the composition and profitability of agricultural investments", *Economic Journal, vol. 103*, pp. 56-78

Rothenberg-Aalami, J. & Pal, J. (2005). Rural telecenter impact assessments and the political economy of ICT for Development (ICT4D), Berkeley Roundtable on the International Economy (BRIE) Working Paper 164. University of California, Berkeley.

Routray, Jayant (2007) *One Village One Product: Strategy for Sustainable Rural Development in Thailand*, CAB Calling, January-March, pp.30-34.

Secretariat of the Pacific Community and UNDP. (2004) *Pacific Islands Regional Millennium Development Goals Report 2004.*

Siddhi P. (2000). *Making solar affordable to the poor*. Presented at Village Power 2000, World Bank, Washington, DC.

U.S. Department of Agriculture, (September 25, 1996). *Rural Empowerment Zones and Enterprise Communities: A Status Report*. Washington: U.S. Department of Agriculture, Rural Development, Office of Community Development.

Wiggins, Steve and Sharon Proctor, (2001). "How special are rural areas? Implications of location for rural development", in *Development Policy Review*, December, 19(4), pp. 427-436.

World Bank, (1976). *The Economic Analysis of Rural Road Projects,* World Bank Staff Working Paper No. 241, Washington, D.C.: World Bank.

____, (2001). *South Asia: A Strategy and Action Plan for Rural Development*, Rural Development Sector Unit, South Asia Region.

____, South Asia Energy, Infrastruct. Unit. (2004). *Access to Electricity: Strategy Options for India*, pp. 1–56.Washington, DC: World Bank.

Index